UNDERSTANDING THE SOCIAL ECONOMY
AND THE THIRD SECTOR

Understanding the Social Economy and the Third Sector

Simon Bridge, Brendan Murtagh and Ken O'Neill

palgrave
macmillan

First published 2009 by
PALGRAVE MACMILLAN

Palgrave Macmillan in the UK is an imprint of Macmillan Publishers Limited,
registered in England, company number 785998, of Houndmills, Basingstoke,
Hampshire RG21 6XS.

Palgrave Macmillan in the US is a division of St Martin's Press LLC,
175 Fifth Avenue, New York, NY 10010.

Palgrave Macmillan is the global academic imprint of the above companies
and has companies and representatives throughout the world.

Palgrave® and Macmillan® are registered trademarks in the United States,
the United Kingdom, Europe and other countries.

ISBN-13: 978–0–230–51813–1 paperback
ISBN-10: 0–230–51813–3 paperback

This book is printed on paper suitable for recycling and made from fully
managed and sustained forest sources. Logging, pulping and manufacturing
processes are expected to conform to the environmental regulations of the
country of origin.

A catalogue record for this book is available from the British Library.

A catalog record for this book is available from the Library of Congress.

10   9   8   7   6   5   4   3   2   1
18 17 16 15 14 13 12 11 10 09

Printed in China

Contents

List of Figures, Tables and Illustrations

Figures

Tables

Illustrations

Preface

This is a book about that section of the economy which is now often referred to as 'the third sector': a name which is intended to distinguish it from the public and private sectors. For many of those interested in it, the most important part of the third sector is the social economy, often because it seems to be the part which offers the most economic and social benefit. Some people refer to this area, or to parts of it, as the voluntary sector or the community sector and there are other concepts associated with it such as social capital.

However, although these and other associated terms are now in relatively wide use, there is no general agreement about what they mean, and there seems to be little clarity about how they are linked. As a result, for those now working in this field, especially when they are new to it, there can be considerable confusion about what is involved. While there has been a third sector in an economy for as long as there have been the two other sectors, much of the language about it is developing only now and, often with government encouragement, a new industry is evolving to promote and support it.

The aim

The aim of this book therefore is to help to make sense of this field by summarising, in an objective framework, what is known about these and similar issues and by indicating some of the main perspectives on them. The book tries to present an overview of the key concepts, to explore the relevance today of the third sector and its components, to explore the varied meanings and definitions of these components and to highlight some of the current key issues in the field, how they are being addressed, and some of their future implications.

Who should read this book?

This book is targeted at policy makers and staff of social enterprise support organisations; at students of the third sector at universities and business schools; at researchers and teaching staff; at social entrepreneurs and those working in the sector; and at funders and potential funders of third sector organisations. It provides a foundation text for those who are studying this sector and a perspective appropriate for both those who might want to engage in it and those who might want to work with, but not necessarily in, it. It has been written in the UK but it also refers to developments in other countries, and much of its content should be relevant elsewhere, where people, for whatever reason, wish to know more about the third sector and its context. It seeks to present them with a sound introduction to the key concepts and issues as a grounding for understanding and work in this area and as a starting point for further explorations of more specialised aspects.

Thank you

In writing this book we have been conscious of many people who have helped and encouraged us, and others who have been tolerant of the time we have devoted to this instead of to other tasks. There are too many to name here but we owe them all considerable thanks.

Simon Bridge
Brendan Murtagh
Ken O'Neill

Acknowledgements

The authors and publisher gratefully acknowledge the following for granting permission to reproduce material in this book and, where indicated, for other help:

Canada, PRI (Policy Research Initiative), What we Need to Know About the Social Economy, A Guide for Policy Research (Ottawa: PRI, 2005) p. 4.

Amy Carter for permission to include the case study on Guludo and for providing material about it.

The Bank of England for permission to quote from The Bank of England, *The Financing of Social Enterprises: A Special Report by the Bank of England*, May 2003.

David Billis and the Association for Research on Nonprofits and Voluntary Action (ARNOVA) for permission to quote from D. Billis 'Sectors, Hybrids and Public Policy: The Voluntary Sector in Context', paper presented at the *ARNOVA 2003 Conference*.

Calouste Gulbenkian Foundation for permission to quote from J. Pearce, *Social Enterprise in Anytown* (London: Calouste Gulbenkian Foundation, 2003).

Cornell University for permission to quote from C. Gunn, *Third Sector Development: Making up for the Market*, Copyright © 2004 by Cornell University.

The Department of Work and Pensions for permission to quote from D. Finn, and D. Simmonds, Intermediate Labour Market in Britain and an International Review of Transitional Employment Programmes (London: Department of Work and Pensions, 2003) © Crown Copyright

HM Treasury for permission to quote from H. M. Treasury, *Credit Unions of the Future: Taskforce Report* (London: HM Treasury, 1999).

Phil Nicholls for permission to quote from *Who Should Run Community Enterprise?*

The Office of National Statistics for permission to quote from *Assessing people's perceptions of their neighbourhood and community involvement* (London: Office of National Statistics, 2002).

Princeton University Press for permission to quote from R. D. Putnam, *Making Democracy Work*, © 1993 Princeton University Press, Reprinted by permission of Princeton University Press.

The Joseph Rowntree Foundation for permission to quote from E. Mayo, T. Fisher, P. Conaty, J. Doling, and A. Mullineux, *Small is bankable: Community reinvestment in the UK*, published in 1998 by the Joseph Rowntree Foundation. Reproduced by permission of the Joseph Rowntree Foundation.

Sage Publications Ltd for permission to quote from R. Forrest, and A. Kearns (2001) 'Social cohesion, social capital and the neighbourhood', *Urban Studies*, Vol. 38.

Simon & Schuster for permission to quote from R. D. Putnam, *BOWLING ALONE: The Collapse and Revival of American Community*, Copyright © 2000 by Robert D Putnam, Reprinted with permission of Simon & Schuster Adult Publishing Group.

Social Enterprise London for permission to quote from *Introducing Social Enterprise* (London: Social Enterprise London, 2001).

Taylor and Francis Books (UK) for permission to quote from:

J. Kendall, *The Voluntary Sector* (London: Routledge, 2003).

A. Amin, A. Cameron and R. Hudson, *Placing the Social Economy* (London: Routledge, 2002) P. Mathias, *The First Industrial Nation: An Economic History of Britain 1700–1914* (London: Methuen, 1983).

Third Sector Magazine for permission to quote from its news bulletins.

The United Nations for permission to quote from *UN Handbook on Non-Profit Institutions in the System of National Accounts* from www.un.org.

Colin Stutt for permission to quote from C. Stutt Consulting, *Finance for the Social Economy in Northern Ireland*, 2004 (www.colinstutt.com) and for his overall help.

Why Address the Social Economy?

Key Concepts

This chapter covers

- the emergence of interest in the social economy, its scale, and why it might have been overlooked in the past;

- the association of the social economy with the concept of social capital, which has in turn been suggested as a requirement for addressing social exclusion;

- the wider concept of the third sector, of which the social economy is a significant part;

- the range of benefits which third sector organisations might have the potential to deliver;

- the agenda, and layout, of this book.

Learning Objectives

By the end of this chapter the reader should

- understand the concept of the social economy, why it might not have been widely recognised in the past, and why interest in it is now growing;

(cont'd)

- be aware of the association being made between the social economy and the concept of social capital, and of the potential benefits of the latter;
- understand the concept of the third sector and how it embraces the social economy;
- appreciate the range of benefits that might be provided by this sector.

Introduction

This book is about an area of human endeavour which has often been overlooked but is now receiving greater recognition. It is an area which has both economic and social impact and it is often referred to as the social economy, which, it is said, 'constitutes a significant movement worldwide'[1] and has 'become a prominent field of public policy innovation, directly linking social policy and economic development'.[2] This link with social policy is often associated with the concept of social capital which the social economy is said to use and to build in the same way that many businesses use and build financial capital. But, although the social economy has been linked to social policy in this way, it is not in the public sector and, despite its links to economic development, it is not in the private sector either. It is therefore said to be, or to form the significant part of, the third sector of an economy. But what exactly are the social economy and the third sector, and associated concepts such as social capital, and how are they related and why are they now of interest? These are the types of question to which this book attempts to provide some answers. There is other written material from which the answers might be sought but it tends to be academic, disparate, partial or scattered. This book attempts to bring key aspects of it together to provide a general introduction to this subject.

Twenty years ago the questions raised in Illustration 1.1 would not have been asked and even ten years ago many of them would have seemed a little strange. People then might have heard references to the voluntary and/or community sector but now, increasingly, it seems that reference is being made to the social economy, to social capital, to the third sector and to other associated concepts also such as social enterprises and social entrepreneurship.

For people new to this field it can be confusing. It is an area which, in many respects, is just starting to be recognised and explored. Therefore new interpretations are emerging for aspects of it, and different levels of recognition are given to areas within it. Because much of this interest has arisen very recently, even the vocabulary used can be confusing as there has not been enough time for a single, or major, usage to emerge. As a result a variety of different expressions can be found, sometimes for the same or overlapping things, as well as a variety of different meanings for some of those expressions.

This book is an attempt to put these concepts into a context and to make some sense of the debate about them by summarising, in an objective framework,

Illustration 1.1   Some Questions

What sort of organisation produces 'The Big Issue', and does it do it for profit or as a public service?

What justification is there for describing a university vice chancellor as an entrepreneur when he is not trying to make a profit for either himself or his backers?

Financial capital is needed by businesses to pay for things like the equipment, material stocks and preparation work they need for the start-up and expansion of their operations, and it can be borrowed or obtained as investments. What, however, is social capital, why might it be needed and where does it come from?

Why does the UK government feel it necessary to have a policy to promote the social economy?

Within the economy there are the public and private sectors, but what is the third sector, and where does the social economy fit into all that?

Why when an economic development agency announced a programme of support for the social economy sector did it claim it would be 'focused on addressing social deprivation'?

And why (a least at the time of writing) is 'Controversy' the second heading in the Wikipedia entry on the social economy?

what has been said about them and by indicating some of the main perspectives and agenda that are to be found.

There is, however, no single obvious point at which to start discussing this subject and, once a start is made, there is then no single logical order in which to proceed. It is a bit like describing our world, the countries in it, and the relationship between them. We are used to maps of the earth which place our own country near the centre, and we may think other maps strange which are centred on other countries. This book does not approach the subject from the viewpoint of just one part of it, but tries to give an overall perspective, so it does not have a predetermined centre point. Indeed there is no predetermined route to follow. If, say, in describing the countries of the world, Portugal were to be taken as a stating point, Spain might be next and then France. After that it could be logical to consider other Atlantic seaboard countries because of their historic connections, or other EU countries because of their political connections, or other Mediterranean countries because of their geographic connections. All these links are relevant but only one can be followed at a time and, whichever is taken first, some of the countries mentioned will have to be re-visited later when the other links are considered.

Some readers may therefore disagree with the order in which subjects are addressed in this book. However, there is no single best way; the choice has been made and this chapter endeavours to provide an introduction to it by looking at some of the key concepts and the words used to label them. It also considers why interest in them has grown recently, not least in government circles, and what they might have to offer. It then indicates the sequence followed in the rest of the book.

The appeal of the social economy

As Illustration 1.2 suggests there is currently considerable interest in the social economy, noticeably in government and research circles, although there is no single clear definition of what it is. The term itself apparently entered the English language only in the late 1980s and early 1990s, having been taken from the French term *l'economie sociale*, and it is generally used to refer to a set of organisations with social purposes which are neither in the public sector nor have the profit-realising objective that typifies the private sector, although they do generate at least some of their income from providing goods or services. We often call such organisations social enterprises and refer also to the social entrepreneurs who have created them and to the social entrepreneurship that is demonstrated in their creation. Associated with them, community enterprise and community business are also referred to alongside the voluntary and community sector, and sometimes

---

Illustration 1.2   Some References to the Social Economy and Associated Concepts

A book published in 2002 about the social economy introduced it in this way:

> Until the 1990s the term social economy hardly featured in English speaking academic and policy discourse, while older terms such as 'third sector', 'non-profit activity', 'community business' or 'voluntary organisation' captured something more modest. They described activity on the margins of a mainstream with primarily a welfare function ... They were not seen as part of the economy (as they were not motivated by job generation, entrepreneurship, meeting consumer demand, or producing profit), nor were they seen as political (promoting citizenship, or empowerment). Their role was to see to the welfare of the marginalised.[3]

In October 2001, however, the UK government launched a Social Enterprise Unit within the (then) Department of Trade and Industry (DTI) (now BERR). In May 2006 this was brought together with the Active Communities Unit in the Home Office to form a new Office of the Third Sector, the creation of which reflected 'the government's recognition of the value, influence and importance of the third sector'.[4] In October 2001 the European Commission also established a Social Economy Unit in Directorate General (DG) XXIII.

According to the (then) DTI in 2002, 'social enterprises create new goods and services and develop opportunities for markets where mainstream businesses cannot, or will not, go'.[5]

Illustration 1.2 (cont'd)

In 2003 the Scottish Executive published 'A Review of the Scottish Executive's Policies to Promote the Social Economy' which set out 'the Government's vision for the social economy ... and the strategic priorities necessary to help the social economy realise its full potential'.[6]

In its Annual Review 2005, Social Enterprise London reported that it had become 'the UK's one-hundredth Community Interest Company' and that it had

- 'built a network of social enterprises, including institutions like Borough Market and "hot spots" like Jamie Oliver's Fifteen';

- 'produced the first Social Enterprise Directory';

- 'launched the Social Enterprise Journal';

- 'and held events to publicise and support social enterprise almost every week of the year'.[7]

In Northern Ireland the organisation that was called the Northern Ireland Co-operative Development Agency is now the Social Economy Agency. In 2006, Invest NI, the Northern Ireland government's business development agency, announced a two-year programme of support for the social economy sector.

---

other terminology is used as well (see Table 1.1). This variety of terms may be a reflection of the interest in the subject although the terms are not only varied but also varyingly defined, and are occasionally the subject of disagreement.

This interest in the social economy and its various ramifications has arisen not because the social enterprises in it are necessarily new types of organisation or are engaging in any new areas of activity, but because there is a new appreciation of the apparent potential of this section of the economy to address some of the problems in, or of, society. Despite this potential, and despite the history of some of the organisations which might now be considered to be in the social

Table 1.1   Some current terminology

Association	Not-for-profit
Charity	Not-for-profit-distribution
Community business	Social enterprise
Community enterprise	Social economy
Community interest company	Social economy business
Community sector	Social economy enterprise
Company limited by guarantee	Social entrepreneur
Co-operative	Social entrepreneurship
Foundation	Third sector
Mutual	Voluntary organisation
Non-profit	Voluntary sector

economy, it was, until recently, often overlooked in economic analysis, at least in the UK, and there are a number of probable reasons for this:

It is a very disparate area. The social economy does not have a clear homogeneity, as is indicated by the differing definitions of it (see Chapter 4) and the variety of social enterprises and other organisations within it.

There was no agreed vocabulary with which to discuss it. It is hard to discuss a subject without having agreed words in common with which to refer to it.

There was little information about it. Many social enterprises have been created, operated and closed without leaving clear records of their presence. They have not been officially categorised and the statistical information on them which has been collected has been fragmentary and incomplete.

Attention has been focused either on the public or on the private sector, or on the comparison between them. The socialist economic systems of formerly 'communist' countries focused on the public sector and their failure was seen by many to demonstrate the superiority of capitalism and of the private sector. At the same time in countries such as the USA and the UK, which actually had mixed economies, there was an emerging political emphasis on the supposed efficiency of the private sector and its economic development potential. There was therefore an emphasis on enterprise and markets and a desire, where possible, to transfer activity from the public to the private sector under the banner of privatisation. All this has tended to highlight the economic value of the private sector, and to contrast it with many parts of the public sector and, as a result, to overshadow other areas which were in neither the public sector nor the private sector.

Social economy organisations rarely make the headlines. Almost all social enterprises and other organisations of which the social economy is comprised are relatively small and few of them receive much publicity, whether for good or bad reasons. It has been the larger private sector organisations which, because of their successes or spectacular failures, have featured in the headlines, often because of the large amounts of money involved. Similarly, large public sector organisations, such as government departments, have also featured in press stories, again often because they have lost money or otherwise been shown to impact on a large scale. In contrast, many social enterprises, because they are small, have not been worthy of individual attention, even when they too have had successes and failures.

However, recently interest in the social economy has grown, as the perception of the benefits and the economic contribution of the area of activity has widened. This is not unlike the rise of interest in small businesses which occurred in the 1980s. There always had been small businesses since businesses began but it was not until the end of the 1970s, when Birch published the results of his research into employment in the US, that significant interest in them as a distinct sector of business began to develop. The second half of the 1970s was a time of rising unemployment and so, when Birch concluded that it was those small firms employing up to 100 people which had in the 1970s created over 80 per cent of the net new jobs,[8] governments took notice. Not least because of that link to employment creation, small businesses became the subject of much attention and many new programmes. Since the link was highlighted, small businesses have arguably become the most researched and supported part of the business spectrum. Some key dates in the emergence of interest in the social economy have been outlined in Table 1.2.

Social enterprises also have an economic impact which, like that of small businesses, had been largely unrecognised for a long time, and they too employ people. Now, though, the scale of the sector is being assessed and some attempts being made to assess its impact. As Chapter 2 will show, social enterprises are not a new phenomenon and, at the beginning of the twentieth century, what has also been referred to as civic society was relied on, in places like the UK, for income and welfare security which the state was not then providing. However, this voluntary provision was uneven and unpredictable, and one consequence of the economic changes later that century, together with the emergence of the welfare state funded by tax revenues from increasing prosperity, was that many welfare functions were taken over by the state. As a result, 'civil society came to be seen as the area of self-help, associational activity and social life, not that of economic activity or

Table 1.2   Some key dates

Emergence of the co-operative movement in the UK	1880s
Possible first use of the term 'social capital' in the US	1961
First European conference of Co-operatives, Mutuals and Associations	1978
Establishment of Social Economy Unit within EU DGXXIII	1989
Establishment of the Social Exclusion Unit to help the UK government reduce social exclusion	1997
OECD report on social enterprises	1999
Social Enterprise Unit set up within the UK Department of Trade and Industry	2001
UK Prime Minister Blair hosts a social enterprise breakfast at 10 Downing Street	2002
UK Department of Trade and Industry publishes *Social Enterprise: a strategy for success*	2002
The publication in Scotland of the Scottish Executive's Social Economy Review	2003
Launch of the *Social Enterprise Journal*, the first journal dedicated to social enterprise	2005
New Office of the Third Sector formed within the UK government's Cabinet Office	2006
Publication by the Office of the Third Sector of *Social enterprise action plan: Scaling new heights*	2006
Publication by the UK government of *The future role of the third sector in social and economic regeneration: final report* to provide 'a vision of how the state and the third sector working together ... can bring about real change' and the announcement of an investment of over £500 million 'to make this vision a reality'.[9]	2007

preparation for it', although this was less the case in other parts of Europe (see Illustration 1.3).[10]

Towards the end of the twentieth century cracks had appeared in the welfare state. It often seemed to be hampered by its associated bureaucracy, it appeared sometimes to encourage dependency instead of enterprise, and it appeared to be unable to reach some areas of social exclusion such as persistent long-term unemployment. In these circumstances the potential of the social economy seemed again to be attractive, in particular its economic contribution including employment and its supposed ability to reach those social parts that other initiatives cannot reach.

Indications of the scale and impact of the sector

It was not that social economy organisations had not employed people before the end of the twentieth century, just that the totality of their economic contribution, and particularly of their employment impact, had not been recognised. Since then it has been estimated that in 1995 there were nearly 1.5 million full-time equivalent employees in the UK's 'non-profit sector'[11] and in 2005 it was claimed that in the UK social enterprises generated about £18 billion in annual turnover and employed more than 775,000 people.[12]

In 2004 the third sector was reported to be the fastest-growing part of the US economy.[13] In Canada a rough estimate in 2005 was that the social economy accounted for about 2.6 per cent of the total Canadian economy, which was larger than aerospace (0.6%), mining (1.0%) and the pulp and paper industries (1.3%) and about the same size as oil and gas extraction (2.5%).[14] The European Commission estimated that in 2007 around 10 million people were employed in the Social Economy in the European Union[15] and in 2006 it was estimated that in France the social economy employed about 7 per cent of the workforce.[16]

The social economy is not the biggest sector of the economy but it is nevertheless a significant sector in many countries. In addition, the social economy appears to be able to provide not just jobs and economic activity but jobs in deprived areas and with associated social benefits. It appears to be able to respond to opportunities to establish economic activity where the private sector could, or would, not operate. As Amin et al. have suggested,[17] as well as this ability to avail of 'market opportunities' to address needs not met by the public and private sectors, there were other expectations of the social economy:

- It had a potential role in building social capital, which was seen as an ability and capacity to enhance economic efficiency and collective engagement.
- It helped to build participatory democracy.
- It supported a counter-culture of survival and transformation on the margins of capitalism.

These are among the reasons why the social economy and the rest of the third sector (see later section in this chapter) matter and why there is interest in them.

It is why in the UK the prime minister described them, in his introduction to the report on the future role of the third sector in social and economic regeneration, as being 'at the heart of society'.[18]

Illustration 1.3   European Recognition

In the late 1980s the Economic and Social Committee of the European Commission commissioned research into the social economy sector which led in 1989 to the establishment of the Social Economy Unit within DG XXIII. Following that move the Commission gave increasing recognition to problems such as social exclusion and the potential of the social economy to address them, and 'the concept of the "third system", was adopted as a formal policy strategy ... although it was deliberately vaguely specified, so that it can explicitly subsume a variety of different terms with broadly the same meaning':[19]

> Third system, third sector, social economy, community development, local development and employment initiatives, local and territorial pacts for employment, endogenous local development, sustainable economy ... the abundance of terms used to describe a group of innovative phenomena shows the current froth around a set of largely unknown realities.[20]

However, although the realities were described as 'unknown', the Commission nevertheless attempted to define the organisations in the 'third system':

> These organisations aim to find solutions rather then [sic] to place themselves in a new market sector;
>
> They often refer to factors such as social solidarity, democratic organisations or the primacy of the individual over capital;
>
> These organisations are *often the result of public/private partnerships and have a close relationship with their local communities;*
>
> The market is not their sole source of income with organisations securing public subsidies, donations or loans – they often have very *mixed income;*
>
> Specific attention is often given to *disadvantaged* people by these organisations;
>
> These organisations are often small-scale structures often with larger numbers of non-active associates or unpaid *volunteers.*
>
> Finally, the most important factor which justifies the growing interest in this type of initiative naturally concerns their close relationship to the development of new types of jobs, mainly linked to satisfying new personal and collective needs which neither the public not the market can currently meet.[21] (emphases in the original)

The association with social capital

The UK government's Office of the Third Sector, announced in 2006, was formed within the Cabinet Office under the Chancellor of the Duchy of Lancaster, whose responsibilities include 'the third sector as well as co-ordinating the government's work to tackle social exclusion'.[22]

'Social enterprises provide a mechanism for bringing excluded groups into the labour market' – Patricia Hewitt, UK Secretary of State for Trade and Industry.[23]

Social enterprises are able to harness the power of local communities, catalysing regeneration and promoting active citizenship – Social Enterprise Coalition.[24]

'Northern Ireland's social economy does a lot more than achieve a good financial balance sheet and employ upwards of 30,000 people. It promotes human and social capital, the glue that holds communities together in time of difficulty and helps them respond positively to change.'[25]

There is a recognition that the process of establishing and operating a business needs more than just money. One formula offered to describe this was 'Success = Idea + Know How + Know Who',[26] and that 'know who' is the ability to network to make contact with and cultivate the people who can help to provide, or to source, information, guidance, sponsorship, support, credibility, control, customers, suppliers and resources. These interpersonal links and the knowledge of who can help to move an issue forward have been labelled 'social capital', which indicates both that it is an essential capital requirement for a successful enterprise and also that it is not part of a business's financial capital. Also, just as successful private sector businesses, once started, can increase their financial capital, so too, it is suggested, successful social enterprises can generate more social capital. The concept of social capital has also been linked to that of civic society in that both refer to people acting together and using networks of people to advance causes (see Chapter 7).

The term 'social capital', it has been claimed, was first used in 1961[27] although the concept behind it was recognised in the nineteenth century. However, it is still a rather indistinct concept, without a single accepted definition. It has been equated not just to the sort of networking and com-munity participation described above, but also to a culture of trust. Never-theless, if it is a capital which is necessary for starting businesses, its apparent lack has been suggested as a reason why it is hard to get enterprises started in deprived areas and why providing financial assistance for such areas is not alone enough. Thus, the argument goes, if the social exclusion of such areas is to be addressed, their social capital needs to be built up and, if the social economy can help to build social capital, it should be promoted and supported.

The assumption of the third sector

> We need to recognise anew ... the importance of the one to one, face to face, not impersonal but personal care, the support from families, neighbourhoods and voluntary organisations that are often the difference between success and failure and the support that demonstrates both the limits of markets and the limits of state action.
>
> So in future I want ... a new compact that elevates the third sector as partner, not as ... a cut price alternative to government, but government fulfilling its responsibilities to fund services and fully valuing the contribution the voluntary sector can make.
>
> From Gordon Brown's speech, as Chancellor of the Exchequer,
> to the Labour Party Conference 2006.

The impression given in almost any traditional economic textbook is that there are two sectors in an economy: the private and the public sector. Even recently a book titled *Modern Economics* still contained the following statement:

> In examining how a mixed economy works, it is convenient to distinguish between the 'private sector' and the 'public sector'. The former consists of those firms which are privately owned. The latter includes government departments, local authorities, and public bodies such as the Environment Agency. All are distinguished by the fact that their capital is publicly owned and their policies can be influenced through the ultimate supply of funds by the government.[28]

There are many organisations, such as social enterprises, which do not seem to fit into either of these categories. They are not public bodies and so do not belong in the public sector, but their capital is not privately owned and, although they may trade, they exist for a social purpose rather than to make money for their owners, and so they do not appear to fit in with private sector firms either. In the past it seems that the dilemma of where they belong in an economy may, to some extent, have been avoided by ignoring them but, now that their impact is being highlighted, that is less easy to do.

These organisations may not be in either the public or the private sector but they, nevertheless, have an economic impact and are part of the economy because they spend money, because many of them employ people and, in some cases, because they generate income by trading. Also, when we start to look for them, we find there are a lot of them. Table 1.3 lists just a few.

Table 1.3   Organisations and activities not in the public or private sectors

Amateur dramatic clubs	Mountain rescue services
Building preservation trusts	National Trust
Co-operatives	Oxfam
Donkey sanctuaries	Professional associations
Enterprise agencies	Quakers
Fair trade companies	Rotary clubs
Golf clubs	Scouts
Hospices	Trades unions
Independent schools	University colleges
St John Ambulance	Voluntary Service Overseas
Knights of St Columbanus	Women's Institute
Lifeboat service	Youth clubs

Note: The organisations and activities in this table are all part of the economy because they trade, buy things and/or employ people. However, if the economy is thought only to consist of the private sector, in which organisations trade in order to make profits for their owners, and the public sector, in which organisations use public funding to deliver government services for the benefit of those who need them, then where do these organisations belong? (See also Table 3.1 for an expanded list.)

All of these organisations have to generate enough income to sustain themselves, but their purpose is not fundamentally concerned with making money. Some of these organisations, such as churches, have been around for a very long time, longer than any private sector businesses, but they have not been widely thought of as comprising a specific sector, possibly because, as noted earlier, of the lack of language with which to make that distinction. Now the words needed are starting to appear, and the terms 'social economy' and 'social enterprise' are just two examples. However, not all the organisations listed are considered by everyone to be social enterprises, or to be in the social economy, but, nevertheless, like the social economy, they do not belong in either of the two previously identified sectors of the economy. Therefore reference is increasingly being made to the 'third sector' to which, it is assumed, such organisations will all belong.

The use in this way of the term 'the third sector', or sometimes 'the third system' or 'the third way', also appears to be quite modern. Organisations are considered to be in this sector, not so much because they all share similar features which suggest that they should be considered together, but because they fit into neither of the other two sectors. Not all these organisations have traditionally seen themselves, though, as being part of the same sector, and some co-operatives apparently still refer to themselves as being in the fourth sector.[29]

The third sector is therefore an inclusive concept designed to cover all those organisations which are in neither the public nor the private sector. The terms 'third system' and 'third way' are also used to refer to this part of the economy, and the organisations in it can be variously described as non-profit, not-for-profit or not-for-profit-distribution (see also Chapter 3). Whatever term is used it covers a wider range of organisations which, taken together, have a significant impact on our lives.

The acclaimed benefits

The above explanation might be summarised as the suggestion that there is, in an economy, a 'third sector', separate from the public and private sectors, which includes a wide variety of organisations established for social and other purposes, such as the pursuit of artistic, sporting, environmental, ethical or cultural objectives. A particular area within the third sector is the social economy, which is said to help to build social capital, which is in turn necessary to help to address social exclusion. However, that might also be said of some other organisations in the third sector, which are all, in any case, considered to be in an economic sector because they have some form of economic impact, and the consequent potential to provide economic benefit.

Thus the third sector has the potential to provide a variety of contributions, the recognition of which explains why interest in it has grown. It is relevant in this introduction to try to list and summarise some of the main benefits claimed for it, although it is not claimed that all organisations in the third sector provide all these benefits, and there are areas of overlap amongst them (see also Chapter 9).

The provision of goods, services and social benefits which the public sector does not adequately provide

Third sector organisations often attempt to meet basic needs and improve people's lives. In the past, hospitals were often in the third sector before there was a public health service, and hospices often still are. Third sector organisations have for a long time been active in the education field and some still run 'specialist' schools such as faith schools and integrated schools.

Third sector organisations may see the need to act to improve things before governments do and, currently, that is particularly noticeable in the area of the environment. Schools and hospitals are also examples of initiatives which were pioneered in the third sector and only later taken over by the public sector once they were shown to be addressing a clear need. Third sector organisations are also active in areas such as arts, culture and sports which people welcome but which often do not offer enough financial return to attract private sector investment. And, of course, while religion has in the past been closely aligned with the state in many countries, and might have been considered to have been part of the public sector, it would now generally be considered to be in the third sector.

The provision of jobs for people who might not otherwise be employed

While the private and public sectors also provide employment, the third sector often provides jobs for people who might not find employment easily in either of the other two sectors. Jamie Oliver's Fifteen Foundation deliberately recruits unemployed young people to train for jobs in its restaurants in order to give them a start which they might not otherwise have got. Other social enterprises deliberately try to employ people from disadvantaged areas or people with particular disabilities. Many of these organisations would be categorised as Intermediate Labour Market (ILM) organisations and often access national and European funding for such initiatives.

The fostering of enterprise and innovation

The social economy is thought to help to foster new and better ways of doing things, particularly in more marginalised areas. The evidence for this is said to be seen in a positive correlation between the strength of social enterprises and that of the local mainstream economy,[30] although such a correlation does not indicate what of this is cause and what is effect. It is thus recognised that many individuals wish to display their entrepreneurial abilities through projects with a social purpose and the third sector can foster such entrepreneurship.

A means for addressing some problems of the welfare state

The third sector is seen to have the potential to complement public service delivery by addressing some needs without the drawbacks which had become apparent in the welfare state system of public sector provision. Amin et al. suggest a number of reasons why the principle of a universal welfare state was, towards the end of the twentieth century, being reconsidered. These included the following:

- Economic growth was faltering and so the employment prospects of the more excluded were reducing.
- Tax revenues were threatened and objections were being raised to the use of tax revenues for universal welfare and income redistribution.
- The welfare state was seen as a choiceless option and more people wanted choice.
- Political parties were starting to reject the idea of the all-providing state and suggested that it fostered a culture of dependency and entitlement.[31]

For reasons such as these the third sector has been seen sometimes as having the potential to provide more efficient and more effective delivery of public services.

The promotion of environmental sustainability, or ethical operations

Whereas some social enterprises are formed specifically to deliver environmental benefits, others at least try to operate in environmentally sustainable ways or to promote ethical behaviour. A building preservation trust, for instance, may have been formed specifically to restore a particular building but it will often try to do so in a way which causes a minimum of consequential environmental damage. Although social enterprises often struggle financially, and so do not want to pay more than absolutely necessary for a good or service, they are not institutionally bound always to select the lowest cost route and they are often closer to those who might be most affected by their actions. Fair trade organisations, for instance, deliberately try to pay an above-market price for their supplies, where the market price is thought to be unfairly low.

The creation of social capital and social cohesion

As indicated above, it has been suggested that social capital is an essential, but often overlooked, prerequisite for success in an enterprising venture, whichever sector it is in. It has also been suggested that it is a lack of social capital that explains why the provision of financial capital, through grants, has often not been enough, on its own, to help ventures in deprived areas. Thus the idea that social enterprises can generate social capital, in parallel with the way that financial ventures can generate financial capital, and that social capital can also help to develop social cohesion, is seen as indicating another important benefit which they have to offer.

Other development help

As well as building social capital it is also argued that the social economy, and other third sector organisations, can offer services to the local economy or help local developments in other ways. The provision of start-up workspace, work preparation training for unemployed people, and child-care provision are all activities often undertaken by social enterprises which can, in turn, benefit other businesses in that area.

The ability to reach parts that other initiatives cannot reach

As well as the provision of both economic and social benefits, there is another feature of at least part of the social economy which is often of interest to governments, and that is its geographic dimension. As their name suggests, community businesses are linked to communities and, although that can refer to an 'interest'-based community, it is usually a place-based concept at least in terms of the employment and other benefits provided by the organisations concerned and it is the locality focus typical of some social enterprises that is 'the thread that connects them to disadvantaged neighbourhoods'.[32] Governments have noted that many social enterprises and/or community businesses have been established in areas of need and it has been said that the major objectives of social enterprises are to provide goods and services which the market or public sector is either unwilling or unable to provide, to develop skills, to create employment and to foster pathways to integration for socially excluded people.[33]

There are several aspects of the social economy which, to some extent at least, have been thought to have an impact on deprivation. As a result, as one analysis suggests,

> It is becoming seen as a holistic solution for social exclusion in a number of ways. First, by encouraging collective self help, confidence and capacity building, and nurturing

the collective values of the economy via socially useful production. Second, by humanising the economy via an emphasis upon autonomy, associated values, and organising the economy at a 'human' scale. Third, by enhancing democracy and participation via a decentralisation of policy to local communities and places. Fourth, by bringing about a greater degree of systemic coherence to the local economy via the local production and consumption of goods and services. Fifth, by acknowledging the relationships between economy, environment, politics, and society.[34]

There has therefore been a tendency to see social enterprise as capable of reaching the parts that other initiatives cannot reach. It is as if it might be a sort of magic bullet for targeting social exclusion and reducing deprivation.

A mechanism for a counter-culture

As the previous point suggests there can be a strong political dimension to some of the benefits claimed for the third sector, or at last for some of its components. The social economy in particular is claimed by some to provide components of a counter-culture to respond to drawbacks of capitalism. Graefe suggests that the social economy was 'once advanced by social democratic and radical academics as a core element of an alternative to neoliberalism',[35] and according to Amin et al.,

> There is a long utopian tradition in favour of the organisation of society around needs, self-autonomy, and social and ecological balance. This utopian view reacts against the capitalist emphasis on individual greed, profit and market value rather than social need. As Fordism slid into crisis, this counter culture gained momentum … (and) some intellectuals even argued that 'the end of work' after Fordism offered a major opportunity to shift social organisation in this direction.[36]

The agenda of this book

If the wording of the above list of benefits suggests that some of what is claimed about the social economy, and about its links and effects, might be more supposition than proven fact, that is intentional. Because the interest in the sector is relatively new, because there has not yet been an enormous amount of research into it (compared to, say, the small business sector) and because it seems to suit some people's agenda but not others', there still appears sometimes to be an element of politics, wishful thinking and controversy in what is said about it. There is disagreement, for instance, about definitions of the social economy and there are disputes about what should and should not be considered to be a social enterprise and what constitutes a 'community' in a community enterprise.

In any emerging field of study it takes time for information gained to be analysed and, despite considerable discussion and research, that information is not always converted into relevant and shared knowledge. Like the example of small businesses already mentioned, when interest in such a field grows, it is not always based on good knowledge and areas of ignorance will remain. There will be a variety of approaches, alternative theories and opinions, and differing vocabularies. In such an evolving field it can be hard to find a general introduction to help newcomers to make sense of the debate and to serve as a starting point for further exploration. This book is an attempt to do that.

The geography of the sector

Because there is such a jumble of definitions and of facts, supposition and wishful thinking, Part I tries to map out the main concepts and the relationships between the social economy and the third sector, and between the third sector and the rest of an economy. In effect, it tries to describe the 'geography' of the field by indicating what is in it and where it is positioned. It starts, in Chapter 2, with an overall look at an economy exploring the way the different sectors in it might have evolved and the key components and concepts in, or associated with, them.

Chapter 3 looks at the third sector within the totality of an economy by examining it alongside the private and public sectors. It explores the range of organisations that operate within it. Chapter 4 examines that part of the third sector which is sometimes referred to as the social economy and considers varied views of what should, or should not, be included within it. It explores the things which those organisations included in the social economy have in common, and those which are said to distinguish them from the rest of the third sector.

The ecology of the sector

Part II looks at some concepts and issues in more detail in what might be described as the 'ecology' of the sector because it looks at how things behave, how they relate to other things and how they might therefore be influenced. Chapter 5 examines the nature of third sector organisations including their legal structures, aims, methods and management; and Chapter 6 considers their funding and includes a critique of sources of finance from micro-level support to venture capital, including the role of social business angels and other funding mechanisms.

A key area of potential linkages is explored in Chapter 7, which explores the concept of social capital and the evolution of some of the theories about it and how it might be linked to a wider socio-political concern for the health of civic society. Governments, and other stakeholders, are often interested in influencing and promoting the development of the third sector, so Chapter 8 explores the main issues associated with this intervention including both why it is tried and what methods have been used to effect it. At the end of this part, Chapter 9 reviews the impact the sector is supposed to have and the evidence for that impact.

The future

Finally, as a conclusion, Chapter 10 offers some thoughts about the future of the sector. It looks at some of the issues, both inside the sector and external to it, which are potentially relevant to that future and considers what their impact might be.

Key Points of Chapter 1

- The social economy has a long history but has, until recently, received relatively little economic attention.
- The language with which to describe the social economy and its components has been limited, but is now starting to evolve.
- The social economy has been linked to social capital, which in turn has been suggested as a key requirement for successful attempts to address social exclusion.
- Organisations which belong in neither the public nor the private sector of an economy are considered to form a third sector. The social economy can be variously considered to be either a part of this 'third sector' or synonymous with it.
- Interest in the third sector is now growing because it appears that

  a) Its size and impact are economically significant.

  b) It, or parts of it, can provide benefits such as the following:

    – complementing public service delivery and providing services and social benefits which might not otherwise be provided;
    – providing jobs for people who might not otherwise be employed;
    – assisting environmental sustainability and ethical business;
    – creating social capital and fostering social cohesion;
    – fostering enterprise and social and economic regeneration;
    – providing an alternative system (which might better suit a political agenda).

  c) It can provide these benefits for areas and parts of the system that other sectors cannot reach. In particular, it is supposed that it can help to reduce social exclusion and counter deprivation.

Questions, Exercises, Essay and Discussion Topics

1. Most colleges were founded and endowed to provide education. They have to secure enough income from their endowments and the services they provide to maintain their operations. They do not remit profit to individuals and they re-use any surpluses to enhance their activities. Are they social enterprises?

2. Does the language currently available provide clarity or cause confusion about the social economy and the third sector?

3. If the social economy and/or the third sector are so beneficial, why have they been overlooked for so long?

4. What might a government hope to get from its support for social enterprises?

5. What would life be like without the third sector?

6. Why might someone want to start a social enterprise?

SUGGESTIONS FOR FURTHER READING

A. Amin, A. Cameron and R. Hudson, *Placing the Social Economy* (London: Routledge, 2002).

J. Pearce, *Social Enterprise in Anytown* (London: Calouste Gulbenkian Foundation, 2003).

References

1. A. Molloy, C. McFeely and E. Connolly, *Building a Social Economy for the New Millenium* (Derry: Guildhall Press/NICDA Social Economy Agency, 1999), p. 5.
2. P. Graefe, 'The social economy and the state: linking ambitions with institutions in Québec, Canada' in *Policy and Politics*, Vol. 30, No. 2 (Bristol, UK: The Policy Press, 2002), p. 247.
3. A. Amin, A. Cameron and R. Hudson, *Placing the Social Economy* (London: Routledge, 2002), p. 2.
4. Letter (undated) issued by the Cabinet Office after the relevant reshuffle to explain the changes.
5. *Social Enterprise: a strategy for success* (London: Department of Trade and Industry, 2002), p. 21.
6. On www.scotland.gov.uk/Topics/People/Voluntary-Issues (accessed 11 July 06).
7. Social Enterprise London, *Annual Review 2005*, on www.sel.org.uk (accessed 20 September 06).
8. For more on this see chapter 1 of S. Bridge, K. O'Neill and S. Cromie, *Understanding Enterprise, Entrepreneurship and Small Business* (Basingstoke: Palgrave Macmillan, 2003).
9. HM Treasury/Cabinet Office, *The Future Role of the Third Sector in Social and Economic Regeneration: Final Report*, HM Treasury, July 2007.
10. A. Amin, R. Hudson and A. Cameron, *Placing the Social Economy* (London: Routledge, 2002), p. 3.
11. J. Kendall, *The Voluntary Sector* (London: Routledge, 2003), p. 23.
12. Taken from the draft speech to have been given by Barry Gardiner, Minister for Competitiveness in DTI, at the BLU/SBS seminar on *Passion, Entrepreneurship and the Rebirth of Local Economies* with Dr Ernesto Sirolli in London on 10 November 2005.
13. C. Gunn, *Third Sector Development: Making up for the Market* (USA: Cornell University, 2004), p. viii.
14. *What We Need to Know About the Social Economy: A Guide for Policy Research*, Canadian Government, Policy Research Initiative, July 2005, p. 3.
15. http://ec.europe.eu/enterprise/entrepreneurship/social_economy.htm (accessed 3 August 2007).
16. GHK, *Social Enterprise: An International Literature Review* (a report for the Social Enterprise Unit) March 2006, p. 18.
17. A. Amin, R. Hudson and A. Cameron, *Placing the Social Economy* (London: Routledge, 2002), pp. 6–8.
18. HM Treasury/Cabinet Office, *The Future Role of the Third Sector in Social and Economic Regeneration: Final Report*, HM Treasury, July 2007.
19. Commission of the European Communities, *The Third System and Employment: A First Reflection* (Brussels: European Commission, 1998), p. 4 – quoted by A. Amin, R. Hudson and A. Cameron, *Placing the Social Economy* (London: Routledge, 2002), p. 21.
20. Ibid.
21. Ibid.
22. From an undated letter about the new Office of the Third Sector issued by the Cabinet Office in 2006.
23. From the introduction to *Social Enterprise: a strategy for success* (London: Department of Trade and Industry, 2002), p. 7.
24. *There's More to Business*, Social Enterprise Coalition. www.socialenterprise.org.uk.

25. P. McGill writing in *Scope* (Belfast: NICVA, September 2000), p. 12.

26. R. Peterson and R. Rondstadt, 'A Silent Strength: Entrepreneurial Know-Who', The 16th ESBS, efmd IMD Report (86/4), p. 11.

27. J. Jacobs, *The Death and Life of Great American Cities* (New York: Random House, 1961).

28. J. Harvey, *Modern Economics* (Basingstoke: Macmillan, 1998), p. 22.

29. C. Gunn, *Third Sector Development: Making up for the Market* (USA: Cornell University, 2004), p. 6.

30. A. Amin, R. Hudson and A. Cameron, *Placing the Social Economy* (London: Routledge, 2002), p. 119.

31. Ibid., p. 5.

32. D. Smallbone, M. Evans, I. Ekanem and S. Butters, *Researching Social Enterprise* (Sheffield: Small Business Service, Research Report RR004/01, July 2001), p. 5.

33. Department of Environment, Transport and the Regions, *Community Enterprise: Good Practice Guide* (London: DETR, 1999).

34. A. Amin, R. Hudson and A. Cameron, *Placing the Social Economy* (London: Routledge, 2002), pp. 19, 20.

35. P. Graefe, 'The Social Economy and the State: Linking Ambitions with Institutions in Quebec: Canada', *Politics and Policy*, Vol. 30, No. 2 (2002), p. 248.

36. A. Amin, R. Hudson and A. Cameron, *Placing the Social Economy* (London: Routledge, 2002), p. 8.

Part I
The Geography of the Third Sector

Part I of this book tries to map out the main concepts associated with, and the relationships between, the social economy and the third sector, and between the third sector and the rest of the economy. In effect it tries to describe the 'geography' of the field by indicating what is in it and where it is positioned.

It starts with an overall look at an economy in Chapter 2. This chapter explores the way the different sectors in it might have evolved and the key components and concepts associated with them. It looks at the way in which they have been presented and contrasts the way they have been defined and/or described by different stakeholders in, or observers of, the sector.

Chapter 3 then looks at the third sector within the totality of an economy by examining it alongside the private and public sectors. It explores the range of organisations which operate within it.

Following that, Chapter 4 examines that part of the third sector which is sometimes referred to as the social economy. It considers varied views of what should, or should not, be included within the social economy. It explores the things which those organisations included in it have in common, and what is said to distinguish them from the rest of the third sector.

What is in an Economy?

2

Key Concepts

This chapter covers

- the emergence, as economies have developed, of different sectors of activity;

- the way that a focus on the private and public sectors has tended to ignore those organisations which belong to neither. They have been said to be in the 'third' sector;

- the evolution of the language for describing these other organisations and their place in the economy;

- the lack of distinct sector boundaries because the sectors themselves are inevitably somewhat fuzzy constructs;

(cont'd)

- economic activity is the result of people trying to satisfy a variety of needs in a variety of ways and it is not predetermined or constrained by artificial sector concepts.

Learning Objectives

By the end of this chapter the reader should

- understand how different economic sectors have evolved;
- appreciate the range of economic activity that does not fall within either the private or the public sector;
- be aware of the limitation of traditional economic language and analysis when considering 'third sector' activities;
- recognise that, in any case, the variety of human needs means that their economic activities are not always going to fall into predetermined categories.

Introduction

Many people will be familiar with the concept that within most economies there are distinct public and private sectors, but not so familiar with the concept that there are parts of economies which belong in neither of those sectors. Those parts which are neither public nor private are now sometimes referred to as the third sector and within it are those activities often referred to as the social economy. However, as Chapter 1 indicated, that vocabulary is of relatively recent origin. Before that, without appropriate words, it was difficult to distinguish, and thus to discuss, third sector activities, and even the distinction between the public and the private sectors of economic activity has arisen relatively recently in the context of human history.

This chapter therefore starts by looking at how distinctions between different areas of economic activity may have arisen. That provides a context in which the third sector, and within it the social economy, can be considered in more detail.

The evolution of an economy

Economics has been defined as 'the study of how people allocate their limited resources to provide for their wants'[1] and an economy is a system within which people do that allocation. But when did the different sectors of an economy evolve? It would seem that, in the early stages of their existence as a distinct species, human beings were all nomadic hunter-gatherers moving around in family bands in search of food. They worked directly to use their resources, such as their time and skills, to provide the food, shelter, warmth and other things that they wanted. This work was probably undertaken on a 'all for one and one for all' basis and, while it might be supposed that individuals would vary in their relative ability to undertake different tasks, there would have been little specialisation and all organised activity must have happened within the family context. Trying to draw distinctions in that situation between public and private sector work would have been meaningless.

Recent observations of surviving hunter-gatherer societies indicate that, although occasionally more food may be obtained than can be consumed in the short term, such surpluses were of little use as they could not be stored and/or protected for any length of time either as an investment for the future or for exchange with others. Probably because food procured by some members of the group could not be put aside to trade for the work of others, it is also found that in such societies there were few or no full-time specialists. Almost everyone engaged in all the work of the society.

The next big stage in economic evolution was the advent of farming and, although observation has also shown that hunter-gatherers may have needed to work for fewer hours a day than farmers, nevertheless farming may have become necessary because it could support greater population densities. With the change from hunter-gathering to agriculture, societies became more settled, surpluses could be stored and guarded, and non-food-producing specialists began to emerge, including eventually rulers and bureaucrats. Families may have grouped together as tribes, and agriculture led to larger, denser and stratified societies,[2] but the kinship basis for groups may have persisted with no significant human organisation existing outside the extended family or tribe. That must have continued as long as tribal society survived and, for instance, even when Christianity first came to Ireland, it was established on a clan basis, although its missionaries, such as Patrick, would have known of the continental model in which bishops, rather than civic leaders, had the overall authority for church functions. One surviving feature from those times, it is suggested, is the traditional Irish Meitheal (lit. 'working party') system of mutual support among farmers, especially at harvest time, which was therefore an early system of co-operative working.[3]

Eventually, even tribes grouped together as larger units and, once the superior authority of kings and other rulers became established, it meant that some activity of, or for, government clearly took place outside the family. This activity of government could be described as work to provide for some of society's needs which was undertaken separately from the work of providing goods, such as food, for consumption. It is here that the beginnings of distinct public sector activity might be found. Today the heart of the public sector is the civil service, and the origins of the British Civil Service, it has been suggested, lie in the court servants that followed the Saxon Kings of England from one resting place to another.[4] It might be argued, though, that they were more personal servants of the monarch than true servants of the public.

Another feature of agriculturally based societies was the emergence of craft workers which led eventually to the establishment of specialised businesses. Many of these would have been family businesses but there were also examples of non-family organisations, such as monasteries, producing goods such as beverages for their own consumption but with a surplus which could be traded with others. Once such ventures grew bigger than the family, or had a regular surplus to trade, they too might be distinguished as a separate economic activity. The East India Company, which derived its powers from a Royal Charter of 1599, is an early example of one such business clearly being established with a separate legal identity (and see Case 2.3 for the example of a company which can trace its origins back as far as 1189). Consequently, at that stage, a distinction could clearly be made between that economic activity outside the family which was organised for private gain and that which was organised for, or by, the state, even if some of our current terminology for these activities had not yet been established.

A snapshot of the economy of England at the end of the seventeenth century can be gained from the work of Gregory King, who was at one time secretary to the Commissioners for Public Accounts and who produced an estimate for the population and wealth of England in 1688 (which is summarised in Table 2.1). It is interesting to note that his main unit for this accounting was the family.

Gregory King does not distinguish between agricultural and non-agricultural labour, which would have been difficult at the time as the 'putting out' system in textiles and other manufacturing sectors distributed industrial work for the underemployed agricultural population to undertake in their homes. Nevertheless perhaps half of the employed population earned their living in agriculture or at least had an attachment to the land, and this proportion would have been much higher in all other countries in Europe except the Netherlands. However, the subsistence sector of the economy appeared to be very small with only a tiny proportion of the population growing and consuming their own food. It would also appear that government expenditure was no more than 5 per cent of national income.[5]

The figures in Table 2.1 show England before the industrial revolution but they do indicate that while at that time traces of family-based subsistence agriculture remained, many people already worked off the land, mostly for someone else, in

Table 2.1   Gregory King's picture of the English economy in 1688

Rank	Families	Individuals	Total income (£)
Lords, knights and gentlemen	16,600	153,000	6,286,000
Professional classes (Church, Navy, Army, office holders)	55,000	308,000	5,280,000
Merchants, traders and shopkeepers	50,000	696,000	4.200,000
Artisans and handicraftsmen	60,000	240,000	2,400,000
Freeholders and farmers	330,000	1,730,000	16,960,000
Labouring and out-servants	364,000	1,275,000	5,460,000
Cottagers and paupers	400,000	1,300,000	2,600,000
Others (common soldiers, common seamen, vagrants)	85,000	250,000	1,550,000

Source: Based on P. Mathias, The First Industrial Nation: An Economic History of Britain 1700–1914 (London: Methuen, 1983), table II, p. 24.

what would now be considered to be the private sector. Only a small proportion worked for the government, in what would now be called the public sector, and much of that employment would have been in the armed services. The industrial revolution, however, caused a huge redeployment from agriculture into industry and by 1801 only about 36 per cent of the labour force was employed in agriculture from which about one-third of the national income was then directly derived. By 1851 those proportions had reduced to about 20 per cent and by 1901 they were only 6–7 per cent.[6] Over the same period, from 1801 to 1901, the proportion of the labour force employed in industry, mining and construction rose from 30 to 46 per cent. In the meantime the proportion working in trade and transport had risen from 11 to 22 per cent but the number employed in public services and the professions stayed the same at about 23 per cent.

As well as agriculture being family based, so too was much of early manufacturing and it was usually financed by re-investment of profits. However, during the nineteenth century, more and more businesses became incorporated and subject to a wider ownership. For instance, only one brewery was listed by the Stock Exchange in 1809 but by 1900 there were 200.[7] That does not mean that all the family businesses disappeared but it does indicate that working for the family had ceased to be the norm for a lot of people.

Public and private sectors, and other activity

It is clear that, by 1900, in the more developed economies most people worked outside the family and that much of this employment, and much economic activity, took place in the private sector with the other significant source of employment apparently being the public services. It seems reasonable therefore to suggest that, between the eighth- and the ninth-century Saxon kings and the eighteenth- and the nineteenth-century industrial revolution, the economy of places like England changed from one in which the vast majority of people provided for their wants through family-based agriculture to one in which there was a distinct private sector. It matched wants with resources through markets for labour as well as for goods and services, together with a public sector which, as well as employing people in the labour market, also used taxation income to provide for other wants.

At the same time as many aspects of economic activity could be separated into distinct public and private sectors, other organisations were also being established outside the family which were run neither for the state nor for private gain. Altruistic charity or other socially beneficial activity carried out neither for direct personal gain nor because of threat or compulsion must have taken place from a very early stage, and establishing permanent sustainable organisations for this might have started with temples and churches. Later, more secular organisations may have emerged. The Romans had colleges for craftsmen, and guilds appeared in Germanic regions as early as the ninth century. The Middle Ages could be said to have had a rich associative life with many countries having forms of corporation, often organised on the basis of trades or professions, and which provided reciprocal mutual support and charity. In England and in much of Western Europe, in medieval times, schools and hospitals were generally run or controlled by the Church. Later, other, secular organisations were founded for such purposes although finding a suitable procedure for creating them officially was not always easy (see Case 2.2). These early schools, universities and hospitals were not state run but, unlike trading companies, they were not established for private monetary gain either, although possibly they did confer on their founders or benefactors gains in conscience, prestige or even favour. (For a well-placed courtier, becoming a benefactor of a college which the monarch was founding might even have had an element of compulsion.) Such activities do not seem to have appeared on the economic 'radar', however, and, even today, economic histories and textbooks often focus largely on the private sector with some reference to the contribution of the public sector.

This involvement of philanthropic individuals and groups in providing for those less well off than themselves was particularly noticeable, in countries like the UK, in the late nineteenth century, which was when the co-operative movement emerged. By the middle of the twentieth century, though, the economies of many developed countries were based on what has been called 'Fordism'.[8] This involved a combination of large businesses producing relatively cheap goods through the economies of scale of mass production, and employing many people for whom they provided jobs for life, together with a welfare state providing many public services funded by the tax revenues from the private sector. By this stage, in many countries, the state had taken over responsibility for many social services such as health and education and most hospitals and schools were in the public sector. Thus there might have seemed to be little need for a third sector.

Despite this, many other areas of activities, such as charity and religion, which were neither public nor private sector had not been taken over by the state. They, together with co-operatives and similar organisations in a number of European countries, continued to exist outside the two sectors, except possibly in 'communist' countries where the public sector took over almost everything. Also, towards the end of the twentieth century, Fordism had become vulnerable to challenges such as rising energy prices, competition from industries in low wage economies, and new technologies. Private sector jobs were being lost while, at the same time, strains were becoming apparent in the bureaucracy of mass state provision of many public services. By the end of the century the ability of the public and private sectors between them to provide for society's needs was thus being questioned and, when the potential contribution of the third sector became apparent, it looked appealing.

The sectors of an economy

Economics may be about allocating resources to address wants, but that has become a very varied activity. In early society all provision for wants was done solely within the family but now not only is some of it done by the private sector and some by the public sector of an economy, but some is also done by a range of organisations which belong to neither of those sectors.

The private sector

In most economies the market has a key role to play in the allocation of resources to meet wants. In such a 'market economy' the allocation of resources is done based on the price consumers are willing to pay, with consumers seeking to pay low prices, other things being equal, and the owner of the resources seeking to produce the goods or services to get as large a reward as possible for their use. This system balances supply and demand and rewards efficiency but is not good for delivering community services such as policing and justice or ensuring that everyone has a basic provision. It also does not address well third-party effects such as pollution.

Nevertheless so many wants are addressed through the market that economic analysis has often concentrated primarily on private sector activity. Private sector organisations are characterised as being owned not by the state but by private individuals or groups of individuals and making profit for their owners by trading in the market place. Such organisations vary enormously in size and scope as the private sector encompasses the following:

- multinational companies;
- larger businesses (established as companies limited by shares);
- smaller businesses (small and medium-sized enterprises – SMEs), including micro businesses, some of which may be companies and some partnerships or sole traders;
- crime and the black economy (crime is an economic activity and is carried out almost entirely for the financial, or other asset, gain of individuals. It may be illegal, but it is still private sector activity).

The public sector

An alternative to a market economy is a 'command economy' in which the production, distribution and pricing of goods and services is decided centrally by an all-powerful planning authority. This can ensure, for instance, that resources are allocated where they are needed, rather than just where they can be paid for. It can provide services such as defence and basic medical care paid for through taxes, but it is bad at matching supply and demand or at providing a very wide range of consumer goods.

A 'command economy' is a public sector economy because government provides the 'all-powerful' planning authority. Even in mixed economies public sector organisations are financed mainly, if not wholly, from the public purse, which is usually derived from taxes. These organisations endeavour to execute government policy and provide services to meet wants in furtherance of that policy. Like private sector organisations, public sector organisations also exist at different levels:

- At an international level there are organisations such as the UN and the EU.
- At the level below that there are national and regional governments and their departments, agencies and executives, including military forces, police services, health services and education systems.

- Then there are local authorities and the activities for which they are responsible, including, possibly, roads, libraries, waste disposal and tourism promotion.
- And then there may be community councils and similar bodies.

The remainder

Most economies are neither purely market economies nor purely command economies. Even in the most capitalist of economies some services, such as defence, are provided on a command basis, and even in communist command economies some individuals still did jobs for each other, even if it was unofficial and discouraged. Most economies are officially mixed economies in which consumer goods are generally provided by the private sector, so decisions on what to produce are directly linked to demand, while services such as defence, policing and justice and basic health and education are centrally provided, together with overall controls on matters like pollution.

Nevertheless the short summary of economic evolution given earlier indicated that in the economies of most societies, in addition to the state (or public) sector and the business (or private) sector, there were a number of other activities. These included the work of those organisations founded for benevolent purposes and the remnants of the original family-based economies, which were not considered to be in either of the two recognised sectors. For this book it is not necessary to establish exactly when distinct public and private sectors emerged, just that they, and the distinction between them, did emerge, and that, even when this did happen, there were already some established activities with an economic impact which fitted into neither of those two categories.

Table 1.3 listed just some of the organisations which fall into neither the public nor the private sector. They range from near–private sector organisations such as co-operatives, some of which do distribute profits to their members (and might therefore be considered really to belong in the private sector), to near–public sector organisations such as hospices and care centres, which deliver services to people on the basis of need and which can be paid for by public funds (and which many people might feel should be undertaken by the public sector itself).

In between those extremes there are a wide range of organisations set up by individuals not by governments, but set up for the purpose of supplying things that people need or want rather than for making money. Charitable organisations clearly come into this category but so too do many other clubs and societies set up to service the requirements of their members. They may not all trade but, if they employ people or otherwise buy things, they have an economic impact. They are therefore part of the economy but not part of either of the two sectors of the economy described above. In consequence they are sometimes referred to as the third sector.

The limitations of language

'The limits of my language', said Wittgenstein, 'mean the limits of my world' and the language we use colours the way we think and filters the way we see things.

For a long time we have had a language of business which has affected the way we think of business and the private sector. Indeed it would seem that it was actually a private sector business, the East India Company mentioned earlier, which introduced to the English language the term 'civil servant'; a term which we now think of as referring to the archetypical public sector employee. At one time those people who worked for companies were referred to as company servants and therefore, when the East India Company wished to distinguish between the soldiers and the administrators who helped it to control much of India, it called the former its military servants and the latter its civil servants. (The East India Company could therefore be said to have had private sector civil servants!) The introduction of this terminology from India into England can then be attributed to Macaulay's essays on Clive and Warren Hastings which were published in 1840 and 1841.[9]

When we consider the variety of organisations that contribute to our economy we have tended to use economic language to describe them. Except in very socialist economies, we have recognised that there are separate private and public sectors in an economy and we have referred to those organisations which are not public sector organisations as businesses. We think of businesses as being limited companies established with the aim and facility to make profits for their owners. We may acknowledge that some businesses are small, even very small, and many businesses are partnerships or sole traderships, rather than limited companies, but we still think that all of them are generally 'there for the money'. To do that, those businesses sell goods or services to customers who pay for them. That is what the private sector is about to most or all of us.

In contrast, the public sector is there to carry out the operations of government. It is there to formulate, facilitate and give effect to government policies and decisions. It has clients and/or consumers of its services but they are not customers as they do not generally pay for all of those services, except indirectly through taxes. The public sector is not there to make money but is paid instead from the public purse to carry out its duties. (If public servants were to accept money from members of the public for services which ought to be free that may constitute bribery and, in effect, be the illegal introduction of private sector practices into the public arena.)

We can also recognise that there is a third sector of the economy but, without a common language for it, it has not been as easy to discuss it. This, together with a failure then to appreciate its merits, has undoubtedly contributed to the lack of attention paid to it. Now, however, terms for it are emerging, although they are not always applied in consistent ways. These are covered below and in the next two chapters.

Mapping an economy

Maps, like models, are not themselves real, but are intended to inform us about reality by illustrating some of its features. In particular they try to show how those features are positioned relative to each other. One attempt to provide a

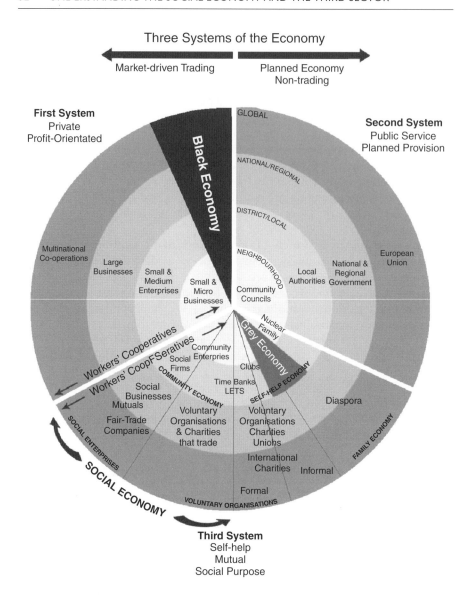

Figure 2.1   Three systems of an economy

Source: J. Pearce, *Social Enterprise in Anytown* (London: Calouste Gulbenkian Foundation, 2003), p. 25.

map of an economy was made by Pearce and it is shown in Figure 2.1. It indicates not just the third sector (or system, as he calls it) and its components, but also where the boundaries are between it and the first two sectors: the public and private systems/sectors.

Another approach is that of Billis (see Table 2.2), who suggests that within an economy there are three 'pure' or 'unambiguous' sectors – business, government

WHAT IS IN AN ECONOMY?   33

Table 2.2   The 'unambiguous' sectors

Core features	Business	Government	Associations
1. Who owns the organization?	Shareholders	Citizens	Members
2. Underpinning governance principles?	Share ownership	Public elections	Private elections
3. What is basis of legitimacy?	Satisfying shareholders and customers	Satisfying voters about public services	Satisfying members about mission
4. What ideas drive priorities and activities?	Market forces and the need to make a profit	Public service and statutory obligations	Persuasion about distinctive mission
5. Distinctive human resources?	Paid employees in managerially controlled firm	Paid public servants in legally backed Bureau	Members and volunteers in democratically elected association
6. Where do other resources come from?	Sales, fees	Taxes	Dues, donations, legacies

Source: D. Billis (2003), 'Sectors, Hybrids and Public Policy: The Voluntary Sector in Context' (draft), Paper presented at the *ARNOVA 2003 Conference*.

and associations – and that all other organisations are hybrids of two or more of these pure forms. He further suggests that each sector can be defined by six questions which have distinctive answers and that each answer is logically linked to other answers, in total representing the 'rules of the game' by which organisations operate.

Billis suggests that hybrids of organisations result when organisations develop characteristics that are found across the sectors (i.e. across the columns in Table 2.2). Table 2.3 presents examples of some of these hybrids:

Then there are continuum models in which it is suggested that there is a continuum between the private sector on the one hand and the government or the public sector on the other hand. An example of this approach comes from Social Enterprise London and is shown in Figure 2.2.

In Figure 2.2 the term 'socially responsible business' is used. Others have made a distinction between socially responsible activity – described as that 'which pursues a financial return on capital, traditionally understood, but within a framework of social and environmental standards' – and socially directed activity, which 'pursues a return on capital where this is more widely defined to integrate social and environmental outcomes'. Socially responsible activity is the realm of most corporate responsibility agendas whereas socially directed activity covers much of 'the work of non-profit organisations and "social enterprises" which generate a degree of earned income in pursuit of a social return'.[10]

The position of the social economy

With the exception of Figure 2.1, these models do not explicitly identify and include the social economy. Chapter 1 introduced the term 'the social economy' and Figure 2.1 suggests that it is an important part of the third sector but

Table 2.3   Examples of hybrid organisations

Government–Association Hybrids (GA)	Quangos (quasi-autonomous non-governmental organisation), non-departmental public bodies (NDPB) or 'local public spending bodies', for example, great national museums and the BBC
Government–Business Hybrids (GB)	Nationalised industries such as British Rail, Coal Industry, British Leyland
Government–Business–Association Hybrids (GBA)	Not-for-profit 'public bodies', such as housing associations, government audited, profit orientated with social mission
Business–Government Hybrids (BG)	Public Private Partnerships (PPP)
Business–Association Hybrids (BA)	Social enterprises, for example, John Lewis
Business–Government-Association Hybrids (BGA)	Private business with shareholders whose business heavily rely on government monitoring and give donations of funds through charitable partners, for example, the National Lottery/Camelot
Association–Government Hybrids (AG)	Association orientated towards government and using paid staff to deliver what we have called public services, and/or local government has its representatives on the management committee of the voluntary organization
Association-Business Hybrids (AB)	Charitable structures which have successful business spin-offs, for example, museums and museum shops, charity shops
Association–Business–Government Hybrids (ABG)	Volunteer organisational structure that was heavily dependent on government funding becomes service provider to government, for example, marriage guidance counselling, charity recruiting staff and holding contracts with NHS/Government

Source: D. Billis (2003), 'Sectors, Hybrids and Public Policy: The Voluntary Sector in Context' (draft), Paper presented at the *ARNOVA 2003 Conference*.

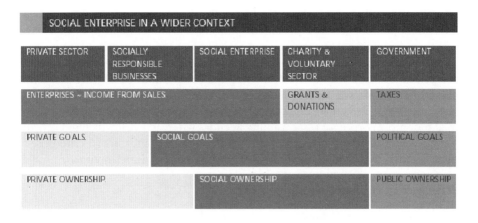

Figure 2.2   The context of social enterprise

Source: Social enterprise London, *Introducing Social Enterprise* (2001).

is not all of it. Most definitions of it also indicate that it does not include all those organisations which are not in either the private or the public sector, but some commentators, nevertheless, use the terms 'social economy' and 'third sector' synonymously. It is therefore difficult to place it precisely in a map of an economy because its position depends on which definition of it is being used. These varying interpretations of the social economy are explored further in Chapter 4. This confusion highlights a dilemma in attempts to delineate this area. Should everything not in either the public or the private sector be considered, by definition, to be in the third sector? Or should the third sector be defined by common characteristics, which some of its component organisations share, although that would still leave out some organisations, which could thus form a fourth sector?

Clear boundaries are not real

As the various continuum models recognise, the boundaries between sectors are never really going to be clear because the sectors themselves are, at least at their margins, rather fuzzy concepts. It might be convenient to consider similar activities as a category but the boundaries indicated between categories are not precise division points. The lines shown on diagrams between the sectors, and between different categories within sectors, are rather like contour lines drawn on a map: they help to indicate where land is rising or falling but you will not find them on the ground. The reality is that different types of economic activity are more like different colours in a spectrum: you can distinguish the main area of one colour from other areas of different colours but in between they blend into each other so there are no precise boundaries where one colour clearly ends and another begins. Also a colour which, for instance, may appear to be a shade of red when contrasted with pale orange may itself appear to be orange when placed beside dark red.

Uncertain areas

The public and private sectors of an economy are defined more or less exclusively as they include only those activities which meet certain criteria. In contrast, the third sector is usually defined inclusively in that it encompasses all economic activity not included in either of the other two sectors. Despite that inclusive approach, and because of the fuzzy nature of the concepts being considered, there are still some areas of uncertainty where it is not clear to which sector an activity should belong. Examples of such border-line cases include the following:

Sole traders and small partnerships. It might be thought that one-person businesses run by people operating as sole traders would be considered to be very small private sector businesses run for the profit of the sole trader. But probably very few people who work as sole traders always allocate their time in the way which best maximises their personal financial return, and the same might also apply to owner-managers of small businesses and to small partnerships. For a sole trader there is no distinction between wages and profits, and many small business owners, while wanting to earn enough money to maintain their lifestyle, will also sometimes do things either free or cheaply for other people or organisations which, for whatever reason, they wish to support. Thus, in their operations, the owners of many small businesses may therefore sometimes behave like social entrepreneurs.

Worker co-operatives. A business might be established as a worker co-operative if its founders wished it to function on co-operative principles applying any surplus for the benefit of the founding community. Yet the format of a worker co-operative can allow it to distribute its surplus to its worker members who are, therefore, in a similar position as shareholders in a private sector business taking personal financial returns from the business's profits.

CASE 2.1

Misplaced Organisations

This case study is about three organisations whose activities would place them in a different sector than that which their form might indicate.

A company limited by guarantee which was really in the public sector!
It might be thought that companies limited by guarantee are archetypal third sector organisations. They are not usually considered to be in the public sector because public sector organisations are usually created by statute and are not bound by company law, and they are not in the private sector because private sector organisations can distribute profits as dividends, which companies limited by guarantee cannot. However, in Northern Ireland, the Local Enterprise Development Unit (LEDU) was set up in 1972 as a company limited by guarantee but it was set up by the Northern Ireland government as its small business agency. It was entirely funded by the Northern Ireland government, which also approved its plans and budgets and appointed its members. In effect, the government also decided who it should appoint as directors and as chairman, with the implied threat that its funding would be withdrawn if it did not comply. Also its Chief Executive had to answer to the Permanent Secretary for the use of the government funding, which was its sole source of income, even though there were times when the Chief Executive was not a director and so could not sign the annual accounts. In practice, if not in theory, LEDU was part of the public sector.

A company limited by shares which was really a social enterprise!
The well-known ice-cream maker Ben and Jerry's was started as a company limited by shares so that the local community could share in its ownership. That might suggest that it was a private sector business. In all other ways, though, it was a social enterprise as it sought not to maximise the financial

CASE 2.1 (cont'd)

return to its shareholders, but to operate ethically for the benefit of the local community. However, when Unilever offered to buy it, and so move it into the private sector, a majority of the shareholders decided to sell their shares to Unilever even though this was contrary to the wishes of the founders.

A public sector organisation which is really a trade association!
The Livestock and Meat Commission for Northern Ireland was founded by statute and is funded by a statutory levy on businesses in the livestock and meat industry. Thus it is considered to be in the public sector. Nevertheless it acts on behalf of the meat-producing and meat-processing businesses in its industry, very like a trade association would act for its members, although, for the latter, membership and associated subscriptions would be voluntary.

A different perspective – the people behind the venture

The sector divisions considered above are based on consideration of the organisations concerned and the purpose of the activity in which they engage. Yet those organisations and their activities are merely the concrete manifestations of the aspirations of the people responsible for starting and running them. It is rather like the way that the mushrooms seen and picked are only the above-ground fruiting parts of the underground mycelia which actually constitute fungi.

Observers have pointed out that, in small businesses research, the emphasis has often been on the enterprise or business created, taking it as the primary unit of analysis. This is not least because it is relatively easy to research businesses as they have a legal existence and data on their activities – including their start-up, operation and, eventually, closure – can be obtained from official records and is the subject of required reports. Nevertheless it has been shown that it can be much more revealing to look instead at the entrepreneur (or entrepreneurs) behind a business. For instance, traditional business-based data will not reveal habitual entrepreneurship, in which one entrepreneur starts several businesses either serially or in parallel, and neither will that reflect an owner's motivations, yet both these factors can be crucial to an understanding of what happens in a business.[11] Similarly much of the analysis referred to in this book focuses on third sector organisations and organisational activity rather than on the people who create and operate those organisations.

If economics is concerned with how people provide for their wants, then it has to be realised that different people have different wants and that realising them can result in very different activities. Maslow's hierarchy of needs suggests that, if people are very hungry, then their main want will be to satisfy that hunger. Once lower-order needs such as hunger and shelter are satisfied, higher-order needs come into play. At the top of Maslow's hierarchy is self-actualisation and here especially different people want to do very different things. Some try to express themselves in art, some in conspicuous consumption, some in learning and discovery, and some through helping others. Many of these wants are not primarily about money and are registered in economic accounts only when money is used as a vehicle through which some or all of the wants might be realised.

People therefore start economic activities, or take up employment, for reasons which may be concerned more with self-actualisation than with personal financial enrichment. The forms those activities take, or the sort of jobs people seek, are related to, and evolve from, those reasons. People do not start activities to be in a particular economic sector; they start activities to meet the needs they perceive, whether that is a need for personal wealth, for the satisfaction of achieving something new, for helping other people or for a mixture of these. It is not necessarily the case that people work in the private sector if they want to make money, in the public sector if they want to exercise power or in the third sector if they want to help others. Where the activity they chose fits into an economic system is something others decide later and is based on arbitrary constructs which do not necessarily reflect the value of the relevant activity to the people concerned. Similarly, choice of which legal form a particular organisation should take is limited by the forms known to be available, none of which may be ideally suited to the founder's purpose.

As noted above, people's objectives are varied, and many people have more than one objective, but realising them involves work. Therefore different people will work in different ways, and sometimes in more than one way in order to achieve different objectives. A politician seeking power may work as an elected representative and find himself or herself in a parliament, which is a public sector organisation. A committed lay member of a church may work for a private sector business during the day to earn enough for the material wants of his or her family, but in the evenings or at weekends may get more satisfaction working on a voluntary basis for the church, which is a third sector organisation. A billionaire, having made a lot of money by starting and growing a successful private sector business, may then decide to put most of that money into a third sector foundation and concentrate on running that to support other worthy causes. It is also clear that the desire of people to do something, and the realisation of that desire through working in a variety of different ways, came long before the resultant activity was classified into different economic sectors. Those sector boundaries, and any subsector boundaries, do not therefore constrain what people want to do, and neither do the sectors necessarily reflect the ways in which people want to work.

Although the fruiting bodies of a fungus are the visible things sometimes called mushrooms, they are by no means the whole of the fungus. Similarly, the organisations actually created are not the totality of the aspirations of their founders. Instead, the legally constituted bodies, the existence and activities of which can be reported and recorded, are the result of the interaction of a number of factors including

- the visions, aspirations, ideas and ambitions of their founders;
- the selection by those founders of methods of operating to realise their purposes;
- the choice by those founders, from the options perceived to be available, of which legal form to use to give their organisations a legal existence.

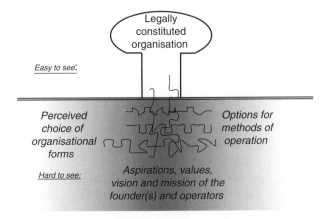

Figure 2.3   What is behind the activity?

However, just as the mushroom is the visible part of the fungus and is thus the part which is used to identify and classify it, it is the registered legal existence of organisations which is relatively easy to measure and record, and so organisational classifications are often based on that. Also, just as an underground fungus will often produce more than one above-ground mushroom, so too a founder's purpose may be realised in more than one business This is recognised in the concept of the habitual entrepreneur (and can also be seen in Case 3.1). So a fuller picture may be gained not from looking at the legal entity but from considering all the relevant factors behind it, as suggested in Figure 2.3. This approach also suggests that, if the label 'social entrepreneur' is applied to someone who starts and/or develops a social economy business, that label is based on the nature of business that is realised and not on the entrepreneur's motivations. An entrepreneur with the same or very similar motivations might instead, or in addition, start a business which is judged to be in the private sector, and in that case he or she would not be described as a social entrepreneur.

The foundation of some social enterprises may be encouraged not because of the enterprise of a founder, but because social enterprise solutions seem to be prescribed by a political agenda. As a result, these ventures may lack the enterprising attributes and resources, such as personal drive and opportunity identification, which are necessary for the success of the enterprise and lack the community links which are necessary for the social side. Amin et al. looked at the social economies in Glasgow and Middlesbrough, where local authorities were to varying extents involved in trying to run parts of the social economy, and concluded that social enterprise solutions can be so prescribed by the agenda of the local authorities that they are simply not possible or relevant in some places. They point out that 'given the UK government's insistence on the greater use of self-help regeneration strategies for the poorest communities, including the greater development of social economy organisations, it may be advocating a solution that relies on the existence of those features of local political, economic, and social life that … the most excluded people and places most significantly lack'.[12]

Because the range of aspirations of the founders (and/or operators) of organisations can be so varied, trying to fit the observed range of activity into categories is always going to be difficult and the resultant boundaries are going to be fuzzy, rather than clear and distinct. Grey areas are inevitable, and they occur not as the result of bad categorisation, but because the resultant activities do not in reality come in neat categories.

Despite any difficulties with boundaries it can be said that there is a lot of activity which is carried out to address wants and has an economic impact, but which has tended not to be recognised in any analysis of an economy which looks only at the public and the private sectors. Thus the varied activity has been grouped as the third sector, which is considered in the next chapter. Some of it has also been labelled as the 'social economy', and that is considered in more detail in Chapter 4.

Key Points of Chapter 2

- There are now perceived distinctions between different aspects of economic activity. However, the traditional focus on the private and public sectors has tended to ignore those activities which fall into neither.

- There is a wide range of activities which belong in neither the private nor the public sectors, and so are said to be in the third sector.

- A common approach to the third sector is an inclusive one which defines it as including everything not in the other two sectors. Other approaches are more exclusive or are based on there being a continuum of activity.

- Reality is less tidy than economic maps might indicate, as what people want to do to address their needs is very varied and is not restricted by economic concepts and definitions. Labels such as 'social entrepreneur' are often based on the nature of the business realised rather than on the motives and behaviour of the person realising it.

CASE 2.2

Establishing an Early Social Enterprise

On 24 May 1514, Henry VIII granted John Dowman a licence to found, in the parish church of Pocklington, a Guild which, according to its original patent, would among other things be able to hold lands with a yearly value of £13 6s 8d and to 'find from time to time one man fitted, and sufficiently learned in grammar, to instruct and educate all and singular scholars who resort to the town of Pocklington for the aforesaid purpose of receiving education'. Pocklington, which was mentioned in the Domesday Book, was then one of the significant market towns in Yorkshire and, at that time, most towns of importance boasted a school. Nearby there was an ancient school at York, where teaching was recorded

CASE 2.2 (cont'd)

in the early eighth century, and Beverly School had also been in existence for a long time as its records were apparently consulted in 1304 to settle a dispute about 'a very ancient custom'. Those old schools were ecclesiastical, for Medieval England had entrusted its education to the Church. However, by the thirteenth century, schools were being founded which were secular both in their purpose and in their government, and, in default of any precedent for creating a special governing body, the roundabout procedure of founding a guild was discovered as a means by which to provide lay governors for such schools. As a result of this foundation early in the fifteenth century Pocklington then had its own grammar school like York, Beverly, Howden, Hemingborough and Hull.

John Dowman (also sometimes known as Dolman) had been a lawyer and churchman of some eminence. He was made a Bachelor of Canon and Doctor of Civil Law by Cambridge University and was Prebend first of Sarum, then of St Paul's and finally of Lichfield Cathedral. When St John's College was founded in Cambridge in 1511 by Bishop Fisher, acting as executor to Lady Margaret Beaufort (the mother of Henry VII), the executors lodged for a time with Dr Dowman, possibly to seek his legal advice. Certainly he made two significant benefactions to St John's College and linked the school he founded to the College by, for instance, obliging the Guild officers to consult the College about the appointment of a schoolmaster.

However, John Dowman's school did not always have an easy existence. In 1547 Henry VIII died and was succeeded by his nine-year old son Edward VI. Edward's ministers followed a reformation policy and, by the Chantries Act of 1547, abolished all the religious guilds and confiscated their property, although the colleges of Oxford and Cambridge were exempted from its provisions. Some provision was made for the temporary continuance of the Guild schools, usually by setting aside a small part of their property to provide maintenance. The result was that some schools disappeared while others survived somehow on a meagre allowance. Pocklington School, however, escaped in an odd way. When he founded it, John Dowman had intended to endow it with some of his property but this was not done. Therefore, when the Guild was abolished, Thomas Dowman, who was the son of John Dowman's first cousin and his heir, offered the property again. He petitioned the Parliament and, in 1551, obtained a private Act of Parliament establishing the Free School of Pocklington. It then flourished, except for occasional lapses, until near the end of the seventeenth century, but then had a century and a half of relative decline, although it did educate William Wilberforce from 1771 to 1776. It was resuscitated in the middle of the nineteenth century by a headmaster who was recorded as having 'rescued' the school from 'the scandalous neglect prior to his appointment'. A Victorian inspector reported that 'the one great want of such a town as Pocklington is one good school which is on a sufficiently large basis to admit the boy who is going to university side by side with the boy who will leave earlier, and which knows how to do full justice to the requirements of both.' He did, however, also criticise it for 'partaking too much of the character of a private school'.

CASE 2.2 (cont'd)

At the start of the twenty-first century the school John Dowman founded still survives in Pocklington as a public school. (NB: The title 'public' for what would now be seen to be a private, fee-taking school is a legacy of the time of the school's foundation when there were no state schools and places in it were open to the public, whereas entry to some other schools was more limited.)

Source: Based on P. C. Sands and C. M. Haworth, *A History of Pocklington School, East Yorkshire 1514–1950* (London and Hull: A Brown & Sons, circa 1951).

CASE 2.3

The Oldest Company in the UK

'The Company and Fraternity of Free Fishermen and Dredgermen of Faversham' was in existence in 1189, if not earlier. It was a 'labour corporation', or trade collective, the profits of which were shared in proportion to the amount of work put in by each individual member. To become a 'freeman' of the Company applicants had to serve a seven-year apprenticeship and be married.

There was good money to be earned from oysters and it is recorded that in the eighteenth century ships from the Netherlands queued to load oysters for the Dutch ports. However, by the beginning of the twentieth century pollution from sewage was beginning to take its toll and in 1903 the oyster beds were declared unfit for use. In 1908 the company was desperate and brought a High Court action against the Council. The Company won and the Council was forced to build a proper sewage treatment plant.

Despite this, as a trade collective, the Company never regained its vitality and in 1930 it was re-established as a conventional limited company in which the former freemen became shareholders. Although the oyster grounds were subsequently let to a neighbouring fishery, they failed after some harsh winters in the 1950s and 1960s. The Company, though, is still in existence and lets the grounds as moorings or for use by wildfowlers. On the strength of its existence in 1189 it claims to be the oldest company in the UK.

Source: Based on information on www.faversham.org, accessed 29 April 2007.

Questions, Exercises, Essay and Discussion Topics

1. Which came first: the public, the private or the third sector? Discuss.
2. Into which of the three sectors (public, private and third) would you place the following and why:

(cont'd)

Sole traders?
Worker co-operatives?
The BBC?
Family economy activity?
Grey economy activity?

3. 'Originally economic activity was neither private sector nor public sector. Thus it must have been in the third sector.' Discuss.

4. Is it possible, on a two-dimensional map, to illustrate all the variants of economic activity?

5. 'The issues which are important in understanding why a business behaves as it does, are not the legal form it has taken and where it might formally be placed on a map of the economy, but are the aspirations, intentions and behaviour of its founder(s) and/or owners/members.' Discuss this in the light of Cases 2.1, 2.2 and 2.3.

SUGGESTIONS FOR FURTHER READING

J. Pearce, *Social Enterprise in Anytown* (London: Calouste Gulbenkian Foundation, 2003).

References

1. J. Harvey, *Modern Economics* (Basingstoke: Macmillan, 1998), p. 7.
2. For further discussion of such implications of farming, see J. Diamond, *Guns, Germs and Steel* (London: Vintage, 1998), pp. 85–104.
3. A. Molloy, C. McFeely and E. Connolly, *Building a Social Economy for the New Millenium* (Derry: Guildhall Press/NICDA Social Economy Agency, 1999), p. 7.
4. P. Hennessy, *Whitehall* (London: Fontana Press, 1990), p. 18.
5. P. Mathias, *The First Industrial Nation: An Economic History of Britain 1700–1914* (London: Methuen, 1983), pp. 24–9.
6. Ibid., p. 308.
7. Ibid., pp. 352–3.
8. See A. Amin, A. Cameron and R. Hudson, *Placing the Social Economy* (London: Routledge, 2002), pp. 2–3.
9. P. Hennessy, *Whitehall* (London: Fontana Press, 1990), p. 18.
10. Based on S. Foster, E. Mayo and J. Nicholls, *Social Return on Investment: Concept Paper* (London: New Economic Foundation, 2002); and D. Aeron-Thomas, J. Nicholls, S. Foster and A. Westall, *Social Return on Investment: Valuing what matters* (London: New Economic Foundation, 2004).
11. For more information, see S. Bridge, K. O'Neill and S. Cromie, *Understanding Enterprise, Entrepreneurship and Small Business* (Basingstoke: Palgrave Macmillan, 2003), pp. 184–7.
12. A. Amin, R. Hudson and A. Cameron, *Placing the Social Economy* (London: Routledge, 2002), p. 81.

Describing the Third Sector

3

Key Concepts

This chapter covers

- the wide range of organisations which have an economic impact which do not belong in either the private or the public sectors of an economy and which have therefore been defined as being in the third sector;

- the other sectoral labels which are often used, such as 'the voluntary sector', 'the community sector' and 'the social economy';

- the way that these labels are sometimes used as if the organisations to which they refer are the third sector, and sometimes as if they are sub-groups within the third sector;

- the varying terminology and the different definitions, sometimes apparently for the same thing, and the reasons why this may, or may not, matter.

(cont'd)

Learning Objectives

By the end of this chapter the reader should

- be aware of the labels used to categorise those organisations which have an economic impact but which are not in either the private or the public sector;

- appreciate that some labels can, and have been, variously used to refer to the whole of this third sector, or to sufficiently large groups of organisations to comprise a third sector in themselves;

- appreciate that some labels, often the same ones, can also be used to refer to subgroups within the third sector, for which there are often no clear boundaries;

- appreciate the need sometimes for care when dealing with different interpretations, particularly when they are based on, or promoted by, different political or economic perspectives.

Introduction

New government lead for third sector, including social enterprise, voluntary and community sector, volunteering and charitable giving

The creation of the Office of the Third Sector within the Cabinet Office reflects the government's recognition of the value, influence and importance of the third sector...

The establishment of the new office is also recognition of how diverse the sector is in its needs and interests.

Heading and extracts from a letter sent out by the Cabinet Office in May 2006.

Chapter 2 showed how, as the private and public sectors of the economy evolved as distinct fields of economic activity, other organisations were created which contributed to the economy but which belonged to neither of those two sectors. Sometimes therefore labelled the 'third sector', these organisations form part of the totality of an economy but have often been overlooked in traditional economics, not least because they are not in the two mainstream sectors. Nevertheless there is a wide range of activities which come into this category.

What is in the third sector?

Sector's Philosophical Pursuit of Proof that it Exists

3 October 2007

The NCVO (National Council for Voluntary Organisations) has embarked on research designed to answer the unanswerable question: what exactly is the third sector?

The idea came about because the research team responsible for producing the umbrella body's UK Voluntary Sector Almanac struggles to decide which organisations to include.

'There is plenty of research about the sector, but definitions vary, so it's hard to compare findings,' said Oliver Reichardt, one of the almanac's authors. 'It's important the sector takes the lead on this, otherwise somebody else will. The Government chose the term third sector, and lots of people are unhappy with it.'

Reichardt said the NCVO was consulting widely over the issue and it could take up to two years to finalise a definition.

If it proves impossible to reach agreement across the sector, he said, the NCVO will probably drop the project altogether.

Whatever the outcome of the research, sector organisations will no doubt continue to ponder their true identity for a while yet.

Source: www.thirdsector.co.uk/News/DailyBulletin/741663, accessed 3 October 2007.

Table 3.1 is an expansion of Table 1.3 but still lists only a few of the organisations and categories of organisation which have an economic impact but which would not generally be considered to belong in either the private or the public sector.

Table 3.1   Third sector activities: An indicative list

Amateur dramatic clubs	Independent schools
Arts and culture organisations	Intermediary funding bodies
Associations*	LETS
Building preservation trusts	Lifeboat services
Business schools	Medical charities
Chambers of Commerce	Mosques
Charities	Mountain rescue services
Churches	Mutuals*
Community enterprises	Rotary clubs
Community heath care bodies	Political parties
Co-operatives*	Professional bodies
Credit unions	Social clubs
Donkey sanctuaries	Social housing schemes
Enterprise agencies	Sports clubs
Fair trade companies	Synagogues
Faith schools	Temples
Family activity (DIY, vegetable gardens, etc.)	Time banks

Famine relief agencies	Trades unions
Foundations*	Universities and university colleges
Freemasons	Voluntary organisations
Golf clubs	Women's Institute
Hospices	Worker co-operatives
Housing associations	Youth clubs

* Associations, co-operatives, mutuals (and foundations) are the categories of organisation included in the classification *Économie Sociale* in some EU member states. Descriptions of them are provided in Chapter 4.

Table 3.2   The main groups of non-profit organisations

The *UN Handbook on Non-Profit Institutions in the System of National Accounts* recommends the International Classification of Nonprofit Organisations (ICNPO) system. It includes 12 major activity groups:

- Culture and recreation
- Education and research
- Health
- Social services
- Environment
- Development and housing
- Law, advocacy and politics
- Philanthropic intermediaries and voluntarism promotion
- International activities
- Religious congregations and associations
- Business, professional associations, unions
- Not elsewhere classified

Source: www.un.org, accessed 15 August 2007.

The range of organisations in this sector is also indicated in Table 3.2, which lists the main classification categories recommended by the United Nations.

Some activities with an economic impact are generally associated with only one sector of the economy. For instance, stock exchange activity is associated with the private sector, government activity with the public sector and religious activity, except in theocracies, with the third sector. Some activities, however, can be found in more than one of these sectors and there are some which can, at least in the UK, be found in all three: The following are examples:

Sport: Sport, when it is done in schools, takes place in a public sector context. Most sports clubs are in the third sector. However, professional coaching is often delivered for private gain and many major football clubs are also clearly private sector organisations.

Business Support: There are, at least in the UK, government-established business support agencies which are in the public sector. Chambers of Commerce and other organisations such as the Institute of Directors are third

Table 3.3   Ownership of forests in England

In 1998 the ownership of forests in England was split between the following:

Ownership category	Percent of forested land
Personal sector (individuals and families)	47
Business sector (for profit)	15
Forestry Commission (public sector)	22
Other public sector including local authorities	9
Charities (often for conservation purposes)	7
Community ownership, common land and unidentified	1

Source: J. Kendall, The Voluntary Sector (London: Routledge, 2003), p. 187.

sector organisations which deliver business support. Much business support is, however, bought from private sector consultancies.

Housing: There is private sector housing provided for sale or rent to make a profit for its builders/owners. There is public sector housing (such as 'council housing' in the UK) which is provided as a public service. There is also social housing provided by housing associations whose board members are volunteers and whose surpluses must be reinvested in housing activities.

Education: Much education is provided by the public sector. However, some independent schools and colleges are third sector bodies and some forms of education, such as private tuition, is provided on a for-profit basis.

Health Care: Like education, health care can be provided by all three sectors. In the UK much health care is provided in the public sector by the National Health Service (NHS). However, there is also a significant provision of supplementary care by third sector bodies such as community health care organisations and St John Ambulance. In addition, some people pay for private sector treatment, possibly because it is quicker or is not available from the NHS.

Forestry: In Britain, environmental charities now own a significant amount of the forested land, as Table 3.3 shows.

Labelling and defining the third sector

A view from the USA

The third sector (is) a label for organizations in the economy that are neither traditional for-profit businesses nor government agencies ....Neither capitalist nor public, the *third sector* is the third element in the mixed economy of the United States. It consists largely of private organizations that act in the economic arena but that exist to provide

(cont'd)

specific goods and services to their members or constituents. These organizations act neither to enrich 'owners' nor to provide high income for top executives. Some are used to protect entrenched interests, and others are used to do social good.

Non-profit organizations fall into two broad categories: some serve only their members, and others perform a broad array of public services. The first group includes social clubs, political parties, labor unions, business associations and cooperatives.

The third sector is a pastiche – a collection of organizations that are usually defined by their *not* being of the larger two sectors but that are otherwise varied in nature.

Source: C. Gunn, *Third-Sector Development: Making Up For The Market* (USA: Cornell University, 2004), pp. vii, 1, 6.

It is already clear that, while this book has tended to refer to the third sector of the economy as the 'third sector', others have given it different labels, including the 'non-profit sector', the 'voluntary sector', the 'voluntary and community sector', the 'social economy' and the 'social enterprise sector' (and it has also been referred to as the third system[1] and the third way[2]). Behind this varied nomenclature it would seem that there have been two broad approaches to definitions about, in or for the third sector and its components:

- *Exclusive*. One approach is more narrow and focused. It seeks to delineate a set of organisations which share certain characteristics, even if those characteristics are quite widely held, and to exclude others which do not. What is included in such a definition is likely to be relatively homogeneous. Definitions of the social economy, of social enterprise or of other components of the third sector are generally of this sort.

- *Inclusive*. The other approach is broader and more embracing. It seeks to include, rather than to exclude, and to integrate, rather than to separate. What it includes may therefore be quite heterogeneous. Definitions of the third sector itself generally fall into this category (see Table 3.4 for some of the categories of organisation which would be included in the third sector in this way).

Definitions of the second, inclusive, sort will tend to be of a higher level and thus similar and compatible as they will all seek to include more or less the same things. In contrast, definitions of the first sort can differ and even be incompatible because they can differ on the characteristics they wish to include and those they wish to exclude. Such differences can arise because definitions are developed for different reasons and because, in any newly developing field of interest, there tends to be an initial proliferation of variations before any common trend or agreed approach has had time to emerge. The result is that, when it comes to

Table 3.4   Categories of third sector organisations and activity

A list of categories of organisations, or of activity, that might be considered to operate wholly, or at least in part, within the third sector, might include the following:

- The social economy (including co-operatives, mutuals, associations and foundations), social enterprises and social economy enterprises.
- The voluntary sector.
- The community sector/economy and community enterprises.
- The family economy.
- The self-help economy.
- Civic organisations.
- Funding intermediaries.
- Member service organisations including clubs, trades unions, business and professional bodies, political organisations.
- Mutual benefit and co-operative organisations, including credit unions, worker co-operatives, consumer co-operatives and agricultural co-operatives.
- Charities.
- The grey economy (but not the black economy, unless the crime is not for personal enrichment – as in the case of Robin Hood?).
- And others such as those sole traders and small businesses who contribute to their community and who take 'a reward for work done' rather than always seeking to maximise personal profit?

things like social enterprises, social businesses, social economy enterprises (SEEs) and community enterprises, there is a plethora of definitions, some overlapping, some disagreeing, some traditional and some fashionable, and some serving special purposes or reflecting different agenda. For some of these expressions and labels, therefore, there is a spectrum of possible meanings and plenty of potential for miscommunication if the meanings intended by the different parties involved in any particular discussion or situation are not made clear.

If the third sector of the economy is defined as encompassing those activities with an economic impact which are in neither the private nor the public sectors, that is a definition which includes all the activities listed in Table 3.1 and is an inclusive one. It emphasises the only feature which all such organisations have in common, which is that they belong in neither of the two other sectors. In the list in Table 3.1 there are many different bodies, some of which have a number of similarities but some of which are very different.

In this field, other, more exclusive categories have been suggested, based on a number of shared characteristics. The definitions advanced for these categories are exclusive definitions and they may be suggested in order to focus on the particular category being defined but they do have the additional effect of indicating sub-sectors within the overall ambit of the third sector. Such is the real or apparent extent of some of these other categorisations that they are sometimes seen either as alternative labels for the third sector or at least as being so distinctive and/or important as to constitute a third sector in their

Table 3.5   Labels for the 'third sector', or for large parts of it

Third sector, Third system, Third way
Non-profit, or Not-for-profit, sector
Social economy, Social enterprise sector
Voluntary sector, Voluntary and community
    sector, Community sector, Community enterprise,
    Community economy
Self-help economy, Family economy
Organised civil society

own right. In that case, because they are exclusive categorisations which do not include some organisations which are not in the public or private sectors, they suggest that, in theory at least, there must be a fourth sector for those excluded categories.

Table 3.5 lists some of the labels given either to the whole sector or to specific sub-categories within it. Some of the terms have been used only to refer to the overall sector and some clearly refer to significant sub-sectors within that overall sector. Nevertheless many of the terms not only have at some time been used more or less interchangeably with one or more of the others but also have sometimes been used to refer to a sub-sector and sometimes to the sector overall. The result is that this is often an area in which the terminology can be confusing as there is no accepted standard practice, as the following examples illustrate (italics added):

In 2003, the *voluntary, third or non-profit* sector occupies centre stage in public policy discussions in the UK.[3]

In what might be called the 'community era' we talked of community action, *community enterprise, and community business*. Today, in the contemporary 'social era', we are more likely to talk of social entrepreneurs, *social enterprise and social business*. Is there some serious significance in this shift in vocabulary from community to social? Does it matter?[4]

Social economy refers to a *third sector* in economics between the private sector...and the public sector.[5]

The *non-profit sector*, usually in the hands of the *Third Sector*, is no longer seen as a residual and poor cousin to the state or the market.[6]

I want a new compact that elevates the *third sector* as partner, not as...a cut price alternative to government – but government fulfilling its responsibilities to fund services, and fully valuing the contribution the *voluntary sector* can make.[7]

Economies may be considered to have three sectors:

- The business private sector, which is privately owned and profit motivated.
- The public sector which is owned by the state and provides services in the public interest.

- The *social economy*, that embraces a wide range of community, voluntary and not-for-profit activities....The *third sector can* be broken down into three sub-sectors: *the community sector, the voluntary sector and the social enterprise sector*.[8]

It is of course possible, as the last quote above illustrates, to see many of these labels, such as the social economy, the voluntary sector and the community sector, as referring to specific sub-sectors within the third sector. John Pearce, in the diagram of the three sectors reproduced in Figure 2.1, has indicated that within the third sector there are a number of sub-groupings including the community economy, the self-help economy, the family economy, the social economy and a grouping of voluntary organisations.

Identifying sub-sectors

In seeking to identify such sub-sectors there are a number of possible bases for distinguishing between different organisations and activities including the following:

- *Legal form*. In the UK many organisations in the third sector have been formed as companies limited by guarantee. However, examples can be found of companies limited by guarantee which are, *de facto* if not *de jure*, public sector organisations (see the example of LEDU in Case 2.1).

- *Purpose and/or potential benefit*. Organisations in this field have been established for a variety of purposes and they can provide a variety of benefits, which are not always the same as their original purposes. An example of a potential benefit which can be particularly attractive to governments is the ability to combat social and economic exclusion, even though that might not be the main reason for starting the activities in question.

- *Size*. Just as in the public and private sectors, third sector organisations can range in size from large and/or international in their coverage to very small and/or local, although at the smallest level it could be hard to draw a clear distinction between a one-person private sole trader and a one-person third sector organisation.

- *Extent of volunteering*. The use of volunteer directors and/or staff is an important aspect of many third sector organisations.

- *Democratic participation*. Many organisations in the third sector have been established to represent or serve particular communities. However, there are differences in the extent to which those communities can or do influence the organisations concerned.

- *Degree of independence from the state*. While it might be thought that all third sector organisations would be independent of the state because they are not in the public sector, there are degrees to this independence. In particular those organisations which are heavily dependent on state funding, whether that is through grants, annual subventions or purchase of services, will be limited in their freedom of action to some extent.

- *Social impact.* The type and extent of social impact of organisations in this sector will be closely linked to their purpose and/or benefits.

- *Economic impact.* The type and extent of the economic impact of the different organisations in this sector of the economy varies substantially.

- *Sources of income.* The sources of income for third sector organisations include 'trading' income earned from the provision of goods and services, grants and donations, and other sources such as investments and membership fees. Not all the organisations in this sector trade, but some do and in this they are to a greater or lesser extent close to the private sector. (However, see also Illustration 3.1.)

Pearce, in producing the map of the sectors reproduced in Figure 2.1, used the dimensions of size and proximity to either the public or the private sector to show how different types of organisation might be positioned relative to one another on a two-dimensional 'map' of the third sector. Other dimensions will produce different spreads. However, in trying to understand the sector it is probably more relevant to look not at how organisations might in theory be categorised but at how they are in practice categorised, and in particular at the most common categorisations which are probably those variously given the labels 'voluntary', 'community' and 'social', each of which is examined below.

Illustration 3.1   Trading: What is so Special About it?

A number of definitions of social enterprises indicate that they derive at least some of their income from trading but why does the trading element seem to be so crucial? If Pocklington School (see Case 2.2) in its early years depended entirely on benefactions and endowments for its income, does that mean that it was not then a social enterprise? Did anything fundamentally change when it began to charge fees and 'traded', and today, as a fee-charging 'public' school is it a social enterprise, even if there is now adequate alternative provision for education in the public sector?

If an organisation with a social purpose receives an endowment and invests it to provide an income to fund its activities, that might not be considered by some to be trading. But the organisation in which the endowment is invested might be a trading organisation and the profits it remits to the investing organisation would be used for a social purpose. Between the investor and the recipient of the investment there are therefore both trading and social purpose, but which organisation, if either, would be the social enterprise?

The voluntary sector

Jeremy Kendall, in the introduction to his book *The Voluntary Sector*, states that 'In 2003, the voluntary, third or non-profit sector occupies centre stage in public policy discussions in the UK.'[9] This clearly suggests that, in that context, the label 'voluntary sector' can be applied to the whole of the third sector of the economy. Later in the book, though, Kendal introduces three definitions of the voluntary sector for use when making international comparisons, but which are less all-embracing. He starts with the 'Broad Nonprofit Sector' (BNS), which includes 'all entities which are formal organisations having an institutionalized character; constitutionally independent of the state and self-governing, non-profit-distributing; and involve some degree of volunteerism'. This, he says, 'is a definition which has been reached through a process of consensus-building within (an international) framework, is relevant for international comparisons, while representing a relatively inclusive definition compared to traditional UK usage'.[10]

Kendal's 'default' definition of the voluntary sector includes 'organizations which are formal, non-profit-distributing, constitutionally independent of the state, self governing and benefiting from voluntarism'.[11] These groups, he suggests, can be seen as comprising a 'broad voluntary sector' (BVS),[12] which includes all organizations in the BNS other than political parties and religious congregations. He then also introduces a definition for the 'Narrow Voluntary Sector (NVS) which includes all organizations in the BVS, less organizations not traditionally thought of as being part of the voluntary sector in the UK. This is primarily because they are seen as effectively being part of the state despite their constitutional status, and/or because they are not thought to be sufficiently altruistic or public-benefit oriented. Excluded on this basis are all universities, schools, sports and social clubs, and trades union and business associations.'[13]

Another definition of the voluntary sector is that provided by the UK's National Council for Voluntary Organisations (NCVO), which aims to 'give voice and support to voluntary and community organisations'.[14] It refers sometimes to the voluntary and community sector and sometimes just to the voluntary sector which it has described as including 'those organisations that are: formal (they have a constitution); independent of government and self-governing; not for profit; and operate with a meaningful degree of volunteer involvement. Examples include housing associations, large charities, large community associations, national campaign organisation etc.'[15]

By remarks such as 'as the boundaries between the public, private and voluntary sectors become increasingly blurred',[16] the NCVO suggests that it might also see the voluntary sector as itself comprising the third sector rather than as just one component of it. Nevertheless these voluntary sector definitions, even the broadest ones, leave out some of the organisations listed in Table 3.1, such as some co-operatives, fair trade companies and business schools which may not have a meaningful degree of volunteer involvement. Therefore, if the voluntary sector is to be considered to be the third sector, these definitions imply either that any organisation without volunteers is in the private or public sector, or that there is still a fourth sector.

Moreover, as Kendal indicates, the language has been changing and, while some people use the recently favoured terms, others still use older terms, and this can lead to confusion. For instance, he acknowledges that 'other language – viz., voluntary and community sector, organized civil society, social economy, third sector or system, and so on – has apparently gained currency in recent years', but he explains that the voluntary sector definitions to which he refers were earlier 'used to conduct statistical mapping, so to change language while leaving the coverage unaltered would be confusing' and that 'the shift in language has largely been an elite-led process, and has not really been adopted on the ground'. 'Certainly', he says, 'in conducting fieldwork… "voluntary sector" was the single most commonly utilised collective noun, usually implicitly deploying our narrow definition.'[17]

Another aspect of the definitions indicated above is that they indicate that voluntary sector organisations are independent of government or the state. Yet the trend in countries like the UK to contract out public services to voluntary sector bodies may have the effect of compromising this traditional identity. Volunteering has also been a key characteristic associated with voluntary organisations but an element of volunteer input is a feature of some organisations not normally viewed as being in the voluntary sector, but which would come under the category of 'associations', such as trade unions, schools with elected governors, housing associations, professional associations, employers organisations and political parties.

The community sector

John Pearce (e.g. in Figure 2.1) uses the term 'community economy', which he sees as overlapping, but not being co-incident with, voluntary organisations. He indicates that the community economy is that part of the social economy 'at neighbourhood and district levels where there is a strong sense of local affiliation' and is comprised of social enterprises which are 'closely linked to their particular locality'.[18] He acknowledges, however, that some definitions of community enterprise have also included those social enterprises 'serving communities of interest' which are not based on geography.

As well as 'community sector' and 'community economy', the term 'community business' has also been used, for instance in the Community Business Scheme, which ran in Glasgow in the 1980s and which was described as the largest social enterprise development programme in the UK. Under the scheme, 'community businesses' were given up to seven years' funding after which they were expected to have become financially independent and community-owned businesses. Although the scheme was extended to cover most of Scotland the greatest level of activity was in Glasgow, where several hundred 'community businesses' were established before it was wound up.[19]

Hayton, who commented on this scheme, suggested that a community business was 'a trading organisation which, through the sale of goods or services, aims to become self-sustaining. Through its activities it creates jobs for those living in particular areas: ones generally characterised by high levels of unemployment and other symptoms of multiple deprivation. Residents of these areas are members of the business, and thus own and control it, although they do not necessarily work in it. Directors are elected from the membership and there is usually provision to co-opt non-executive directors. Trading profits are either reinvested or are spent on projects of benefit to the local community.'[20] Based on these characteristics, he found that many of the enterprises established were not actually community businesses. The 'businesses', he reported, fell into the following four groups:

- Community businesses owned and controlled by local residents with a remit to create jobs for local people by setting up commercially viable trading organisations.

- Enterprises that were essentially conventional private sector companies with ownership and control vested in those who owned the company rather than the wider community.

- 'Businesses' that were Urban Programme-funded projects that had been set up to run for the duration of the grant.

- 'Businesses' whose objective was to create a service for a community rather than jobs. Effectively these were voluntary sector projects which, after an initial period of public subsidy, were able to survive as they relied upon unpaid labour. They had no intention of becoming commercially viable.'[21]

Another illustration of the earlier use of the term 'community business' is provided in Case 3.2, which, drawing directly from contemporary documents, describes LEDU's Community Business Programme in the language which was used when it was launched at the end of the 1980s. This study too demonstrates that the term 'community business' was then in common use, and that the third sector was also then being referred to, but not apparently social enterprise, social entrepreneurship or the social economy. Although it was expected that the businesses supported by the programme would have community links (but see Illustration 3.2), those so-called 'community businesses' represented a category of organisation which was essentially the same as, rather than distinct from, the category which would now often be referred to as social enterprises.

Although the LEDU case suggests that many enterprises which were called community businesses might today be referred to as social enterprises, nevertheless the definition given earlier by Hayton does emphasise the relationship between the business and the community it serves. It is that relationship which, for many people, makes a business a community business, but there can be different degrees of community involvement as Illustration 3.2 describes.

Pearce suggests (see Figure 2.1) that community economy organisations are generally small, being comparable in size to SMEs and micro businesses in the private economy, while other social economy organisations can be larger. He makes a distinction, therefore, between community enterprises, which have a distinctly local quality, and social enterprises, which are not bound to place and can have regional, national and even international reach. This distinction is set out in the Table 3.6.

The following observations on the degree of community involvement in so-called 'community enterprises' were made in 1991:

> There are many differing views on who should run community ventures. One way to look at the problem is to classify the available choices by the degree to which residents of a community exert influence over the project or enterprise. As the table shows, at one end of the scale (community provision) members of the local community play no part whatsoever. At the other end (community control) local residents are encouraged to become members of the venture and in this way exercise complete ownership and control.

Community control

The project is controlled by a board which is either appointed directly, or heavily influenced, by the main funders, which will be composed almost entirely of business or professional people and is only accountable to the funders. The project will be run on the basis that the board know what is needed in the area. Also any assets will normally revert to the funders when the lifetime of the project is complete.

Community consultation

The project is controlled by an appointed or self-selected board or committee. The main funders influence the choice of controlling group, which tends to be composed almost entirely of business or professional people. The controlling group attach some importance to consulting the community and do this through public meetings, questionnaires or more informal contacts. Attempts may be made to distribute progress reports to the community, but there is no effective system of accountability to the community. The community has no claim on the assets whether during the lifetime of the project or on dissolution.

Community co-option

Some local residents are intentionally co-opted onto a self-selected board or committee but form only a small (and often non-vocal) minority. However, because there are local representatives on the board/committee it tends not to undertake consultation or establish an effective process for accountability. The community again has no claim on the assets either during the lifetime of the project or on dissolution.

Community management

Local residents are encouraged to take over the management of the project. The board or committee must operate, however, within the budget provided and adhere to the guidelines laid down by the funders. While there is a budget there are usually no assets involved.

Illustration 3.2   (cont'd)

Community representation*

While local residents are not members of the enterprise, care is taken to ensure that the controlling board/committee is clearly representative of a cross section of local interests, groups and estates. People with helpful specific skills are invited to join and there is a strong desire to implement some effective system of accountability to the local community for whom the assets are held 'in trust'.

Community control

Local residents are encouraged to become members of the enterprise and the members directly elect the board/committee on a one person, one vote basis. There is direct accountability, and powers of co-option allow people with specific skills to become members of the board/committee. The assets are controlled by the members.

Issues raised

These observations suggest that the actual degree of community influence in a project may depend on the balance struck between any conflicting wishes of the funders and the community. Funders may seek to impose conditions on the use of their money and, as customers who are prepared to pay for what they want, they are entitled to seek to impose their own conditions, especially when they relate to the responsible use of that money. If the conditions proposed are too onerous then the group concerned has the options of seeking to renegotiate them or to refuse the deal on offer.

Note: * This, it is suggested, is often the most appropriate structure for enterprises in areas where there is little history of direct community involvement or where the nature of the project is too general to attract local membership.
Source: Based on an article by Phil Nicholls, 'Who Should Run Community Enterprise?', in *Newsview*, Issue 2, which was published by Community Business Northern Ireland in November 1991.

However, Pearce detects a shift in the vocabulary of what was the community development field behind which it is possible to discern three strands of changing thought:

- a shift from an emphasis on collective action to that on entrepreneurialism;
- a shift from an emphasis on ownership and accountability to a focus on what the organisation delivers; and
- a shift from a political perspective to one emphasising technical approach aimed at getting the job done.[22]

Table 3.6   Community and social economy

Community enterprise	Social enterprises
Community ownership company	Building society
Community based housing association	Charity trading arm
Community benefit corporation	Consumer retail society
Community business	Credit union
Community co-operative	Fair trade company
Community credit union	Housing association
Community development corporation	Intermediate labour market
Community development finance initiative	Marketing co-operative
Community housing trust	Mutual co-operative society
Community interest company	Public interest company
Community trading organisation	Social business
Community trust	Social firm
Employee-ownership business	Workers' co-operative
Housing co-operative	
(Local) development trust	
Local Exchange Trading Scheme	
Neighbourhood co-operative	
Neighbourhood enterprise	
Social co-operative	
Social firm	
Time bank	
Voluntary enterprise	
Workers' co-operative	
Neighbourhood, Local, District	Regional, National, International

Source: J. Pearce, *Social Enterprise in Anytown* (London: Calouste Gulbenkian Foundation, 2003), p. 29.

One aspect of this changing vocabulary, suggests Peace, is that whereas 'in what might be called the "community era" we talked of community action, community enterprise and community business. Today, in the contemporary "social era", we are more likely to talk of social entrepreneurs, social enterprise and social business.'[23]

The social economy

The social economy constitutes a broad range of activities and practices which have the potential to provide opportunities for local people and communities to engage in all stages of the process of local economic regeneration and job creation, from the identification of basic needs to the operationalisation of initiatives. The sector covers the economic potential and activities of the self-help and co-operative movements, i.e. initiatives which aim to satisfy the social and economic needs of local communities and their members. The sector includes co-operatives; self-help projects; credit unions; housing associations; partnerships; community enterprises and businesses.[24]

The social economy is often the focus of attention for many people interested in the non-private and non-public sector of the economy. While many different definitions have been offered for the social economy and/or its constituent organisations, these are generally exclusive definitions and it is clear that, like the definition of the voluntary sector given above, they do not include all the organisations covered by inclusive third sector definitions. (For instance, a Canadian study specifically states that 'the non-profit and voluntary sector ... is considerably larger than the social economy'.[25]) Nevertheless the term 'social economy' is sometimes used as a label for the third sector, presumably on the basis that those organisations it does not include are assumed to be relatively insignificant or that what it does include is relatively so important and homogeneous as to constitute the sector in its own right. Although the labels 'voluntary' and/or 'community sector' are also on occasion used in the same way, the social economy is so often given such prominence that the different definitions of it and the concepts associated with it are given more detailed consideration in Chapter 4.

The social enterprise sector
A term associated with the social economy is the 'social enterprise sector', which is also discussed in Chapter 4. Some sources, such as, for instance, Pearce in Figure 2.1, present the social enterprise sector as a significant component of the social economy. Others seem to use the term almost as a label for the whole of social economy. For instance, in the Foreword to the UK government's *Social Enterprise: a strategy for success*, Tony Blair, who was then Prime Minister, states that when he hosted a social enterprise breakfast at No. 10 he met 'people from every part of the social economy'.[26] The social enterprise action plan later produced by the UK Cabinet Office's Office of the Third Sector states that 'Britain's social enterprise sector is one of the most successful and vibrant in the world.'[27] However, while the action plan refers frequently to social enterprise and social enterprises, it does not use the term 'social economy' but does refer occasionally to the social enterprise sector and to the third sector. The latter, it indicates, embraces social enterprises together with voluntary and community organisations, charities, mutuals and co-operatives.

Do the different definitions matter?

This chapter, and the next one, include a lot of definitions, including definitions for different aspects of the third sector and different definitions for the same aspect. It can be argued that these differences are not important because most people working in the area understand broadly what the third sector and its components are and do not need to define them more precisely. Also most people starting or running a third sector organisation are far more concerned with how well their organisation is performing than with how it might be categorised by bureaucratic or academic rules and principles.

However, the definitions do matter to some people and they are worth considering for a number of reasons:

- *Consistent research.* Definitions matter to researchers in this field who need to use clear definitions for what they are researching if they are to get consistent results and who need to know whether their definitions are the same as those used by other researchers to see if their results are suitable for comparison. Researchers, though, are also attracted to definitions which make measurement easy. Thus a UK-wide survey of social enterprises, conducted for the Small Business Service, did not claim to describe the total population of social enterprises according to any of the usual definitions but instead focused on those organisations registered as industrial and provident societies or as companies limited by guarantee (but excluding those companies in standard industry classifications deemed unlikely to include much social enterprise activity).[28]

- *Measuring the scale or impact of the sector.* Measuring the scale or impact of the social economy, or of a sub-sector of it, may be an example of research but it has a particular relevance to areas such as government policy because the bigger the impact of a sector appears to be, the more governments tend to be interested in it. Definitions therefore matter because wider definitions will indicate a bigger impact and it is argued that the third sector has not, in the past, had the development support it merited because it was not measured as there was no agreed definition of what it was.

- *Targeted policy.* If policy makers are considering support for a sector or sub-sector they will need to define who they wish to help with that support.

- *Fair and consistent disbursement of support.* The application of support policy can involve the provision of advice and information, grant or loan schemes, or tax incentives or concessions. If that policy is targeted then the people who are tasked with providing advice, awarding grants or loans, or approving tax incentives or concessions need to be clear which organisations would be eligible for that support in order to be fair and consistent when excluding organisations which apply but are not eligible.

- *The choice of legal form for organisations.* One consequence of limiting support to tightly defined sectors is that organisations may select, or change, their legal form in order to try to qualify for such support.

- *Politics or ideology.* Operators in, or advocates of, particular sections of the third sector sometimes wish to advance those specific sections for political or ideological reasons, and different definitions are likely to reflect different perceived roles that those sections are expected to perform (see also section 'Paradigm differences' in Chapter 4). As Wikipedia's entry on the social economy says, under the sub-heading of 'Controversy',

Defining the limits of the social economy is made especially difficult by the 'moving sands' of the political and economic context. Consequently organisations may be 'part in, part out', 'in this year, out the next' or moving within the social economy's various sub-sectors.

There is no single right or wrong definition of the social economy. Many commentators and reports have consciously avoided trying to introduce a tight definition for fear of causing more problems than they solve.[29]

- *The different definitions exist.* Whether they matter or not, the different definitions do exist, and it is therefore helpful to those who may come across them to know that they exist and to know that different labels can sometimes be given to the same thing, and that the same label can sometimes be given to different things. Without that sort of understanding, writings about the sector can appear to be very confusing.

- *The differences can be illuminating.* The differences between the different definitions can help to highlight key aspects of some of the organisations in the third sector.

Illustration 3.3   A View on Definitions

It is perhaps best to step back from these attempts at encompassing definitions and follow Amin et al.'s[30] view that the social economy is 'centred around the provision of social and welfare services by the not-for-profit sector'. In this view, 'social economy organisations are understood to represent a break from the "binary choices" of conventional socio-economy strategies that present market and state as mutually exclusive spheres of economic growth and social regeneration'. This starting point has three benefits. First, unlike the definitions reviewed by Mendell and Levesque, it highlights a distinction between the social economy and cognate terms like 'the voluntary sector' or the 'not-for-profit sector'. While it is the organisations within these sectors that are felt to break with the 'binary choices' of market and state, it is primarily those that provide social and welfare services that are interpellated by the term 'social economy'. Second, while this conceptualisation follows the third sector in being defined by what it is not (namely the state or the market), it gestures towards a certain number of economic institutions and practices related to the delivery of those services. Third, it leaves space for politics (as Bourque would wish) to define both the relevant range of organisations included in the social economy and the parameters of the services to be delivered. Thus, in Quebec, many not-for-profit groups have refused to be considered part of the social economy, and have demanded alternative policies to support 'autonomous community activity'. Similarly, as we will see below, both social movements and state officials seek to give concrete meaning to the 'social economy' by proposing relevant policies and institutions. While politics means comparisons between countries will suffer from

> ### Illustration 3.3   (cont'd)
>
> the unevenness given to the definition of the social economy across space and time, within any political space the term will delimit a sphere of activities and policies based on debates and struggles between social forces.
>
> *Source*: P. Graefe 'The social economy and the state: linking ambitions with institutions in Quebec, Canada', *Policy & Politics*, Vol. 30, No. 2, p. 249.

The fourth sector

If the third sector of an economy is defined inclusively as encompassing all those activities with an economic impact which are not included in either the public or the private sector, then there will be no fourth sector. If, though, the third sector is defined exclusively by common characteristics then it is likely that there will be some things not included, which might then be presumed to be in the fourth sector.

Indeed the term 'fourth sector' is occasionally used. 'For some it is used to identify a segment for co-operatives, for others it points to a "household" sector.'[31] Similar to the 'household sector' concept, Wikipedia suggests that the fourth sector is sometimes considered to be 'the informal sector, where informal exchanges take place between family and friends'.[32]

In conclusion

It is clear that the terminology used when talking about this area of an economy frequently does not help as there is no universally agreed set of definitions. Instead there are a variety of different terms and many of those terms can themselves have a variety of meanings so that it is often not immediately clear, when different people use different terms, whether they mean the same thing, or separate things, or whether one of the things referred to might be a subset of the other. For instance, terms like 'the social economy', 'the voluntary sector' and 'the community sector' might be used as labels for what is considered to be the third sector of the economy, or they might be used to refer to different or overlapping sub-sectors within the third sector. Care is thus required.

Care is particularly necessary when dealing with those different definitions or interpretations which are based on, or promoted by, differing political or economic views. Some commentators have sought to avoid tight definitions in order not to offend others by excluding organisations they favour. Other proponents might be suspected of proposing very specific definitions in order to exclude organisations of which they disapprove or because they suit the causes they wish to promote. And, of course, as in many areas of society, fashions change and what it was at one time popular to promote can later lose favour. It is for reasons such as these that seeking to define the third sector and its components can be controversial.

Key Points of Chapter 3

- There are many organisations, in a wide range of categories, which do not belong in either the public or the private sector and so might be considered to be in the third sector, if it is defined inclusively.

- Terms such as 'the voluntary sector', 'the community sector', 'the voluntary and community sector' and 'the social economy' can be confusing because sometimes they have been used as labels for what is considered to be the third sector of the economy and sometimes they might be used to refer to different or overlapping sub-sectors within the third sector.

- Terms such as 'the voluntary sector', 'the community sector', 'the voluntary and community sector' and 'the social economy' are commonly defined exclusively and thus, when they are used synonymously with the third sector, they imply that here is a fourth sector which contains those organisations which they exclude.

- Care is thus required when dealing with the terminology in this field.

CASE 3.1

Several Ventures – One Aim

In 2002 Amy Carter, with her partner Neal Allcock, wanted to alleviate poverty and promote cultural and biological diversity by opening a number of tourist lodges around the world. These lodges would be developed and run to complement and help the local environment and people and to raise the international standards by which 'ethical' tourism companies are measured.

Amy and Neil opened their first lodge at the end of 2004 at Guludo Beach in the north of Mozambique on the shore of the Indian Ocean (www.guludo. com). This location was chosen because of its extreme poverty and excellent tourism potential. Adult life expectancy was under 40 years and under-5 infant mortality was almost 30 per cent. The average amount of schooling received was a year and a half, but most women did not get any education at all. Food shortages at the end of the dry season caused death by starvation, and malaria struck when the rains started. HIV and water-borne diseases were the other major causes of premature death. When Amy and Neal looked at Guludo, at WWF's suggestion, they found that less than a quarter of the eligible children attended primary school and no children from there went to the secondary school. Boys' parents could not afford schooling or needed their sons in the fields and girls were 'sold' into marriage at puberty, many having children when they were as young as 13 years. There had been no jobs near Guludo since the Portuguese left 32 years ago.

CASE 3.1 (cont'd)

By the end of 2006 Amy's and Neal's efforts had achieved the following:

- 1160 families had participated in malaria workshops and received mosquito nets.
- 300 people had clean water.
- 300 children (80 per cent of those eligible) had enrolled for primary school and would all join the Global Angels feeding programme (one good meal a day for a year).
- 5 children in Guludo had received scholarships to attend secondary school.
- 5 new shops had opened.
- 3 craft co-operatives had been established with over 27 members.
- 60 people had received employment and training.
- Marine conservation projects in the region had started.

All this enterprise secured for Amy the New Statesman 'Young Social Entrepreneur of the Year 2006' award but if you look for all this activity in one business you will not find it, because Amy and Neal established three separate businesses:

- Bespoke Experience Limited is a fair trade tourism business which was established as a company limited by shares and therefore one from which its owners can take profits in the form of dividends. Bespoke Experience markets the venture and sells its holidays and looks after corporate functions such as PR, insurance and finance.
- Bespoke Experience in turn set up a wholly owned Mozambican company called Guludo Experience Limitada (GEL), which bought the rights to a 40-hectare beach-side concession in the recently established Quirimbas National Park and constructed an 18-person luxury lodge called Guludo Beach Lodge. In 2006 work started on Bespoke's second lodge, Mipande, which is 15 km southwest of Guludo in a breath-taking area of coastal forest and complements the beach holiday offered in Guludo. These lodges are constructed using local materials, techniques and labour and they employ local people (who are, if necessary, given the training they need to avail of such employment) and buy locally, all for a fair price. Thus the lodges are developed in a way which ensures that the guests' presence and their activities benefit the local community.
- Amy and Neal also founded the charity SERF (Social and Environmental Regeneration Fund) to work with communities in and around the lodges to relieve poverty and protect the environment. Bespoke Experience gives SERF

CASE 3.1 (cont'd)

5 per cent of its accommodation revenue to which are also added other donations, often from guests staying at the lodges. SERF is established in England as a company limited by guarantee and a registered charity and it aims to be a model of excellence for working with rural communities in the areas of health, education, enterprise development, environment management and research.

Source: Correspondence with Amy Carter.

Points raised

Bespoke Experience is a fair trade company but it can still distribute profit to its shareholders and might therefore be considered to be in the private sector. GEL might also be supposed to be in the private sector but it too has a clear social objective. SERF is a charity which does not itself trade at all and so, according to many definitions, would not be considered to be a social enterprise, although it is in the third sector. Looked at from an organisational perspective, Bespoke Experience, GEL and SERF are different organisations with different formats and different aims, and Bespoke Experience and SERF are even in different sectors of the economy. However, all three organisations came from the same aspirations of Amy and her partner and so, from their perspective, they are just different manifestations of the same purpose. Using the fungus analogy suggested in Chapter 2, they are like three mushrooms growing from the same mycelium but appearing above the ground on different sides of a somewhat arbitrarily placed dividing fence.

As Amy herself puts it,

> Through these companies Bespoke has created a unique business model where all three organisations are legally and financially separate, but SERF operates as Bespoke's 'charity department' and GEL acts as Bespoke's 'lodge operations department'. Bespoke acts as lodge owner and carries out sales, marketing, PR, and corporate functions.

This case thus demonstrates that to understand what is going on it is often necessary to follow the entrepreneur, not the business.

CASE 3.2

LEDU's Community Business Programme

From 1972 to 2002 the Local Enterprise Development Unit (LEDU) was Northern Ireland's government-funded small business agency. In the middle of the 1980s, as part of the Northern Ireland Department of Economic Development's Pathfinder initiative, LEDU examined ways of extending its enterprise, as opposed to just small business, development activity.

CASE 3.2 (cont'd)

One proposal which was put to LEDU in 1986 was based on what was described as a 'Third Sector' approach to business. It pointed out that large sections of Northern Ireland's population lived within large peripheral housing estates and inner city ghettos which had become economic wastelands inhabited by dispossessed and frustrated families totally dependent on the welfare state, which itself reinforces dependency. This circle, it was suggested, was viciously self-perpetuating and the waste of human resources was tragic, irrational and cruel, and therefore, in seeking to engender an enterprise culture throughout Northern Ireland, there was a need to target innovative social and economic programmes that would impact significantly in those areas that needed to benefit most.

Already, the proposal claimed, many local community groups were exploring the possibility of an approach whereby local communities sought to establish their own businesses. The rationale behind that strategy, it said, combined social and economic criteria, leading to local communities establishing trading organisations and creating jobs locally by providing goods and services needed by local people and retaining profits within local communities which could be used to fund further economic and social development projects.[33]

LEDU sought to support and expand this approach by establishing a programme of support for community businesses. Its original 'Community Business Proposal' sought 'to contribute to resolving existing economic difficulties by utilising the resources and skills that exist in the community and putting them to work. The people that make up communities', it was suggested, 'have the motivation and willingness to help themselves' and 'Northern Ireland has some well established community-based businesses' which 'have developed without an overall support system and by direct community action'.[34]

As a result, a pilot 'Community Business Programme', funded by the International Fund for Ireland, was launched in 1989. Participating groups worked with a Community Business Worker who provided training in assessing local needs, finding and testing ideas, market research, costing, business planning, management skills and legal matters. Once committed to working on the programme, groups were eligible for a formation grant to cover early costs such as surveys, visits and meetings. The project also provided funding for the preparation of business plans and a contribution towards the first-year costs of a full-time manager.

Although the programme did not attempt to define a community business, it did limit its support to enterprises which were, or would be, in some way community based, and which did not distribute profits to individuals but instead provided the community in question with some form of benefit such as jobs or skills.

CASE 3.2 (cont'd)

After the end of the pilot programme the initiative was continued, probably more because it was aimed at disadvantaged communities (and so appeared to be very compatible with the Northern Ireland government's 'Targeting Social Need' objective) than because it had achieved any clear positive results. Nevertheless LEDU took over the funding of the programme which was relaunched in 1992 still as the Community Business Programme. It continued until LEDU itself was subsumed into Invest NI in 2002. When that happened the programme was taken over and, in effect, repackaged as Invest NI's Social Entrepreneurship Programme, which was announced in 2006.

Points raised

- At the time the programme was designed and developed, which was in the late 1980s and early 1990s, the term commonly used for a business which, unlike private sector businesses, did not distribute profits to individuals and had social aims linked often to a particular community, was 'community business'. In 1991, for instance, Northern Ireland, as well as having a Community Business Programme, also had a 'Community Business Week', which was fostered by 'Community Business Northern Ireland'. The concept of a community business was not closely defined however.

- The term 'third system' was also then in use, but there was no mention of the social economy or social enterprise.

- By 2006 the terminology had changed and the 'Community Business Programme', in essence, had become the 'Social Entrepreneurship Programme', which now assists 'social economy enterprises'.

Questions, Exercises, Essay and Discussion Topics

1. Of the three organisations described in Case 3.1, which, if any, are in the third sector?

2. Is there a better name for the third sector?

3. The term 'community sector' is just an older name for the third sector. Discuss.

4. If the terms 'voluntary sector', 'community sector' and 'third sector' are used to describe different things, what are the differences between them? What do they nevertheless have in common?

5. If there is a fourth sector, what might be in it?

======= **SUGGESTIONS FOR FURTHER READING** =======

A. Amin, A. Cameron and R. Hudson, *Placing the Social Economy* (London: Routledge, 2002).

J. Kendall, *The Voluntary Sector* (London: Routledge, 2003).

J. Pearce, *Social Enterprise in Anytown* (London: Calouste Gulbenkian Foundation, 2003).

References

1. For instance, EU DGV pilot action, *Third System and Employment* and reports produced for it, 1999.
2. For instance, 'A Third Way between state and market', A. Amin, A. Cameron and R. Hudson, *Placing the Social Economy* (London: Routledge, 2002), p. 11.
3. J. Kendall, *The Voluntary Sector* (London: Routledge, 2003), p. 1.
4. J. Pearce, *Social Enterprise in Anytown* (London: Calouste Gulbenkian Foundation, 2003), p. 66.
5. From the Wikipedia entry on social economy (www.wikipedia.org, accessed July 2006).
6. A. Amin, A. Cameron and R. Hudson, *Placing the Social Economy* (London: Routledge, 2002), p. vii.
7. From the speech of Gordon Brown, Chancellor of the Exchequer, to the Labour Party Conference on 25 September 2006.
8. www.wikipedia.org/wiki/Social_Economy, accessed 7 December 2006.
9. J. Kendall, *The Voluntary Sector* (London: Routledge, 2003), p. 1.
10. Ibid., p. 21.
11. Ibid., p. 6.
12. Ibid.
13. Ibid., p. 21.
14. www.ncvo-org.uk, accessed 8 December 2006.
15. www.wikipedia.org/wiki/Social_Economy, accessed 7 November 2006.
16. *A Manifesto for Voluntary Action,* www.ncvo-org.uk, accessed 8 December 2006.
17. J. Kendall, *The Voluntary Sector* (London: Routledge, 2003), p. 6.
18. J. Pearce, *Social Enterprise in Anytown* (London: Calouste Gulbenkian Foundation, 2003), pp. 28–9.
19. As reported in A. Amin, A. Cameron and R. Hudson, *Placing the Social Economy* (London: Routledge, 2002), p. 63.
20. K. Hayton, 'Scottish community business: An idea that has had its day', *Policy and Politics*, Vol. 28, No. 2 (2000), p. 195.
21. Ibid., p. 196.
22. Based on J. Pearce, *Social Enterprise in Anytown* (London: Calouste Gulbenkian Foundation, 2003), p. 66.
23. J. Pearce, *Social Enterprise in Anytown* (London: Calouste Gulbenkian Foundation, 2003), p. 66.
24. A. Molloy, C. McFeely and E. Connolly, *Building a Social Economy for the New Millenium* (Derry: Guildhall Press/NICDA Social Economy Agency, 1999), p. 11.

25. *What We Need to Know About the Social Economy: A Guide for Policy Research* (Canada: Policy Research Institute, July 2005), p. 4.

26. *Social Enterprise: a strategy for success*, Department of Trade and Industry, 2002.

27. Cabinet Office: Office of the Third Sector, *Social enterprise action lan: Scaling new heights* (London: HM Government, 2006), p. 3.

28. IFF Research Ltd, *A Survey of Social Enterprise Across the UK*, research report prepared for the Small Business Service (SBS), July 2005.

29. wikipedia.org/wiki/Social_Economy, accessed 7 November 2006.

30. A. Amin, A. Cameron and R. Hudson, 'Welfare as work? The potential of the UK social economy', *Environment and Planning A*, Vol. 31, No. 11 (1999), p. 2033.

31. C. Gunn, *Third Sector Development: Making up for the Market* (New York: Cornell University Press, 2004), p. 189.

32. www.wikipedia.org/wiki/Social_Economy, accessed 7 November 2006.

33. Based on an article by Paul Sweeney in *Pathfinder Enterprise* published by the Department of Economic Development in about 1988.

34. Based on a funding submission by LEDU to the International Fund for Ireland, 1987.

The Social Economy and Social Enterprises

Key Concepts

This chapter covers:

- the emergence of the concept of the social economy and why it is currently of interest;
- various approaches to the social economy, and to its components, and the lack of a single common interpretation of it;

(cont'd)

- different views on social enterprises and their relationship to the social economy;
- the archetypical components of the social economy (co-operatives, mutuals, associations and foundations) and other categories within it;
- some indications of the scale of the social economy.

Learning Objectives

By the end of this chapter the reader should

- understand how the concept of the social economy has emerged and why the social economy might currently be of interest;
- appreciate that there is a diversity of definitions which have been advanced for the social economy, sometimes reflecting different paradigms;
- appreciate that there are coherent traits, values and organisational formats which mark out social enterprises as components of the social economy;
- understand what co-operatives, mutuals, associations and foundations are;
- be aware of some of the other components of the social economy;
- appreciate that some parts of the social economy, such as LETS and community credit, will not register in formal economic measures and that a corollary of this is that a desire for measurable economic outputs from support schemes may actually hinder community involvement;
- appreciate the scale of the social economy.

Introduction

As Chapter 3 explained, the social economy has often been the focus of attention for those people interested in the wider aspects of the economy beyond just the private and public sectors. As it also explained, 'the social economy' is a term which can be used to refer to either a distinct and very significant part of the third sector of an economy or a part of the economy which is itself sufficiently prominent to be considered to be the third sector. In either case it is thought by many people to be very important both economically and socially.

The social economy is usually defined by shared characteristics, an approach which serves to include some organisations and to exclude others. The organisations which are included in it have been grouped into a number of subsets or categories, and it was around three of these categories in particular – co-operatives, mutuals and associations – that the concept of the social economy seems first to have been formulated. Because it was recognised that they shared a number of characteristics but did not fit into either the public or the private sector of an economy, these organisations were considered to be a third section of the economy and were, in French, referred to as *l'économie sociale*, from which the English term 'the social economy' was derived.

Once the concept of the social economy started to be recognised, arguments were advanced that other organisations should be grouped within it. To the original three categories of co-operatives, mutuals and associations were later added foundations and, according to some authorities, more recently those organisations referred to as social enterprises, social businesses or social economy enterprises. The result has been a number of exclusive definitions which, although being relatively wide, have not included all the organisations which are in neither the public nor the private sector. That has in turn led to arguments that the social economy is not itself the whole of the third sector or that there must therefore be a fourth sector (see Chapter 3).

Because of this ambiguity, and because of its perceived importance, this chapter examines the social economy, considers the variety of views of what is considered to be in it, and explores the different subsets of organisations generally considered to be among its components.

The emergence of the social economy

Moulaert and Ailenei[1] have described how the term *économie sociale* became accepted after it was first used in 1830 by the French economist Charles Dunoyer. They suggest that the emergence of the social economy as a specific concept, in France and at that time, was the result of institutionalisation and a theoretical assessment of practical experiences.

Those experiences might be said to have had their roots in aspects of Egyptian, Greek and Roman life and later in the guilds that appeared in Northwest Europe in medieval times when a rich associative life was evident. This was the case in other parts of the world also, including medieval Byzantium, Muslim countries and India, in which 'associations' were formed in order to organise and protect communities of interest. Moulaert and Ailenei quote several authors who contend that the social economy has a history of emergence and re-emergence linked to a series of economic and social crises. Many of the guilds and other associations, they suggest, were created to provide assistance, mutual support and charity in the uncertain times of the early middle ages. The changes later brought about by the industrial revolution led to a decline in craft-co-operatives and created renewed interests in 'utopian socialism' and the values of co-operation and mutual support. The French revolution, it has been argued, fostered political equality but not material equality, and because material inequalities remained, mutual support organisations (*mutuelles*) appeared in the middle of the nineteenth century. In the last quarter of that century agricultural and savings co-operatives were formed in response to the needs of small producers affected by increasing accumulation and the economic power of the bigger businesses thus created. In France, it might be said, republican ideals generated distinctive interests in associations as a buffer between individuals and the state, whereas in England, ideas around communitarianism strongly influenced the co-operative movement.

Based on an assessment of such experiences, in particular in France, the concept of *l'économie sociale* came to be seen as encompassing the co-operatives, *mutuelles* and associations mentioned above. Chapter 2 indicated that, when the private and public sectors evolved as separate parts of an economy, there was still a wide range of activities which belonged in neither of those two sectors and so they are said to be in the third sector. That approach to the third sector defines it as including everything not in the other two sectors. The approach to the social economy described above is different as it is based on including only certain categories of organisation which have a number of shared characteristics. However, today, according to Moulaert and Ailenei,

> The social economy represents a wide family of initiatives and organisational forms – i.e. a hybridisation of market, non-market (redistribution) and non-monetary (reciprocity) economies showing that the economy is not limited to the market, but includes the principles of redistribution and reciprocity.[2]

Although the social economy may have been first conceptualised in the nineteenth century there have been crises since then which have further stimulated its development. In the twentieth century, the economic collapse of 1929–1932 led to the formation of consumption co-operatives for food and housing,[3] and further initiatives in 1970s Europe have been seen, on the one hand, to be a reaction to the crises in the mass production system and, on the other hand, to be a response to the overburdening of the welfare state.[4] Indeed Amin et al. trace the most recent interest in the social economy to the end of full employment and the crisis in welfare provision which started in the 1970s. This 'post-Fordist' environment, they suggest, was characterised by

- rising global energy prices;
- rising imports from low wage counties and flexibly organised new economies;
- wage drift and sustained opposition from organised labour;
- decreasing return on sunk capital;
- growth of new technologies and organised principles no longer dependent on economies of scale;
- falling demand for mass-produced goods and the rise of customised consumption;
- waning support for mass representative democracy; and
- strains on government to provide expensive welfare services and the rise of new right market ideas on the management of the relationship between the state and the economy.[5]

Teague points out that, in this context, governments and policy makers have sought too much from the sector by combining its roles in business incubation, social repair and welfare delivery.[6] However, this latest crises of state management, Amin et al. suggest, simultaneously renewed interest in the potential of the social economy as a place of work and provider of welfare services. For instance, the European Commission established its Social Economy Unit, within DGXXIII, in 1989 and the importance of the social economy was formally recognised by the European Union in its 1994 White Paper on *Growth, Competitiveness and Employment*. This paper indicated that the EU saw the 'third sector' as a potentially important contributor to the growth of employment and as means of avoiding dual labour markets, twin-speed societies and urban segregation. By the end of the 1990s attention was being paid to the social economy in many of the EU member states, including the UK (see Chapter 8), and it would seem that this re-emergence of the social economy as a subject of interest can be linked to economic and social change resulting, at least in Western Europe, from the late-twentieth-century 'post-Fordist' changes to manufacturing strength and the welfare state environment. From different shades of political opinion the social economy is, in many quarters, now attracting considerable attention.

What is the social economy?

> The social economy is an imprecise term –
> but in general can be thought of as those organisations who (sic) are independent of the state and provide services, goods and trade for a social purpose and are not profit distributing.[7]

There are, between some different stakeholders, deep theoretical and policy differences as to what constitutes the social economy and what its ultimate political purpose is.[8] The classification *économie sociale* used in some EU member states has typically specifically included three categories of organisation – associations, co-operatives and mutuals – and was expanded in the early 1990s to include foundations also. (These categories are sometimes referred to as CMAFs: co-operatives, mutuals, associations and foundations.) However, as the quotation above indicates, at least in UK government circles, the social economy is defined only very loosely in terms of some characteristics of the organisations within it. The European Commission also does not formally define the social economy but, presumably based on the *économie sociale* classification, has indicated that

> The so-called social economy, including co-operatives, mutual societies, non-profit associations, foundations and social enterprises provides a wide range of products and services across Europe, and generates millions of jobs.[9]

and that

> The importance to the European economy of co-operatives, mutual societies, associations, foundations and social enterprises (which together are sometimes referred to as the Social Economy) is now receiving greater recognition[10]

The latter reference adds that

The social economy is found in almost all economic sectors. Cooperatives are particularly prominent in certain fields, such as banking, crafts, agricultural production and retailing. Mutual societies are predominately active in the insurance and
mortgage sectors, whilst associations and foundations figure strongly in the provision of health and welfare services, sports and recreation, culture, environmental
regeneration, humanitarian rights, development aid, consumer rights, education,
training and research. Some Social Economy bodies work in competitive markets
while others work close to the public sector. Cooperatives, for example, which
are formed on the basis of fulfilling the interests of their members (producers or
consumers) play an important role in several markets and contribute to effective
competition.[11]

In the UK, the Industrial Common Ownership Movement (ICOM), the fed-
eral organisation of UK co-operatives, has argued that the social economy sector should be thought of as a continuum in an approach similar to the French
économie sociale,[12] and Molloy et al. presented this diagrammatically, as shown
in Figure 4.1.

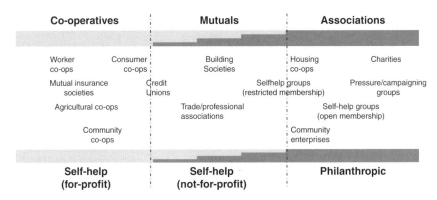

Figure 4.1   Traditional components of the social economy

Source: A. Molloy, C. McFeely, and E. Connolly, *Building a Social Economy for the New Millenium* (Derry: Guildhall
Press, 1999), p. 12.

The approach in Figure 4.1 presents the social economy as a sector encompassing a range of organisations, with agencies positioned in different places
in the range depending on their economic rationale and constitutional status. Cooper[13] defined the social economy as areas of activity that overlapped
between the private, public and voluntary sectors and saw it as flexible
but characterised by a number of a common features. These are shown in
Table 4.1.

Another approach is that of Sattar and Mayo,[14] who suggest that the social
economy can de described using three 'I's:

- *Identity* covering those for whom there is a convergence of interest and sense of identity as a social economy distinct from other sectors of the economy;
- *Institutions* covering the three main institutional categories of co-operatives, mutuals and voluntary associations; and
- *Intention* covering economic activities pursued with a social or ethical intention.

Table 4.1   Common features of the social economy

Values	Characteristics	Organisations	Activities
Democratic	Economically active	Co-operatives	Creating and
Collective	Mutually supportive	Community	managing workspace
Co-operative	Community or	businesses	Developing property
Mutual	common ownership	Charitable trading	Training
Sustainable	Community benefit	LETS	Job creation schemes
Equitable and open	Common	Credit Unions	Providing local
	use/distribution of	Community based	services
	surplus	development trusts	Running commercial
	Community based	Ethical	services
		banks/community	Providing social
		finance schemes	housing
		Industrial and	Providing low cost
		provident societies	personal loans

Source: Based on M. Cooper, 'The development of the third sector in Bristol', *Local Economy*, Vol. 14, No. 4 (1999), pp. 348–349.

Paradigm differences: What is the social economy's role?

Basing descriptions of the social economy on objective assessments of what is in it, as this chapter has tried to do, might appear to be logical, but it is not the sequence that often appears to be followed. Instead, assessments of what is considered to be in the social economy are, in effect, based on definitions subjectively derived from the function that it is expected or hoped that the social economy will serve.

One of the reasons advanced for the lack of a single, generally accepted, definition of the social economy is that it is due, at last in part, to the various different traditions and policy emphasis that exist. Amin et al., for instance, have identified 'considerable international differences in the ways in which the social economy and its relationship to market, state and civil society are envisioned'. In the United States, they suggest, which, compared to many European countries, has a weak welfare state playing a largely residual role, the sector is shaped by 'bottom-up' community development processes fronted by a voluntary sector now only loosely connected with political activism. In Western Europe, the tendency towards a withdrawal of state funding has encouraged stronger community economic development and enterprise linked to an expanded role for the third sector more generally. France could be seen perhaps as the paradigmatic model of a state-supported social economy in which the social enterprise has been accorded a specific legal status. But within Europe there are significant variations between a French–German–Belgian tradition of strong social economy providers recognised and regulated by national governments and a weaker Mediterranean model where formal recognition and development of a social economy distinct from strong charities is, at best, embryonic. The Anglo-Saxon model has a particular emphasis on tackling social exclusion, has become strongly spatialised and, in the UK, has been closely connected to the New Labour ideas of building a Third Way between the market and the public sector. Amin et al. also find potential in Nordic interpretations of the social economy as there the presence of large public sectors and comparatively strong welfare systems create the conditions for the social economy to play a strong role in the progressive politics of redistribution.[15]

The different roles that social enterprises in these different traditions have played, or are expected to play, not only lead to different definitions reflecting those different roles but also lead some people to focus on the social economy and some on social enterprises. Peter Lloyd, for instance, has identified two very different schools of thought, one of which he identifies as of a US/UK approach and the other as of a European approach. The European approach, he suggests, is a social economy approach which does not hold back from offering a challenge to the post-1980s hegemony of liberal market forces as the only grand narrative and takes a whole society perspective instead of just a business-focused one. In contrast, the US/UK approach is a social enterprise approach as it starts with the enterprises of which the social economy is composed, and defines them as businesses operating in a market context but using surpluses to achieve social objectives. Lloyd suggests that this difference reflects a fundamental difference in paradigm between a European political economy approach and the narrow market-based approach arising from Anglo-Saxon neo-liberal traditions.[16]

Graefe has suggested that the situation presents three potential economic development scenarios in late welfare state countries. The first is a neo-liberal one, where the market place is pre-eminent and where the social elements of the economy are pushed aside, and the second involves a return to traditional social democratic forms based on reconstructing the welfare state. However, neither of these, he suggests, is either likely or practicable, leaving a third option to connect market and non-market components of the modern economy:

> It is in this context that the social economy finds its full expression: as part of renewed social democratic strategy that includes work-time reduction, greater workplace participation, and the provision of services that meets new demands and needs. On the one hand, the social economy can meet new needs by mobilising resources latent within communities, and by building new solidarities. On the other hand, this social provision bypasses the Taylorist welfare state and is based on more participatory forms of organisation and decision making. More broadly, as economic success increasingly comes to rely on extra-economic resources (such as social capital), strategic spaces are opened for a vision of development that integrates social priorities at every stage.[17]

The different definitions officially advanced largely follow the different roles officially assigned to the social economy and, it is suggested, the argument over the role of the social economy can, at times, be reduced to three broad choices:

- An economic/entrepreneurship approach, which sees social economy organi-sations as 'businesses' that can assist community regeneration, and puts an emphasis on their financial sustainability. Social enterprises will function, it is believed, where the private sector will not, or at least not until some pump-priming has been done by the sector to make it attractive for private interests. It could be argued that the UK DTI perspective on the sector held this view but that subsequently it has been softened with the relocation of the Social Enterprise Unit to the Cabinet Office.

- A socio-economic policy approach, which sees the sector as 'patching up' the inadequacies of the welfare state, while still confining it to a marginal role in the economy. The sector should confine itself to 'the parts that government cannot (or will not) reach' and thus it is characterised as a 'low cost provider', supplementing rather than complementing the welfare state.

- A political/ideological approach which envisages a social economy sector significantly strong to lever institutional change and to promote more demo-cratic structures and citizen participation in decision-making.

Typically, an emphasis on the first, or on the second, of these roles will lead to a focus on social enterprises and to definitions of them which emphasise their business attributes. The third one, however, leads to a focus on the social econ-omy and to definitions which emphasise the democratic nature of its compo-nents. For instance, the first and second might be associated with the US/UK approach, which, Lloyd suggests, has, in the UK, produced the (then) DTI definition of a social enterprise, which is as follows:

> A business with primarily social objectives whose surpluses are principally reinvested for that purpose in the business or in the community, rather than being driven by the need to maximise profit for shareholders and owners.[18]

The third is closer to the European approach, which Lloyd illustrates with a definition from Laville, for whom social enterprises are

> Enterprises initiated by groups of citizens who seek to provide an expanded range of services and more openness to the community – they place a high value on indepen-dence and economic risk taking.[19]

This difference in approach, it would appear, can be seen not just between countries but also between different stakeholders. Policy makers, it has been suggested, generally want to fund social enterprises whereas practitioners often want to develop a social economy.

The lack of a clear generally accepted terminology for the social economy may reflect not just different national paradigms but also changes in perception, and of language, over time. Within the UK, it has been suggested, the vocabulary shift, from 'community businesses' to 'social enterprises' (and now to 'third sec-tor'?), might reflect a pragmatic change in the emphasis, in the management and perhaps in the values of the sector. Factors such as the poor experience of some Scottish community business projects in the early 1990s, the political impact of

Thatcherite ideas on market efficiency and performance, and the appeal of high performing entrepreneurs might all have had an impact. The community and co-operative organisations created at local level had been seen by some as part of a process of seeking different economic forms as an alternative to the dominant system but now, according to Pearce,

> Much contemporary debate on social enterprise tends...to be satisfied to identify sectors within the twenty-first century mainstream economy where it is considered appropriate for social enterprises to operate. That means taking on tasks which governments are insisting the public sector should no longer fulfil but in which the private sector has no interest because they are not really profitable. Social enterprises thus become the problem fixers.
>
> There is a danger therefore of social enterprises being boxed into that corner of the economy which deals only with the most disadvantaged in the poorest areas mopping up the problems of society as cheaply as possible by using voluntary and work-for-the-dole labour. In this scenario, the social economy would continue to be no more than the prop which underpins the 'real' economy – very much the third sector, subservient to the public and to the private, pre-eminent sector. Not a third system and no longer an agent for change.[20]

In soliciting support for the Social Economy, we do not argue that it is a panacea which will permanently eradicate unemployment. We do, however, argue that a national policy and strategic framework for the development of the Social Economy will have significant impact in assisting the disadvantaged and most marginalised into economic activity. The nature of the Social Economy is such that it addresses the issues of long-term unemployment and social deprivation while offering a viable and coherent area of economic activity in its own right.

Source: A. Molloy, C. McFeely and E. Connolly, Building a Social Economy for the New Millenium (Derry: Guildhall Press/NICDA Social Economy Agency, 1999), p. 7.

Social enterprises

The different models of the social economy which are summarised above seem to treat social enterprises differently. The European approach starts with the social economy which, the EU indicates, includes co-operatives, mutual societies, associations, foundations and social enterprises. Thus by specifying social enterprises alongside co-operatives, mutual societies, associations, foundations it suggests that organisations in the latter categories, while being at the core of the social economy, are not themselves social enterprises. The US/UK approach, however, in effect starts with social enterprises and seems to imply that the social economy amounts to the sum of all the social enterprises within it, which implies that co-operatives, mutual societies, associations and foundations are social enterprises because they are in the social economy.

One way of avoiding the issue of whether social enterprises include co-operatives, mutual societies, associations and foundations is to talk instead about 'social economy enterprises' as a generic term. The European Commission, for instance, under the heading of 'Social Economy Enterprises', indicates that there are certain common characteristics shared by what it then calls social economy entities:

- Their primary purpose is not to obtain a return on capital. They are, by nature, part of a stakeholder economy, whose enterprises are created by and for those with common needs, and accountable to those they are meant to serve.

- They are generally managed in accordance with the principle of 'one member, one vote'.

- They are flexible and innovative – social economy enterprises are being created to meet changing social and economic circumstances.

- Most are based on voluntary participation, membership and commitment.[21]

This approach to defining not the social economy *per se* but some or all of its components is common. Those components have been variously labelled 'social enterprises', 'social economy enterprises' (SEEs), 'social economy entities', 'social economy organisations' and/or 'community enterprises' or 'businesses', and it is upon definitions of them that many approaches to the social economy are founded. The European research network, EMES, has, for instance, proposed a definition of social enterprise which is based on four economic and five social criteria, and which can provide a useful framework for differentiating definitions of social enterprise across Europe (see Illustration 4.1).

Illustration 4.1   The EMES-Proposed Definition of the Social Enterprise

Economic criteria

1) Continuous activity of the production and/or sale of goods and services (rather than predominantly advisory or grant-giving functions).

2) A high level of autonomy: social enterprises are created voluntarily by groups of citizens and are managed by them, and not directly or indirectly by public authorities or private companies, even if they may benefit from grants and donations. Their shareholders have the right to participate ('voice') and to leave the organisation ('exit').

3) A significant economic risk: the financial viability of social enterprises depends on the efforts of their members, who have the responsibility of ensuring adequate financial resources, unlike most public institutions.

Illustration 4.1   (cont'd)

4) Social enterprises' activities require a minimum number of paid workers, although, like traditional non-profit organisations, social enterprises may combine financial and non-financial resources, voluntary and paid work.

Social criteria

5) An explicit aim of community benefit: one of the principal aims of social enterprises is to serve the community or a specific group of people. To the same end, they also promote a sense of social responsibility at local level.

6) Citizen initiative: social enterprises are the result of collective dynamics involving people belonging to a community or to a group that shares a certain need or aim. They must maintain this dimension in one form or another.

7) Decision-making not based on capital ownership: this generally means the principle of 'one member, one vote', or at least a voting power not based on capital shares. Although capital owners in social enterprises play an important role, decision-making rights are shared with the other stakeholders.

8) Participatory character, involving those affected by the activity: the users of social enterprises' services are represented and participate in their structures. In many cases one of the objectives is to strengthen democracy at local level through economic activity.

9) Limited distribution of profit: social enterprises include organisations that totally prohibit profit distribution as well as organisations such as co-operatives, which may distribute their profit only to a limited degree, thus avoiding profit maximising behaviour.

Source: EMES (2001) The Emergence of Social Enterprises in Europe, Brussels, EMES; http://www.emes.net.

In 1997 the European Network for Economic Self Help and Local Development analysed the variety of social enterprises in European countries and identified some common principles, which in turn led to working definitions of social enterprises. The common principles were as follows:[22]

- They seek to tackle specific *social aims by engaging in economic and trading activities.*
- They are *not-for-profit organisations,* in the sense that all surplus profits generated are either re-invested in the economic activities of the enterprise or are used in other ways to tackle the stated social aims of the enterprise.

- Their legal structures are such that all assets and accumulated wealth of the enterprise do not belong to any individuals but are held in trust to be used *for the benefit of these persons or areas* that are the intended beneficiaries of the enterprise's social aims.
- Their organisational structures are such that the full participation of members is encouraged on a *co-operative basis* with rights accorded to all members.
- It is a further characteristic of the social enterprise that it encourages *mutual co-operation* between social enterprises and with other organisations in the wider economy.

Oatley identified six characteristics shared by organisations in the social economy:[23]

- A combination of social, ethical and economic purposes and values.
- Benefits for members or community rather than to reward investment.
- 'People centred' rather than 'investment centred'.
- Participative values.
- Independent and self-governing.
- Where trading takes place it is to address the aims of the organisations.

Pearce also suggests that there are six defining characteristics of a social enterprise (italics in original):

- Having a *social purpose or purposes;*
- Achieving the social purposes by, at least in part, *engaging in trade* in the market place;
- *Not distributing profits* to individuals;
- Holding assets and wealth *in trust for community benefit;*
- *Democratically* involving members of its constituency in the governance of the organisation; and
- Being independent organisations *accountable* to a defined constituency and to the wider community.[24]

Other definitions of social enterprises include the following:

- *UK Government Definition:* 'A social enterprise is a business with primary social objectives whose surpluses are principally reinvested for that purpose in the business or in the community, rather than being driven by the need to maximise profit for shareholders and owners.'[25]
- *SBS Definition:* (The UK's Small Business Service [SBS] is now the Enterprise Directorate in the Department of Business, Enterprise and Regulatory Reform [BERR].) 'Social enterprises are competitive businesses, owned and trading

for a social purpose. They seek to succeed as businesses by establishing a market share and making a profit. Social enterprises combine the need to be successful businesses with social aims. They emphasise the long-term benefits for employees, consumers and the community.'[26]

- *OECD Definition*: 'Any private activity conducted in the public interest, organised with an entrepreneurial strategy but whose main purpose is not the maximisation of profit but the attainment of certain economic and social goals, and which has a capacity for bringing innovative solutions to the problems of social exclusion and unemployment.'[27]

Comparing definitions

Using a set of criteria based mainly on the EMES proposal, Table 4.2 presents a comparison of some of the definitions of social enterprises, or social economy component organisations, given above. This comparison suggests that, even for the limited number of definitions chosen, there is little that they agree is an essential criterion except that of having a social purpose. Even the re-investment of profits is not always an absolute requirement as both the (then) DTI and the EMES definitions allow some profit distribution, the OECD definition does not disallow it and some other definitions clearly include those co-operatives which distribute profits to their members. However, the definitions, in general, do suggest that there are some coherent traits, values and organisational formats which mark out social enterprises, and the social economy of which they are a significant part, as a distinctive economic, social and cultural sphere of activity.

Other approaches and definitions

Another way of thinking about social enterprises is to look at their areas of work. Pearce identifies four main activity areas, which include the following:[28]

- local development and regeneration such as the management of workspace units, training programmes, business support, physical development and environmental work and housing provision;
- working for the state, which involves the delivery of state services, asset transfer of local resources such as play grounds or community facilities although, as we show later, this raises important concerns about the sector providing cheap alternatives to welfare provision;
- providing services to the community such as local retraining, a community café or second-hand store; and
- Market-driven businesses that look like organisations in the first sector and which emphasise their profitability as well as their social mission.

Pearce also highlights the diversity of the sector which embraces both small and very large businesses such as the Cooperative Bank, large housing associations

Table 4.2 A comparison of definitions of social enterprises or social economy component organisations

Criteria	Source of definition							
	DTI	EMES	European network for economic self-help	European Commission	Laville	OECD	Pearce	SBS
Social purpose	Primarily social objectives	An explicit aim of community benefit	Seek to tackle specific social aims	Created by and for those with common needs	An expanded range of services	Organised for certain economic and social goals	Has a social purpose or purposes	Owned and trading for a social purpose
Community		Involves people of a community with shared needs			More openness to the community			
Democracy		Decisions not based on capital ownership		Generally managed in accordance with the principle of 'one member, one vote'			Democratically involves members of its constituency in its governance	
Participation and accountability		Users are represented and participate in governance	Structures encourage full participation of members	Mostly based on voluntary participation and are accountable to those they are meant to serve	Initiated by groups of citizens		Accountable to defined constituency and wider community	
Profits	Surpluses principally reinvested for the social objectives	Limited distribution of profits	All surplus profits re-invested in the enterprise or used to tackle its aims	Primary purpose is not to retain a return on capital		The main purpose is not profit maximisation	Does not distribute profits to individuals	For the benefit of employees, consumers and the community

Table 4.2 (Continued)

Criteria	Source of definition						
	DTI	EMES	European network for economic self-help	European Commission	Laville	OECD	Pearce	SBS
Trading		Continuous activity for the production/ sale of goods/ services	Tackle aims by engaging in economic and trading activity				Engages in trade (at least in part)	Seek to succeed by establishing a market share and making a profit
Autonomy		A high level of autonomy			A high value put on independence		Is an independent organisation	
Risk		Viability depends on members' efforts			A high value put on economic risk-taking			
Employment		A minimum number of paid workers						
Assets			Assets held in trust for the benefit of those addressed by the aims				Holds assets in trust for community benefit	
Others			Encourages mutual co-operation with others in the local economy	Flexible and innovative – created to meet changing social and economic circumstances		Capacity for innovative solutions to social exclusion and unemployment		

and, in the UK, a growing credit union sector. Some enterprises are staffed entirely by voluntary staff whilst others have large workforces of paid employees. Similarly, a large number are dependent on grant aid or regular fund-raising whilst others can be financially self-sustaining and the relationship amongst these types of income streams can vary over time. Linked to this, social enterprises tend to be people rather than profit centred although, as is noted in Chapter 5, this is a constant tension in the operation of social enterprises and community businesses. A number of initiatives in the social economy demonstrate the value of alternative economic models including informal trading schemes and time banks, whilst others apply more formal business models to deliver social gain.

Illustration 4.2   Other Definitions of Social Enterprises

Other definitions of social enterprises, collected by Pearce, include the following:

- Social enterprises:

    Are not-for-profit organisations.

    Seek to meet social aims by engaging in economic and trading activities.

    Have legal structures which ensure that all assets and accumulated wealth are not in the ownership of individuals but are held in trust and for the benefit of those persons and/or areas that are the intended beneficiaries of the enterprise's social aims.

    Have organisational structures in which full participation of members is encouraged on a co-operative basis with equal rights accorded to all members.[29]

- ... organisations who are independent of the state and provide services, goods and trade for a social purpose and are non-profit-distributing.[30]

- Social enterprises are competitive businesses, owned and trading for a social purpose. (They) have three common characteristics:

    Enterprise orientation – [are] directly involved in producing goods or providing services to a market ... seek to be viable trading concerns, making an operating surplus.

    Have explicit social aims ... have ethical values ... are accountable to their members and the wider community for their social, environmental and economic impact.

    Social ownership – are autonomous organisations with governance and ownership structures based on participation by stakeholder groups ... profits are distributed as profit-sharing to stakeholders or used for the benefit of the community.[31]

Illustration 4.2   (cont'd)

- Social enterprises try to make a profit, but they operate on a not-for-personal-profit basis, applying any surplus they create to furthering their social objectives. They put people first and, through their economic activities, seek to deliver employment opportunities and other social, environmental, or community benefits.[32]

Further definitions are as follows:

- Social Economy Enterprises are community owner/co-operative businesses, trading for economic and social purposes. They seek to succeed as businesses by establishing a market share and making a profit. They combine the need to be financial successful businesses with social objectives. They emphasise the long-term benefits for employees, consumers and the community.[33]

- The term 'social economy organisations' is occasionally used to include SEEs and other organisations in the social economy that carry out other activities, such as the provision of advice to governments and services to SEEs.[34]

- Social economy enterprises are organisations democratically governed by their members or the stakeholders they serve that use a combination of market (sales revenue and paid labour) and non-market (government funding, private philanthropy and volunteer labour) resources to produce and deliver goods and services in the market place based on a combination of the common interests of members and concern about the well-being of others. They are citizen-led, community-based organisations that deliver goods and services locally, sometimes as part of a network of similar organisations that provide financial, strategic and technical support.[35]

- SEEs are businesses that trade in the marketplace in order to fulfil economic and social aims. They bring people and communities together for indigenous economic development and social benefit. They have three common characteristics:

    Enterprise Focused. They are directly involved in the production of goods and the provision of services to a market. They seek to be viable trading concerns, making a surplus from trading.

    Social Aims. They have explicit social aims such as job creation, training and the provision of local services. They have ethical values including a commitment to local capacity building. They are accountable to their members and the wider community for their social, environmental and economic impact.

    Local Ownership. They are autonomous organisation with governance and ownership structure based on participation by stakeholder groups (users or clients, local community groups, and so on) or by trustees. Profits are distributed as profit sharing to stakeholders or used for the benefit of the community.[36]

- Social Enterprise = (social improvement and verification) + (competition and innovation).[37]

Illustration 4.2   (cont'd)

And some definitions of a community enterprise or business are as follows:

- A community enterprise is a non-profit-making organisation which is controlled and run by local people in the community. It is sustainable in the sense that it manages to raise enough funds through its activities or through fundraising in order to make ends meet financially.[38]

- A community business is a sustainable commercial enterprise which is owned and controlled by the local community. It aims to create jobs and related training opportunities and to encourage local economic activity. Profits are used to create more jobs and businesses and to generate wealth for the benefit of the community.[39]

- ... Community enterprise organisations working for sustainable regeneration in their community through a mix of economic, environmental, cultural and social activities. They are independent, not-for-private-profit organisations, locally accountable and committed to involving local people in the process of regeneration.[40]

- A community co-operative is a multifunctional business run for local benefit and directly owned and controlled by the community in which it operates. Some of its activities may be social in character, but it must make a profit overall.[41]

There is, in the definitions of social enterprises given in Illustration 4.2, a shared concern for a social purpose, collective ownership, but combined with a business mode of operation. Profits are made but recycled within the organisation and not paid as a dividend for private gain. There are, however, subtle differences between the different definitions, and the list emphasises the plurality of definitions with community businesses being more closely linked to area-based regeneration specifically and to 'locality' more generally. Some attach priority to training and job creation although the definitions highlight the interchangeability of terms and concepts. This approach also underscores the tripartite functional distinction between the enterprise focus, social objectives and democratic local ownership.

Other components of the social economy

As well as social enterprises the EU description of the social economy specifically includes co-operatives, mutuals, associations and foundations. There are also other categories of organisation and enterprise which can be included such as LETS and intermediate labour markets (ILMs). These categories, and some sorts of organisation within them, are therefore considered here.

Co-operatives

Co-operatives are democratic shareholding organisations run for and by their members on the basis of one member one vote, rather than on capital shareholding, and have a range of social purposes, which may include the increased control by people working in the enterprise, equal opportunities and ethical trading. Members may be employees in a worker co-operative, savers and borrowers in a credit union, tenants in a housing co-operative, businesses in a marketing co-operative or customers in a consumer co-operative (see Illustration 4.3).

Illustration 4.3   The Core Values of Co-operatives

The International Co-operative Alliance has articulated the core values of co-operatives as a set of seven principles:

1st Principle: Voluntary and Open Membership
Co-operatives are voluntary organisations, open to all persons able to use their services and willing to accept the responsibilities of membership, without gender, social, racial, political or religious discrimination.

2nd Principle: Democratic Member Control
Co-operatives are democratic organisations controlled by their members, who actively participate in setting their policies and making decisions. Men and women serving as elected representatives are accountable to the membership. In primary co-operatives members have equal voting rights (one member, one vote) and co-operatives at other levels are also organised in a democratic manner.

3rd Principle: Member Economic Participation
Members contribute equitably to, and democratically control, the capital of their co-operative. At least part of that capital is usually the common property of the co-operative. Members usually receive limited compensation, if any, on capital subscribed as a condition of membership. Member allocate surpluses for any or all of the following purposes: developing their co-operative, possibly by setting up reserves, part of which at least would be indivisible; benefiting members in proportion to their transactions with the co-operative; and supporting other activities approved by the membership.

4th Principle: Autonomy and Independence
Co-operatives are autonomous, self-help organisations controlled by their members. If they enter into agreements with other organisations, including governments, or raise capital from external sources, they do so on terms that ensure democratic control by their members and maintain their co-operative autonomy.

5th Principle: Education, Training and Information
Co-operatives provide education and training for their members, elected representatives, managers and employees so they can contribute effectively to the development

---

Illustration 4.3   (cont'd)

of their co-operatives. They inform the general public – particularly young people and opinion leaders – about the nature and benefits of co-operation.

6th Principle: Co-operation among Co-operatives
Co-operatives serve their members most effectively and strengthen the co-operative movement by working together through local, regional, national and international structures.

7th Principle: Concern for Community
Co-operatives work for the sustainable development of their communities through policies approved by their members.

Source: International Cooperative Alliance (1994) Draft Statement on Cooperative Identity, Geneva, ICA.

The International Co-operative Alliance, to which many co-operatives belong, states that

> A co-operative is an autonomous association of persons united voluntarily to meet their common economic, social and cultural needs and aspirations through a jointly owned and democratically-controlled enterprise.[42]

Consumer and producer co-operatives

Broadly there are two major classes of co-operatives: those which are consumer or user led, in which the consumer is the primary stakeholder; and those which are producer or supplier or employee led, where whoever produces the goods or services is the primary stakeholder. Retail co-operatives fall within the first category, whilst agricultural co-operatives and worker co-operatives fall into the second group.

Service and care co-operatives

In a study for the UK Co-operative Council (UKCC), ICOM pointed out that there were a number of interlinked policy and funding changes that were increasing the importance of co-operatives in the delivery of core services. These included

- the withdrawal of the state from key areas of welfare;
- the promotion of the third sector in the delivery of social programmes;
- a return to community ownership and consumerist management principles; and
- greater reliance on self-help in the processes of industrial change in advanced Western societies.[43]

There is an interesting structural variation within care co-operatives that high-lighted the complexity of the constitutional and financial profile of the sector. In the agency co-operative model, carers are self-employed and pay the co-operative a commission for centralised services such as administration and locating work (a form of employment agency). In the worker co-operative (or 'principle' model), where the co-operative itself employs its members to deliver the service, the carers are employees of the co-operative. Each one has different implications for VAT, income tax, national insurance contributions and the corporate financial growth of the sector.

Credit unions

Credit unions are co-operative financial institutions that are owned and con-trolled by their members and operate on a number of principles which include the following:

- Only people who are credit union members could borrow.
- Loans will be made for prudential productive purposes.
- A person's desire to repay will be considered more important than the ability to repay.

Credit unions are sometimes categorised as co-operatives and sometimes as mutuals. They are mutual organisations in that they exist for their members and, in the UK, they are not incorporated under co-operative legislation. However, they are defined by HM Treasury as 'co-operative organisations' (which encourage their members to save regularly and enable them to bor-row at lower interest rates than those normally charged by other financial institutions).[44]

Credit unions in the UK are registered and regulated by the Registry of Friendly Societies under the Industrial and Provident Societies Acts of 1965–1968 and the Credit Union Act of 1979. Members save by subscribing for non-transferable shares deposited within the credit union and may take out loans at a maximum rate of interest of 1 per cent per month. The objectives of credit unions as defined by the 1979 Act are as follows:

- the promotion of thrift among the members by the accumulation of savings;
- the creation of sources of credit for the benefit of members at a fair and reasonable rate of interest;
- the use and control of members' savings for their mutual benefit; and
- the training and education of the members in the wise use of money and in the management of their financial affairs.

In 2006 there were nearly 800 credit unions in the UK and that number was growing by about 50 new credit unions per year.

Mutuals

Mutuals are organisations, such as insurance mutuals, health mutuals and building societies, which are formed to provide benefits for their members. They were important before the advent of the welfare state, enabling people, for instance, to protect themselves against adversity with mutual insurance schemes. The building societies and mutual insurance companies are the major mutuals which still exist, although this is changing as many building societies become banks in the drive to find new markets and capital. Co-operatives and mutuals are very similar structurally, having a common ancestry in the village and trade-friendly societies of the past.

Mutuals exist for the benefit of their members and are non-profit-making organisations as any surplus they make is returned to their members. Mutual societies were historically formed to overcome social or economic injustice confronting the poorer members of communities and for the purpose of trying to improve their members' lives. Friendly societies, which are mutual organisations, were originally formed to help poorer people save for funeral expenses and witnessed considerable growth following the Industrial Revolution in the nineteenth century. In the absence of a welfare state or social protection systems, friendly societies were used by people to save, to build retirement capital or as a form of insurance against illness or an inability to work. At their peak in 1945, they provided for the needs of 8.75 million private subscribers in the UK through 18,000 branches of societies.[45]

Many mutuals have operated in the life insurance sector with profits being rebated to the clients in the form of dividend distributions or reduced future premiums rather than as a financial profit to investors. However, without shareholders, mutual companies lacked access to equity markets to grow and financial deregulation in both the USA and the UK led many large insurance companies and building societies to de-mutualise and to offer shares to current policy holders as a replacement for their stake in the company.

Associations

Associations are organisations which operate within a set of rules but are normally unincorporated. In the UK being unincorporated means that they are not incorporated as companies but do often have some other form of registration which

---

CASE 4.1

An Example of a Mutual

The Communication Workers Friendly Society (CWFS) was founded in 1895 by the Postman's Federation to provide assistance to its members during illness or death. It was originally known as the Mutual Benefit Society. As the Society expanded, it changed its name to the Union of Communication Workers Insurance Society (UCWIS) and was run as part of the Union of Communication Workers (now CWU). With the introduction of the 1992 Friendly Society Act

CASE 4.1 (cont'd)

and changes to financial regulations, CWFS became an independent organisation which operates separately from the Communication Workers Union (CWU) and is responsible for its own decision-making. CWFS is run by a Board of Directors, consisting of nine elected members of the Society and the Society provides affordable financial products with an ethos of mutuality and friendliness. It encourages savings and accepts much lower premiums from savers than mainstream insurance companies. CWFS currently provides a range of products with the benefit of having deductions made directly from pay, including Life & Savings Plan, Sickness Benefit Scheme and Children's Savings Plan. At the end of 2005, CWFS had more than 27,000 members and total assets of over £110 million. As a friendly society providing financial advice and services, CWFS is authorised and regulated by the Financial Services Authority (FSA).

According to CWFS,

> A mutual, mutual organisation, or mutual society is an organization (which is often, but not always, a company or business) based on the principle of mutuality. Unlike a true cooperative, members usually do not contribute to the capital of the company by direct investment, but derive their right to profits and votes through their customer relationship. A mutual exists with the purpose of raising funds, from its membership or customers, which can then be used to provide common services to all members of the organization or society. A mutual is therefore owned by, and run for the benefit of, its members – it has no external shareholders to pay in the form of dividends, and as such does not usually seek to maximise and make large profits or capital gains. Mutuals exist for the members to benefit from the services they provide. Profits made will usually be re-invested in the mutual for the benefit of the members, although some profit may also be necessary in the case of mutuals to sustain or grow the organisation, and to make sure it remains safe and secure.[46]

Source: http://www.cwfs.co.uk/societies.aspx, accessed 2007.

means that they can exist as a legal entity.[47] In the UK many voluntary sector organisations have been associations but there are also associations which might not be considered to be in the voluntary sector, such as trade unions, trust hospitals, schools with elected governors, housing associations, professional associations, employers' organisations and political parties. As with other subsets of the social economy, associations vary in their size, sectoral coverage and purpose.

Housing associations

Within the UK one of the most active manifestations of social economy associations is the housing association sector. This movement stemmed from the rise in homelessness in the 1960s and the perceived need for a new rented sector to fill the gap left by the decline in private renting. Since the early 1990s housing associations have been the main providers of new social rented housing in England, primarily as homes for rent for disadvantaged groups such as the homeless, elderly and disabled, young single people, low income families and members of minority groups; but also low cost home ownership housing, mainly through shared ownership schemes. Housing associations vary greatly in size, ethos and tenant group, and new development schemes are financed by both public subsidy and private borrowing.

Since the 1988 Housing Act, housing associations have had to rely more heavily on private sector loan finance and this has caused tensions especially with matters such as development costs and the need to service the interest charges on private sector finance. Partly in response to this vulnerability and partly to deepen their remit, many associations have ventured into new 'business areas' such as care services, especially for the elderly, community development and training.

Among the characteristics of housing associations which they share with many other social economy organisations are the following:

- They have a 'mixed' funding capability and can match government grants with resources raised by the private sector.
- They have traditionally targeted excluded and marginal groups but some of them have developed mainstream roles especially in the management of stock transferred from local authorities.
- Most are governed by management committees rather than by elected representatives or local councils.
- They are registered charities.
- They have originated from a combination of charitable and entrepreneurial backgrounds rather than past involvement in municipal socialism.
- Many of them have a strong local orientation offering decentralised and sensitive management of geographic communities or communities of interest.

As the 1990s progressed under the Thatcher administration, more emphasis was placed on the role of local authorities as strategic *enablers* not involved in the operational delivery of policies, including social housing.[48] Large Scale Voluntary Stock Transfer enabled tenants to have their houses managed by different landlords, which in particular benefited existing and new housing associations. Malpass[49] pointed out that in 1992 the housing association sector in Great Britain consisted of 733,000 dwellings but that it grew quickly as a result of both investment and stock transfer, and by 2002 it had more than doubled in size, reaching around 1.7 million units. The creation of about 200 new Registered Social Landlords has added to both the stock and the size and capacity of the largest associations. The Labour government supported stock transfer, which grew steadily after their election in 1997. However, many commentators feel that the transfer of housing has failed to deliver the levels of involvement aspired by those actively in the process and that in some cases local authorities retained strong control over community-based housing organisations.[50] Moreover, others pointed out that this approach was less about developing the social economics of housing and more about rolling back the welfare state and the 'demuncipal-ization' of social housing.[51] Gibb made a crucial point in asserting that part of the problem has been that stock transfer to community level tends to treat the challenge of regeneration in relative isolation from wider economic dynamics.[52] Mooney and Poole thus argued that for transfer to be successful it should be less about simply managing the stock and more about the centrality of housing as a regenerator in the most disadvantaged areas of the UK.[53]

It is also interesting to note that, although associations are often considered to be archetypical components of the social economy and therefore clearly to belong in the third sector, in Northern Ireland, in compliance with Section 75 of the Northern Ireland Act 1998, housing associations have been officially designated as public authorities along with public sector bodies such as civil service departments.

Charities

This is not necessarily the right place to discuss charities, but Figure 4.1 suggests that charities could be considered as a subset of the social economy within associations. This might be an appropriate place for some of the better-known charities such as, in the UK, Oxfam, Dr Barnardo's and the RSPCA, which are philanthropic rather than self-help, and are clearly neither co-operatives nor mutuals. However, charities as a whole are a much broader group.

Being a charity is not a distinct form of legal existence. In the UK any organisation can apply for charitable status provided its purposes or aims are for public benefit. Before the Charities Act 2006 charities had to have objects which fell within one or more of the four broad categories of the relief of the poverty, the advancement of education, the promotion of religion and other purposes beneficial to the community which were recognised as charitable. The Charities Act 2006, which applies in England and Wales, specifically included public benefit in the definition of a charitable purpose but introduced a more extensive list of charitable purposes. This list came into effect on 1 April 2008 and includes

a) the prevention or relief of poverty;

b) the advancement of education;

c) the advancement of religion;

d) the advancement of health or the saving of lives;

e) the advancement of citizenship or community development;

f) the advancement of the arts, culture, heritage or science;

g) the advancement of amateur sport;

h) the advancement of human rights, conflict resolution or reconciliation or the pro-motion of religious or racial harmony or equality and diversity;

i) the advancement of environmental protection or improvement;

j) the relief of those in need, by reason of youth, age, ill-health, disability, financial hardship or other disadvantage;

k) the advancement of animal welfare;

l) the promotion of the efficiency of the armed forces of the Crown, or of the efficiency of the police, fire and rescue services or ambulance services;

m) other purposes currently recognised as charitable and any new charitable purposes which are similar to another charitable purpose.[54]

Organisation with such purposes do not have to register as charities but may find that, on balance, it is advantageous to do so. Being a registered charity can help an organisation to attract volunteer help and it can help fund-raising because it can reassure potential donors. At least in the UK it also allows the charity to recover the income tax paid on 'gift aid' and can also have other tax advantages as it provides relief from a number of other taxes. There are disadvantages such as the limits it places on certain forms of political and campaigning activity and the extent on which charities can trade. Charities do not have to have a particular legal form and can be either incorporated bodies, such as companies and industrial and provident societies, or unincorporated bodies such as clubs and friendly societies.

The more famous charities might be thought to concentrate on things such as the relief of the poor, the sick, the aged, the destitute or animals, but, at least in the UK, many other organisations are charities including many housing associations, religious bodies, building preservation trusts, think tanks, education organisations, arts bodies and medical research establishments – to list but a few. Many areas within the third sector can therefore, if suitably presented, be accepted as charitable and charities are not found only within a limited part of the third sector spectrum.

Foundations

According to a communication from the European Commission on promoting the role of voluntary organisations and foundations, the latter, like voluntary organisations, undertake a wide range of activities but are legally a more homogenous group and are essentially for public benefit, whereas voluntary organisations can be essentially for private benefit. For the purposes of the communication, foundations are described as

bodies with their own source of funds which they spend according to their own judgement on projects or activities of public benefit. They are entirely independent of government or other public authorities and are run by independent management boards or trustees.[55]

Foundations have been a long-established format for philanthropic giving as the example of the Carnegie Trust fund (see Case 4.2) demonstrates. From an

American perspective, Gunn[56] describes foundations as private entities given special non-profit status for their charitable or philanthropic distribution of money. They have investment portfolios which are used to generate a profit from money put into trust for the wider public or specified beneficiary groups. Because they rely on the stock market, the performance of foundations and the profits they yield for redistribution varies considerably. Large American foundations set up by millionaire business philanthropists such as Ford, Kellogg and Gates have seen the value of their investment rise and fall as the market ebbed and flowed throughout the unpredictable late 1990s. Gunn points out that in 1998 the top 1 per cent of foundations controlled 60 per cent of all foundation assets.[57] Other entities in the non-profit sector include corporate foundations and community foundations. The former are used by large corporations to help even out the distribution (and tax benefits) of their charitable giving over years of relative high and low income. (In the USA, corporations get the same tax relief as individuals for their gifts to foundations.) Case 4.3 describes development trusts in the UK which are examples of community foundations.

Intermediate labour markets and transitional employment programmes

An Intermediate Labour Market (ILM) has been defined as 'a diverse range of initiatives that typically provide temporary waged employment in a genuine work environment with continuous support to assist the transition to work'[58] and their principal characteristics have been identified as follows (and see Illustration 4.4):

CASE 4.3

Development Trusts

The United Kingdom has more than 400 Development Trusts, which Carpenter has defined as 'community-owned enterprises that make profits through, property or trading and reinvest them for social benefit'. The *Regeneration and Renewal* survey showed that the average value of selected Trusts' assets increased by 17 per cent between 2006 and 2007. Government policy to encourage the transfer of land and buildings owned by local authorities to community organisations has helped to stimulate the growth of Development Trusts. The proportion of Development Trusts delivering public sector contracts has increased steadily over the last year. For example, Coin Street Community Builders in London has assets of £26.1 million in 2007 up from £18.3 million in 2006 and has developed a strong portfolio of government contracts although of the 15 top performing Trusts 10 make a financial surplus and five do not.

Source: J. Carpenter, The Development Trust Survey, 2007, *Regeneration and Renewal,* 19 September, pp. 18–20.

- The main aim is to give those removed from the labour market a bridge back to the world of work by improving participants' general employability.
- The core feature is paid work on a temporary contract (often up to 12 months), together with training, personal development and job search activities.
- In order to limit the risk of replacing 'real' jobs, the work is in additional economic activities, ideally of community benefit.
- Projects and programmes rely on packages of funding from various sources including New Deal, the European Social Fund (ESF) and local regeneration funding.[59]

A distinction is drawn between ILMs and Transitional Employment Programmes. The latter emerged in the USA and the UK as a new generation of initiatives aimed at tackling long-term unemployed and hard-to-reach people in the labour market. However, unlike traditional job creation programmes

> *TEPs (Transitional Employment Programmes) typically target the hardest to place unemployed and combine short periods of paid work experience with additional support and job placement services aimed at getting participants into regular jobs. TEPs also make more extensive use of private sector job placements but unlike conventional employment subsidies the goal of the programme is to offer temporary, relevant and realistic work, rather than a contract of employment and continuing employment with a particular employer.*[60]

Illustration 4.4   Intermediate Labour Markets in the UK

Finn and Simmonds surveyed ILM initiatives in the UK and highlighted their labour market and regeneration potential. The overall average for job outcomes across all the ILMs surveyed was 43 per cent. This average, however, disguised a wide range of job outcome rates. For example, the average for non–New Deal ILMs was 67 per cent, and this may partially reflect the relatively higher employability of some recruits. In addition,

- The survey showed that in 2003 the turnover of ILMs had increased by almost 120 per cent since 2000, and the number of ILM jobs had increased to just over 7000. In total, there was an estimated minimum of 8700 ILM jobs in the UK.

- The duration of ILM jobs was mostly between 26 and 52 weeks, and the average length of stay varied from 65 to 75 per cent of the contract length, suggesting that around 12,000 people passed through ILMs in 2002/3.

- This growth had mostly come from local partners and local organisations identifying ILMs as a tool to improve job outcomes and achieve regeneration and social objectives. At the national level there had been no specific actions by government to stimulate the growth of ILMs, but neither had it sought to restrict their development.

- The motivation and ability to start and maintain an ILM came mainly from local conditions and local capacity although the availability of European funding and the flexibility of New Deal had enabled this increase.

- The majority of ILMs were based on New Deal 18–24 and 25+ age ranges, and all of the larger ILMs were based on New Deal. A large majority of ILMs were with less than 100 jobs, but there were a few very-large-area-based ILMs, where there was a central organisation which co-ordinated, enabled or directly funded local ILMs within the wider area.

- The largest single funding source was European funds.

Source: Based on D. Finn and D. Simmonds, Intermediate Labour Market in Britain and on International Review of Transitional Employment Programmes (London: Department of Work and Pensions, 2003), p. 57.

Community trading schemes

Local Exchange Trading Schemes (or Systems) (LETS) are an example of community credit schemes. LETS are local, non-profit-making exchange systems for a range of goods and services without money. Members of a scheme can earn credits, usually made equivalent to the currency of the country, by doing work for other people in the network and can spend those credits acquiring services

---

CASE 4.4

Intermediate Labour Market Case Studies

The following is an indication of the variety of ILM approaches across Europe and the way in which they are applied in local settings.[61]

Glasgow Works was started in 1994 to engage long-term unemployed people in work and training on projects with a local social benefit, delivered as a partnership between the state, the private sector and specialist voluntary sector organisations.

Rotterdam Works was started in 1989 from a jobs-pool which targeted older people, the unskilled and migrants, and at the time of reporting about 3200 jobs were created.

Atlantis is a Berlin-based not-for-profit company that links the production of ecologically orientated goods and services with ecologically oriented training and jobs. 400 jobs were created.

The *Wise Group* in Glasgow has been described as one of the biggest and best-known social economy projects in UK.[62] The Group, which comprises a series of not-for-profit businesses, was started in the early 1980s and its core businesses include Heatwise, which concentrates on home insulation and heating systems and home security and safety, and Landwise, which concentrates on environmental upgrading. The Wise Group carries out its activity by recruiting, training and managing a workforce drawn from the long-term unemployed. An evaluation[63] highlighted its distinctive approach in linking training to real job opportunities. Welfare payments are topped up during training in order to deliver the following benefits:

- It gives people a period of employment in their own right.
- It keeps them in contact with the habits of work.
- It improves their skills to keep them closer to the labour market.
- It prevents them dropping into unemployability.

---

they need. LETS are defined by Information on Regeneration for Community Organisation (IRCO) as follows:

> LETS are currency systems which measure the exchange of goods and services between people in a local community. They do not involve the exchange of actual money, but are purely accounting systems which keep information on transactions which are accounted for in a local currency.[64]

Marshall and Macfarlane[65] examined creative ways of relieving social exclusion by exploiting the potential of the non-wage element of the household economy but emphasised that LETS were best used complementarily to state distribution activities including benefit take-up campaigns, the informal economy, volunteering and self-help such as local credit unions. A major area of concern in the operation of LETS and related tradable schemes is the issue of measurement and in particular valuing the contributions made within the sector. Nevertheless, for a number of commentators and supporters of the sector, a distinctive edge for the social economy lies in its ability to provide an alternative to the formality of financial markets.

Williams and Windebank[66] argue that formal recognition of 'mutual aid' linked to the development of social capital is an urgent and realisable agenda for depressed local communities. They have proposed an Active Citizens Credits (ACC) Scheme, which could build mutual aid and in so doing provide

CASE 4.5

Some Problems of Formal Measurement and Targeted Assistance

LETS involve the exchange of the outputs of work but without the exchange of real money. They do not provide formal paid jobs and do not therefore show up on the employment 'radar'. They are an example of social economy activity which does not register in formal measures of an economy such as GDP and employment and this raises problems in recognising the scope of the social economy sector because the formal economy does not recognise the economic value of community activity:

> It recognises only cash, trade and employment as economic, not life support systems and natural assets.[67]

In an understandable desire to use public resources efficiently many official initiatives in disadvantaged areas have focused on specific issues such as unemployment and tried to set targets which were both specific and measurable.[68] That might lead, however, to a focus on identified symptoms and on specific and measurable interventions to address them, rather than on uncertain causes and on holistic but less measurable cures. Initiatives which, for example, seek to address unemployment as an identified problem will not recognise the value of organisations such as LETS because their outputs do not register in official measurements and do not include formal employment.

Chanan is critical of approaches that rely too much on jobs because they ignore the monetary value of other sectors of the economy and because spatial development goes beyond employment generation. She has pointed out that an emphasis on employment objectives has sometimes held back community involvement because, even in disadvantaged areas, the unemployed are a minority of the population. Moreover, employment often absorbs a large proportion of the local development budget and the broad involvement of disadvantaged localities needs the participation of a cross section of the population, not just the unemployed.[69] She concludes that 'in order to fully come into its own, the social economy must liberate itself from the short-term politico-economic equation of social policy with employment policy'.[70]

a complementary social inclusion policy. The ACC Scheme would provide a means of recording, sharing and rewarding participation in mutual aid and provide credits for a more expansive definition of work. Williams and Windebank found little empirical evidence of mutual aid outside kinship exchange but suggested that its development contains short-term potential in lower income neighbourhoods where the wait for full employment is likely to be a long one.

The scale of the social economy

The following statistics provide some indication of the scale of the social economy (and see also Chapter 9):

> The European Commission estimated that by 2007 approximately 10 million people were employed in the social economy in the European Union, that co-operatives had a total of 78 million members and that at least 109 million Europeans were insured with mutual insurers.[71]

> One country in which the social economy is well established is France, where it is estimated[72] that the social economy employs some 7 per cent of the workforce.

> The (then) DTI estimates that in the UK there are around 15,000 social enterprises representing 1.2 per cent of all enterprises in the UK. Over 775,000 people work for those enterprises surveyed, including almost 300,000 volunteers. They generate just under £18 billion in annual turnover.[73]

> The European Confederation of Workers' Co-operatives, Social Co-operatives, and Participative Enterprises (CECOP) is an international non-profit association with its headquarters in Brussels representing small and medium-sized worker-controlled enterprises across 42 member countries of the Council of Europe. CECOP's members include 37 national and regional federations of co-operative enterprises representing around 83,000 enterprises employing 1.3 million workers.[74]

> In 2005 almost 400 credit unions were members of the Association of British Credit Unions Ltd (ABCUL) and they provided financial services to over 404,000 people.[75]

> In the United States, credit unions have a membership of 86 million. As of the end of 2005, the National Credit Union Administration insured more than $515 billion in deposits in 8695 non-profit co-operative US credit unions.[76]

> The rapid growth of credit unions in other parts of the world led to the creation in 1970 of the World Council of Credit Unions, which further encouraged its global spread and it now covers 79 countries with 34,000 financial co-operatives.[77]

Conclusions

The social economy is widely recognised as an important part of an economy: so important that some people consider it to be the third sector of an economy alongside the public and private sectors. However, although definitions of it vary, it does not include all the organisations and activities which are outside the private and public sectors. Therefore, either it alone is not the whole of the third sector or, if it is so described, there must be a fourth sector.

This chapter has reviewed efforts to define the social economy and its components, especially social enterprises. Different approaches come from different histories of development, cultures and political economies, and make it difficult to articulate a clear set of rules governing its composition and structure. Nevertheless, this review highlights the essential distinction between the social economy and the market and public sectors. There are common traits, values and organisational formats which mark out the social economy as a distinctive economic, social and cultural sphere of activity. Collective ownership, non-profit distribution, democratic governance arrangements, the inclusion of multiple stakeholders in planning and control, a clear social benefit, but with recognisable systems of trade and exchange relations are some of the recurring themes in the social economy sphere. These characteristics and the relationships amongst them are explored in greater detail in the second part of the book.

Although there is some coherence across the different descriptions of the social economy and/or its components there are different concepts of the role. Two broad paradigms have been identified: an US/UK approach, which tends to focus on social enterprise as an alternative form of business ownership and/or aim; and a largely European approach, which sees the social economy not as a supplement to public and market-focused private sectors, but as an alternative political or ideological approach.

In a related context, there are different views expressed as to whether it is about developing new forms of business, delivering low cost substitutes for failing welfare state provisions, being a vibrant part of the economy, supplying complementary public services or providing a vehicle for social transformation.

Key Points of Chapter 4

- The concept of the social economy seems to have emerged first in France in the first half of the nineteenth century. The emergence, and re-emergence, of the social economy in different periods of history has been linked, it is suggested, to a series of economic and social crises.

- In the European tradition the archetypical components of the social economy are co-operatives, mutuals, associations and foundations to which is also added the category of social enterprises. However, describing the social economy, and social enterprises, is a somewhat complex and contested area.

(cont'd)

- Different approaches to the social economy and social enterprises have arisen in countries with different economic, political and institutional histories. Two broad paradigms have been identified and a wide range of definitions offered. The definitions do, in general, indicate that there are common traits, values and organisational formats which mark out the social economy as a distinctive economic, social and cultural sphere of activity.

- Some parts of the social economy, such as community credit, do not involve the exchange of real money and do not create formal jobs, so the benefits they produce will not therefore register in formal economic measures. A corollary of this is that a desire for measurable economic outputs from support schemes can actually hinder community involvement.

Questions, Exercises, Essay and Discussion Topics

1. Within the social economy reference is often made to the term 'Triple Bottom Line'. What do you think this means?

2. Why has the social economy developed differently in different countries and over time?

3. Why is the search to define the social economy so difficult?

4. What do you regard as the critical characteristics of social enterprises?

5. Does locality matter in the development of the social economy?

6. 'In essence, the social economy sector is about effective co-operation, interdependence and the active participation of citizens in the social and economic well-being of local communities. It is concerned with creating an egalitarian, inclusive and full democratic society that promotes social justice, fundamental equality, and equality of opportunity.'[78] Would all social economy stakeholders agree? Discuss.

SUGGESTIONS FOR FURTHER READING

A. Amin, A. Cameron and R. Hudson, *Placing the Social Economy* (London: Routledge, 2002).

A. Molloy, C. McFeely and E. Connolly, *Building a Social Economy for the New Millennium* (Derry: Guildhall Press/NICDA Social Economy Agency, 1999).

J. Pearce, *Social Enterprise in Anytown* (London: Calouste Gulbenkian Foundation, 2003).

J. Blake, *Charitable Status, A Practical Handbook* (London: Directory of Social Change, 2008 – published in association with Bates, Wells and Braithwaite).

References

1. F. Moulaert and O. Ailenei, 'Social economy, third sector and solidarity relations: A conceptual synthesis from history to present', *Urban Studies*, Vol. 42, No. 11 (2005), pp. 2037–53.
2. Ibid., p. 2044.
3. Ibid., p. 2041.
4. Ibid., pp. 2037–53.
5. A. Amin, A. Cameron and R. Hudson, *Placing the Social Economy* (London: Routledge, 2002), pp. 3–4.
6. P. Teague, 'Developing the social economy in Ireland?' *International Journal of Urban and Regional Research*, Vol. 31, No. 1 (2007), pp. 91–108.
7. Policy Action Team 3, HM Treasury, *Enterprise and Social Exclusion*, 1999 (www.hm-treasury.gov.uk/docs/1999/pat3.html, accessed 1 March 2000), paragraph 5.2.
8. E. Hunt, 'The normative foundations of social theory: An essay on the criteria defining social economics', *Review of Social Economy*, Vol. LXIII, No. 3 (2006), pp. 423–48.
9. http://ec.europa.eu/enterprise/entrepreneurship/social_economy.htm, accessed 3 August 2007.
10. http://ec.europa.eu/enterprise/entrepreneurship/coop/index.htm, accessed 3 August 2007.
11. http://ec.europa.eu/enterprise/entrepreneurship/coop/index.htm, accessed 3 August 2007.
12. Guide to Co-operative and Community Business Legal Structures (London: IOCM, 1999).
13. M. Cooper, 'The development of the third sector in Bristol', *Local Economy*, Vol. 14, No. 4 (1999), pp. 348–59.
14. D. Sattar and E. Mayo, *Growth Areas of the UK Social Economy* (London: UK Social Investment Forum, 1998).
15. A. Amin, A. Cameron and R. Hudson, *Placing the Social Economy* (London: Routledge, 2002), pp. 9–11.
16. P. Lloyd, in *Rethinking the Social Economy*, CU2 Contested Cities – Urban Universities (eds) (Belfast: The Queen's University Belfast, 2006), pp. 9–18.
17. P. Graefe, 'The social economy and the state: Linking ambitions with institutions in Quebec, Canada', *Politics and Policy*, Vol. 30, No. 2 (2002), p. 250.
18. Department of Trade and Industry (DTI), *Social Enterprise: a strategy for success* (London: Department of Trade and Industry, 2002), p. 14.
19. P. Lloyd, in *Rethinking the Social Economy*, CU2 Contested Cities – Urban Universities (eds) (Belfast: The Queen's University Belfast, 2006), p. 14.
20. J. Pearce, *Social Enterprise in Anytown* (London: Calouste Gulbenkian Foundation, 2003), pp. 69–70.
21. http://ec.europa.eu/enterprise/entrepreneurship/coop/index.htm, accessed 28 March 2007.
22. European Network for Economic Self Help and Local Development, *Key Values and Structures of Social Enterprise in Western Europe: Concepts and Principles for the New Economy* (Berlin: Technologie-Netwzwerk with European Network for Economic Self Help and Local Development, 1997).
23. N. Oately (1999) 'Developing the social economy', *Local Economy*, Vol. 14, No. 4 (1999), pp. 339–45.
24. J. Pearce, *Social Enterprise in Anytown* (London: Calouste Gulbenkian Foundation, 2003), pp. 31–2.
25. Cabinet Office/Office of the Third Sector, *Social Enterprise Action Plan: Scaling New Heights* (London: Cabinet Office, 2006), p. 10.
26. Reported as being available on the SBS website in 2001 by D. Smallbone, M. Evans, I. Ekanem and S. Butters, *Researching Social Enterprise* (Sheffield: Small Business Service, Research Report RR004/01, July 2001), p. 14.

27. Organisation for Economic Co-operation and Development (OECD), *Social Enterprises* (Paris: OECD, 1999), p. 10.

28. J. Pearce, *Social Enterprise in Anytown* (London: Calouste Gulbenkian Foundation, 2003), pp. 51–5.

29. The Concise Project, *Key Concepts, Measures and Indicators* (Concise Project, Middlesex University, 2000).

30. Policy Action Team 3, *Enterprise and Social Exclusion, Report of the National Strategy for Neighbourhood Renewal: Policy Action Team* 3 (London: HM Treasury, 1999).

31. Social Enterprise Coalition, *Introducing Social Enterprise* (London: Social Enterprise Coalition, 2001).

32. Social Economy Consortium, *Opening the Gateway to Birmingham's Social Economy* (Birmingham: Social Economy Consortium, 2001).

33. Social Economy Agency, *Defining and Explaining Social Economy Structures, Briefing paper for Assembly Members* (Derry: Social Economy Agency, Northern Ireland, 2001), p. 2.

34. Policy Research Initiative, *What We Need to Know About the Social Economy: A Guide for Policy Research* (Canadian Government: Policy Research Initiative, 2005), p. 2.

35. Ibid., p. 11.

36. From Social Economy Agency, *Defining and Explaining Social Economy Structures, Briefing paper for Assembly Members* (Derry: Social Economy Agency, Northern Ireland, 2001).

37. L. Black and J. Nicholls, *There's No Business Like Social Susiness: How to be Socially Eenterprising* (Liverpool: The Cat's Pyjamas, 2004), p. 16.

38. Voluntary Action Lochaber, *All You Ever Wanted to Know about Community Enterprises* (Lochaber: Voluntary Action Lochaber, 2002).

39. *Definition of Community Business* (West Calder, Community Business Scotland, 1991), as quoted in J. Pearce, *Social Enterprise in Anytown* (London: Calouste Gulbenkian Foundation, 2003), p. 33.

40. Development Trusts Association, *Annual Report 2000* (London: DTA, 2000).

41. Highlands and Islands Development Board, *Community Co-operatives* (Highlands and Islands Development Board, 1977), as quoted in J. Pearce, *Social Enterprise in Anytown* (London: Calouste Gulbenkian Foundation, 2003), p. 33.

42. International Cooperative Alliance, *Draft Statement on Cooperative Identity* (Geneva: ICA, 1994), p. 1.

43. Based on UKCC *Co-operating in Care. A Study of Care Co-operatives* (London: ICOM, 1998).

44. HM Treasury, *Credit Unions the Future Taskforce Report* (London: HMT, 1999), p. 7.

45. http://en.wikipedia.org/wiki/Mutual_organization.

46. http://www.cwfs.co.uk/societies.aspx, accessed 2007.

47. For instance, in Northern Ireland the Fold Housing Association is not a company but is registered under the Industrial and Provident Societies Act (NI) 1969. However, its sister organisation in the Republic of Ireland, Fold Ireland, is a 'not-for-profit company formed by guarantee of the members and without a shareholding' (see www.foldireland.ie, accessed 27 April 2007).

48. A. Holmans, M. Stephens and S. Fitzpatrick, 'Housing policy in England since 1975', *Housing Studies*, Vol. 22, No. 2 (2007), pp. 147–62.

49. P. Malpass, *Housing and the Welfare State* (Basingstoke: Palgrave Macmillan, 2005).

50. M. McKee, 'Community ownership in Glasgow: The devolution of ownership and control, or a centralising process?' *European Journal of Housing Policy*, Vol. 7, No. 3 (2007), pp. 319–36.

51. P. Malpass and L. Cairncross, *Building on the Past: Visions of Housing Futures* (Bristol: The Policy Press, 2006).

52. K. Gibb, 'Transferring Glasgow's council housing: Financial, urban and housing policy implications', *European Journal of Housing Policy*, Vol. 3, No. 1 (2003), pp. 89–114.

53. G. Mooney and L. Poole, 'Marginalised voices: Resisting the privatisation of council housing', in Glasgow, Local Economy, Vol. 20, No. 1 (2005), pp. 27–39.

54. *Charities and Public Benefit: Summary Guidance for Charity Trustees*, www.charitycommission.gov.uk, accessed 19 April 2008.

55. *Communication from the Commission on Promoting the Role of Voluntary Organisations and Foundations in Europe* on http://ec.europa.eu/enterprise/library/bib-social-economy/orgfd-en.pdf, accessed 27 April 2007.

56. C. Gunn, *Third Sector Development* (New York: Cornell University Press, 2004).

57. Ibid., p. 28.

58. D. Finn and D. Simmonds, *Intermediate Labour Market in Britain and on International Review of Transitional Employment Programmes* (London: Department of Work and Pensions, 2003), p. 4.

59. B. Marshall and R. Macfarlane (2000), *The Intermediate Labour Market: A Tool for Tackling Long-Term Unemployment* (York: Joseph Rowntree Foundation, 2000).

60. D. Finn, and D. Simmonds, *Intermediate Labour Market in Britain and on International Review of Transitional Employment Programmes*, 2003, p. 4.

61. A. McGregor, Z. Ferguson, I. Fitzpatrick, M. McConnachie and K. Richmond, *Bridging the Jobs Gap: An Evaluation of the Wise Group and the Intermediate Labour Market* (York: Joseph Rowntree Foundation, 1997).

62. A. Amin, A. Cameron and R. Hudson, *Placing the Social Economy* (London: Routledge, 2002), p. 35.

63. A. McGregor, Z. Ferguson, I. Fitzpatrick, M. McConnachie and K. Richmond, *Bridging the Jobs Gap: An Evaluation of the Wise Group and the Intermediate Labour Market* (York: Joseph Rowntree Foundation, 1997).

64. Information on Regeneration for Community Organisation, *Briefing Paper 9 on LETS* (London, ICRO, 1997), p. 1.

65. B. Marshall and R. Macfarlane (2000) The Intermediate Labour Market: *A Tool for Tackling Long-Term Unemployment* (York: Joseph Rowntree Foundation, 2000).

66. C. Williams and J. Windebank (2000) 'Beyond social inclusion through employment: harnessing mutual aid as a complementary social inclusion policy', *Policy and Politics*, Vol. 29, No. 1 (2000), pp. 15–28.

67. Ghanan (1999) Employment policy and social economy: promise and misconceptions *Local Economy*, Vol. 14, No. 4 (1999), p. 361.

68. The Green Book recommends that 'Targets should be SMART: i.e. Specific, Measurable, Achievable, Relevant and Time-bound' (HM Treasury, *The Green Book: Appraisal and Evaluation in Central Government*, The Stationery Office, 2003).

69. G. Chanan, 1999, ibid., p. 365.

70. Ibid., p. 367.

71. http://europe.eu.int/comm/enterpriSocial Economy/, accessed 2007.

72. GHK, Social Enterprise: *An International Literature Review* (London: Social Enterprise Unit, DTI, 2006), p. 18.

73. Quoted by Anne-Marie Davison in NI Economic Bulletin 2006, p. 123.

74. http://www.cecop.coop accessed/, accessed 2007.

75. http://www.abcul.org, accessed 2007.

76. Current data from http://en.wikipedia.org/wiki/Credit_union.

77. http://en.wikipedia.org/wiki/Credit_union.

78. A. Molloy, C. McFeely and E. Connolly, *Building a Social Economy for the New Millennium* (Derry: Guildhall Press/NICDA Social Economy Agency, 1999), p. 9.

Part II
The Ecology of the Third Sector

Part I of this book looks at the concepts of the social economy and the third sector and mapped out the relationships between them, and between the third sector and the rest of an economy. In effect it tries to describe the 'geography' of the sector by indicating what is considered to be in it and where it is thought to be positioned relative to the rest of an economy.

Part II looks in more detail at what might be described as the 'ecology' of the third sector because it concerns how organisations in it behave, how they relate to each other and to other sectors of the economy, and how they might be influenced.

Chapter 5 explores key aspects of the nature of third sector organisations including their formation, legal structures, aims, methods and management.

Chapter 6 examines not only the sources of finance available to, and used by, third sector organisations, but also the diverse financial needs of organisations in the sector, including the need for financial skills.

A key area of potential linkages is then explored in Chapter 7, which looks at the concept of social capital and at the evolution of some of the theories about it and how it might be linked to a wider socio-political concern for the health of civic society.

Governments, and other stakeholders, are often interested in influencing and promoting the development of the third sector. Chapter 8 explores the main issues associated with this intervention including both why it is tried and what methods have been used to effect it.

Concluding this part, Chapter 9 reviews the impact the sector is supposed to have and the evidence for that impact.

The Nature of the Third Sector

Key Concepts

This chapter covers

- what third sector organisations are actually like, rather than what theoretical attempts to categorise them might suggest they are like;
- key aspects of third sector organisations;
- some of the issues that these aspects can raise for third sector organisations;
- how, in these aspects, third sector organisations compare and contrast with private sector organisations.

Learning Objectives

By the end of this chapter the reader should

- appreciate the main characteristics shared by most third sector organisations, but not most public or private sector organisations;
- appreciate that third sector organisation do not all share all the characteristics identified;
- be aware that some third sector organisations can share some characteristics with some private or public sector organisations;
- understand that third sector organisations do not always behave as theory might suggest they should;
- be aware that there is considerable heterogeneity across third sector organisations;
- be aware that a range of methods are now available to help third sector organisations to account for and report their achievements.

Introduction

Part I of this book explored the position of the third sector in an economy and looked at the variety of organisations within it and the various ways in which they can be categorised. There is a wide variety of organisations within the third sector, and the categories of organisations as well as the vocabulary and definitions used for the sector are still evolving and can be confusing. Table 4.2 presents a comparison of definitions which suggests that, even within the rather narrower focus of just the social economy, there is little agreement on what characteristics the organisations within it share. Nevertheless third sector organisations do share a number of characteristics, even if they do not all share all of them. This chapter explores key aspects of third sector organisations in order to indicate the extent to which there might be some shared characteristics.

This chapter, in effect, looks at what third sector organisations are actually like, rather than at what theoretical attempts to categorise them might suggest they are like. The issues considered here can help to provide an understanding of the distinctions and similarities across the third sector organisations, and how they compare and contrast with private or public sector organisations. Some aspects of third sector organisations are addressed in more detail elsewhere in this book, however. For instance, the type of activity the organisations engage in, or at least the sectors they operate in, was considered in Chapter 3 and finance for third sector activities forms the subject matter of Chapter 6 and so these issues are not covered again here.

Founders

An appropriate starting point for considering third sector organisations is their foundation. Yet seeking to characterise the typical founder of a third sector organisation is like trying to define the typical entrepreneur. Both groups of people reveal great heterogeneity coming from all races, social classes, gender and ages. Indeed, according to many observers, the founders of third sector organisations are just as much entrepreneurs as those who found private sector organisations. It is clear that, across third sector founders, there is no stereotypical person or personality. They range from people such as Mother Teresa, Dr Barnardo, General Booth, Bill Gates and Bob Geldof, who are on the international stage, to the worker priest, reformed alcoholic and housewife abuse victim, who simply operate within their local communities.

Evidence suggests that very often third sector organisations, and in particular social enterprises, are promoted, established and/or directed by groups of people, rather than by individuals, and those groups may be formed from categories of people such as

- people who work or live in areas of long-term disadvantage and seek to address some of its problems, for instance by establishing a training service for long-term unemployed;

- groups of like-minded people who organise to meet a community need, solve a problem, take advantage of an opportunity or fill a gap in provision, for instance by preserving a historic local building from demolition;

- people within the public sector who seek to encourage the establishment of social enterprises and social partnerships to achieve better local economic or community development, for instance by funding home-based palliative care for cancer sufferers;

- people in established third sector organisations, such as charities and voluntary organisations, who seek to develop alternative or supplementary ways of meeting their objectives, for instance by developing a trading arm;

- owners or managers in value-driven businesses seeking to establish third sector businesses to fulfil their social obligations. Examples of this are the numerous trusts established by international companies to support further the arts or educational and social opportunity for disadvantaged groups or young people. This is sometimes referred to as Corporate Social Responsibility (CSR) and is often interpreted as reflecting enlightened self-interest on the part of the founding organisations.

CASE 5.1

An Italian Example

In 1998 the association Città Futura was founded by a group of young adults who dreamt of changing the course of history in their southern Italian home-town – Riace. During the previous two decades the inhabitants, who kept the town alive by living in its historical centre, gradually migrated elsewhere. Today Riace counts less than 600 people, compared to 3000 in the 1960s. As a consequence many houses/buildings have been closed and boarded up, the economy lags and state subsidies are the only resource for many. Crime had become the main worry for the remaining inhabitants.

Città Futura now aims at recovering the historic centre, promoting tradi-tions and ancient trades and putting an end to unauthorized building which often has ruined the local coast line. In order to take the first step towards this goal – the restructuring of houses in the historic town centre – Città Futura approached Banca Etica, the first ethically oriented bank in Italy. In the year 2000 the bank acknowledged the initiative's importance and granted the asso-ciation a loan.

Currently 11 house-hotels (houses converted into 'hotels') have been opened which are able to provide accommodation for 55 people within the medieval setting of the old town. Furthermore, an old mill has been transformed into a weaving factory, which has not only created new employment opportunities, but also offered visitors an alternative tourism experience.

Source: Unpublished Canadian Government draft report.

Objectives

The aims, and the nature of the objectives, of social enterprises or other third sector organisations are often used in studies in this field as the primary, or only, criteria to distinguish such organisations from other ventures. Social aims and objectives are not, though, a unique characteristic of third sector organi-sations as, for instance, the example in Case 3.1 illustrates. Many commercial organisations in the private sector will have some sort of social impact on the communities in which they are operating by, for example, providing employ-ment and training or through local purchasing. Typically, though, these social impacts are not explicitly stated by the businesses concerned as being among their objectives.

In the third sector, on the other hand, social aims are typically either the primary aims or are among the primary aims of organisations in what the lan-guage of current times refers to as 'the triple bottom line': alluding to social and environmental objectives as well as, and underpinned by, financial objectives. Sometimes an ethical objective is also added, thus making a 'quadruple bottom line'. The term 'people, planet and profit' is also entering common parlance as an alternative expression, highlighting the breadth of aims.

The non-economic objectives of third sector organisations can be very varied, ranging from saving souls in the case of churches, to protecting the vulnerable from harm in the case of charities for children, to achieving democracy in the workplace through workers' co-operatives, or supporting the disadvantaged through credit unions.

Objectives in the social economy

In the case of many social enterprises, the terms 'non-profit', 'not-for-profit' (or sometimes more accurately 'not-for-profit-distribution-to-individuals') or 'more-than-profit' are commonly used. This indicates that any profits, or surpluses, are not for distribution to the shareholders or other owners for personal gain but are to be re-invested into the enterprise, or otherwise used, to help it to meet better its social, environmental or ethical objectives. It can also simply mean that the enterprise concerned does not seek to maximise a financial surplus and so arranges to supply its goods or services at prices which are consistent with that aim. In the USA a social enterprise may be incorporated as a for-profit or non-profit organisation and the term 'not-for-profit' is common. Pearce defines non-profit distribution as 'any profit recycled into the enterprise or into the local community rather than distributed to members',[1] recognising the importance of making a profit and focusing attention on how it is used.

In essence, it can be said that, at least from a common UK and US perspective, the typical social enterprise is a business in a market context that has different and more socially informed values than the typical private sector business, and that uses any profits it does make to pursue objectives other than owner or shareholder value. The popular shorthand phrase is that social enterprises are 'market led but values driven'.[2]

The Social Enterprise Coalition (SEC) stresses that

social enterprise is not defined by its legal structure but rather by:

- its nature, its social aims and outcomes;
- the basis on which its social mission is embedded in its structure and governance; and
- the way it uses the profits it generates through its trading activities. In particular, the concept of the multiple 'double or triple bottom line' is used to capture the approach and aims of social enterprises to meet financial, social and often environmental goals.[3]

Objectives for the social economy

When considering the aims for social enterprises or the social economy collectively, or as a sector, differences of purpose and scope can arise.

As elaborated upon in Chapter 4, the European 'political economy' approach to the social economy would adopt a wider 'whole society' perspective as opposed to it being viewed as merely 'an alternative business form'. It is about the role of social enterprises as an 'integral component of the social economy' and is essentially people (citizen) driven. It is about 'openness, sharing, mutuality, multi-functionality and above all an ethos of independence that gives it a right to promote the cause of the citizenry. It fills gaps, shaves the edges of poverty and exclusion, gives meaning to social life, builds social capital and social discourse.'[4]

Overall

The common characteristic of the aims of third sector organisation lies not so much in what those aims are, but in what they are not. Those aims are not, or at least not primarily, concerned with enhancing the financial wealth of the organi-sations' owners, which is a key characteristic of the private sector. Nevertheless, because they do not have recourse to public sector financing sources such as taxation, third sector organisations do need to generate enough income to cover their costs if they are to sustain their existence.

Legal structures

Third sector organisations have developed differently in different countries, often because of the different regulatory frameworks that exist and the different forms of legal entity that are available. From one country to another the same legal form may not be available to all third sector organisations and in some countries third sector organisations might have a choice of legal form available to them. So it is important to recognise that third sector organisations are not typically defined by their legal status.

In the UK there is not a single legal definition of the more limited term 'social enterprise' and many social enterprises regard their legal form or model as merely the vehicle for their activities, not the defining feature. The European Commis-sion description of the term 'social economy' mentions organisations registered as co-operatives, mutuals, associations and foundations along with social enter-prises. The social enterprise sector, in the UK, operates under a complex legal, and regulatory, framework and the choice of legal form is not narrowly restricted but is often determined by the nature of the activities being undertaken by the social enterprise, the requirements of the key stakeholders, the appropriate gov-ernance structure and, crucially, the ability to access the required finance.

A third sector organisation, depending on what sort of organisation it is, may operate as a charity, a trust, an industrial and provident society, a co-operative, a company limited by shares, a company limited by guarantee, a public limited company, an unlimited company or a partnership. It is sometimes possible to combine forms by, for instance, being both a company limited by guarantee and a registered charity, or by a group structure in which a charity might have a trading company limited by shares as a wholly owned subsidiary. This is often done to facilitate a variety of activities while taking advantage of tax exemptions and various forms of support (see Table 5.1). In general, in the UK, non-profit organisations may operate 'business' ventures directly through wholly owned subsidiary companies provided the activities of those subsidiary companies do not conflict with the aims of the parent organisations and remit to the latter any profits made.

Table 5.1   Possible forms of legal existence for non-public sector organisations in the UK

This table is a summary, and inevitably a simplification, of what can be quite a complex legal situation. For instance, the separate categories shown are not always mutually exclusive as, for instance, some trusts are established as companies limited by guarantee.

Organisations with the following forms will usually be in the third sector

Company limited by guarantee	A company with members whose liability is limited to the extent of the guarantee that they agree to contribute towards its debts, should that be necessary. An upper limit of one pound per member is, however, often set for this potential contribution. The social or public interest is usually underpinned by a constitutional requirement that profits are not paid out to members.
Trust	A trust is a legal means by which control of property is given to a person or institution for the benefit of others (the community), for example a development trust which is typically community owned and combines community effort with business expertise to foster economic, social and environmental renewal.
Industrial and provident society (IPS)	Organisations registered under the Industrial and Provident Societies Act become corporate bodies whose members benefit from limited liability. There are two types of organisations which can thus register: co-operative societies whose activities will be primarily for the benefit of the members (see below), and societies formed to benefit the community at large.

NB Charity: A charity is not a distinctive legal form. An organisation, whether incorporated or not, can apply to be registered as a charity by the Charities Commission (in GB) if its objectives and activities are charitable. Being a charity has not only tax advantages but also regulatory constraints. The requirements for registration, however, mean that those organisations which are registered as charities will be in the third sector (see also section on Charities in Chapter 4).

Organisations with the following form could be in the third sector or the private sector

Co-operative	A co-operative is an association of people united voluntarily to meet their common economic, social and cultural needs through a jointly owned and democratically controlled organisation formed for the primary benefit of its members, not the wider community. Co-operatives are registered under the Industrial and Provident Societies Act, but to be registered as bona fide co-operatives they have to fulfil a number of conditions, the first four of which reflect the International Co-operative Alliance's statement on the co-operative identity and relate to the community of interest, the conduct of business, the control of society and limits on interest on share and loan capital.
	Many co-operatives are in the third sector but those which limit their membership to their own workers and share the profits among those workers can be considered to be in the private sector.
Unincorporated	An unincorporated body may operate as an organisation but does not have a legal existence independent of its members. Thus a club which is unincorporated might have a bank account, buy or sell goods, and even employ people. But it is the members who would be legally liable for any problems.

Table 5.1   (Continued)

Organisations with the following forms will usually be in the private sector

Public limited company	A company limited by shares, a portion of which must be publicly available for purchase.
Private company limited by shares	A company limited by shares which are not publicly available for purchase.
Unlimited company	Differs from the limited company in that the liability of its members is unlimited in return for which it is relieved of some regulatory constraints.
Partnership	Formed under the Partnership Acts, the owners (partners) may have limited or unlimited liability. They are commonly used by the professions in a position of trust, for example, architects, lawyers and accountants.

Because of the variety of possible legal structures they take, third sector organisations are subject to a variety of regulatory and tax regimes. This means that their registrations and taxation affairs are recorded in a variety of different categories, some of which may also include private sector organisations. This makes it difficult to determine even the number of third sector organisations.

There is evidence that some countries are introducing legislative and regulatory changes in their efforts to facilitate the development of the social enterprise sector and in particular to enhance opportunities for innovation and cohesion. They seek 'pathways of adaptation rather than multiple legal forms'.[5] Recent examples include the following:

- In July 2005, in the UK, Community Interest Companies (CICs) were introduced (see Illustration 5.1). A CIC can be structured as a private company limited by guarantee or by shares or as a public limited company (plc.). This makes it possible for a social enterprise to raise finance from private investors and to reward them by returning some of the profit as dividend payments. (The overwhelming part of any surplus must still go to the community. Private investors cannot gain from any capital appreciation in a project.)

- In July 2001, in France, the category *Société Co-opérative d'Intérêt Collectif* (SCIC – Co-operative Society of Collective Interest) was introduced. SCICs have a new legal status, introduced by amending existing co-operative legislation. It serves to shift the emphasis from an organisation's corporate status to a focus on its objectives. Thus it enables an association to change into a co-operative without having to alter its legal form. In contrast to existing co-operative legislation, it introduces a multi-stakeholder dimension – at least three different interest groups (including users and employees) must be represented in the membership and, therefore, in the decision-making process. It is contended that the existence of the new legislation assists new enterprises to start-up as it 'makes it easier to mobilise new partners. Roles and objectives are clearer and public authorities seem more prepared to buy into the equity than they would to become a member of an association'.[6]

Illustration 5.1   The Community Interest Company

In the UK on 1 April 2005 the Secretary of State for Trade and Industry appointed the first Regulator of Community Interest Companies and on 1 July 2005 the legislation on the creation and operation of CICs came into force in Great Britain (and on 6 April 2007 in Northern Ireland). CICs were created for people who want to conduct a business or other activities for community benefit. In effect, they are bespoke limited liability companies under which social enterprises can trade.

Around 900 CICs were registered by March 2007 with numbers growing quite rapidly, embracing small shops to multi-million turnover operations.

A CIC can be a private company limited by guarantee, or by shares, or a public limited company. To be a CIC, a company must

- *Be registered as a CIC*. A CIC must be registered in the same way as a normal company with the same incorporation documents but supplemented by a Community Interest Statement. (Charities cannot be CICs but can form a CIC for trading purposes.)

- *Meet the Community Interest Test*. The primary purpose of a CIC is to benefit the community, rather than individuals. A community for CIC purposes can embrace either the community or population as a whole or a definable sector or group of people either in the UK or elsewhere. It is expected, however, that the community will be wider than just the members of the CIC. (As a co-operative aims to provide benefits for its members, it would need to demonstrate the wider community benefits.) The Regulator will decide from the submitted Community Interest Statement whether a company meets the Community Interest Test.

- *File an annual CIC report*. A CIC must file an annual CIC report with its accounts. The purpose of this CIC report is to show that the CIC is still satisfying the Community Interest Test.

- *Have an 'Asset Lock'*. 'Asset Lock' is a term used to cover the provisions designed to ensure that the assets of the CIC are, subject to meeting its obligations, either retained in the CIC and used for community purposes, or transferred to another asset-locked body. In the case of a CIC which is a company limited by shares the payment of dividends to shareholders is permitted but is limited by a dividend cap which has three elements:

  - a maximum dividend per share which limits the amount of dividend to a maximum percentage of the paid-up value of that share;

  - a maximum aggregate dividend which limits the total dividend declared to a maximum percentage of the profits available for distribution;

  - a limited ability to carry forward unused dividend capacity from year to year.

Illustration 5.1   (cont'd)

Moreover, this precludes any return to such shareholders attributable to capital appreciation on an asset. The asset-lock is attractive to funders. If the CIC ceases, assets must be distributed to the community.

Source: Based on *Community Interest Companies Briefing Pack*, prepared by the Regulator of Community Interest Companies, Companies House, Cardiff, as distributed in 2007.

Do CICs change the rules?

There has been no legal provision in the UK preventing third sector organisations incorporating as companies limited by shares or preventing private companies limited by shares from acting as though they were third sector organisations. However, third sector organisations have often found it helpful if they were incorporated, or otherwise registered, in a way which helped to indicate their third sector status. This has often been the case, for instance, when those organisations have sought funding support from public sector grant schemes or private trusts which frequently limit their support to companies limited by guarantee or to charities.

Companies limited by guarantee are precluded from remitting any profit they make to individuals such as their members, and typically their directors have acted in a voluntary capacity as the articles of association have prevented the payment of directors. Funders liked this because they felt that it served to prevent their funds being passed on to other supporters as dividends or directors' emoluments, but it could also have the counter-effect of lessening the ties between those supporters and/or directors and the companies concerned. If directors are not remunerated they may feel that their contribution is not valued, or is not as important as their input to other companies which do reward them. Also, if companies are not paying their directors, they can find it hard to demand a proper performance from those directors, such as, for example, regular attendance at meetings.

CICs can be seen as an attempt to bridge this gap by providing funders with an assurance that the companies concerned are acting in the community interest while, at the same time (at least in the case of CICs which are companies limited by shares) allowing some payments to be made to directors and/or investors and thus enabling the companies concerned to demand an adequate performance in return.

GHK in its report[7] argued that it is not necessary to have a multiplicity of legal forms. It noted that in France 'care has been taken in the legislation to provide migration pathways through which existing organisations can easily adapt themselves to new needs'. For the UK, this would mean 'creating bridges' from guarantee companies, charities, IPSs, share companies and partnerships 'so that any of them could easily become a social enterprise'.

Intermixed with these explicit legal structures, are a wide range of social enterprise categories such as the following:

1. Charities Trading Arms – trading companies owned by the charity, set up to enable them to meet their objectives by generating additional income.
2. Community Businesses – a business that serves a geographical community or a community of interest (e.g. refugees).
3. Co-operatives – associations of persons united to meet their common economic, cultural and social needs through jointly owned enterprises.
4. Credit Unions – a financial co-operative owned and controlled by its members providing access to finance and opportunities to save.
5. Development Trusts – community based and owned, they permit local communities to bring about social, economic and environmental renewal.
6. Employee-owned Businesses – they are often formed to create and preserve jobs in areas where jobs are scarce or under threat.
7. Housing Associations – the main providers of new social housing, they are run as businesses but do not trade for profit. Any surplus is reinvested and the association is guided by a volunteer committee or management board.
8. Intermediate Labour Market (ILM) Companies – provide training and work experience for the long-term unemployed.
9. Social Firms – small businesses created to provide integrated employment and training to people with disabilities and disadvantages.

Ownership

The concept of ownership of many third sector organisations is not straightforward. In the case of a company limited by shares it is clear that the shareholders are the company's owners with the extent of their ownership being determined by the number (and type) of shares they hold. As owners they are entitled to sell their shares in the company and, together, can sell the whole of the company and keep the proceeds of the sale.

In the case of a company limited by guarantee, the ultimate authority in the company is its members and it is they who elect its directors, usually on the basis of one vote per member. Those members, while they may control the company in that way, are precluded from selling off the company and/or its assets and keeping the proceeds. In that sense they are not its owners, but then neither is anyone else. Industrial and provident societies are in a similar position in that the people who control the organisation are not entitled to sell it.

Often the people who control third sector organisations are community based. They may be individuals appointed from within the relevant community, elected community representatives or representatives of other community bodies. In this way there may be an attempt to achieve a genuine sense of local ownership and to ensure that the organisation values and embraces concepts such as democracy, sharing, empowerment, mutuality and locality. However, its legal form and the structure and composition of the controlling team do not of themselves ensure the incorporation and maintenance of these values in an organisation. The process of leading and managing the organisation plays a vital role in determining the culture and values it embraces.

CASE 5.2

A Possible Drawback of Community Participation

The Northern Ireland Hospice is a company limited by guarantee. Its members, who normally pay a small annual subscription, elect the Hospice's Council of Management at the Annual General Meeting. The Council is the responsible body for the governance of the Hospice and the employment of its staff. The Hospice was established as a charity in 1981 and began to receive patients in 1983. In 1997, the Council of the Hospice decided to set up a new service for life-limited children and appointed a Project Director for this Children's Hospice. However, in 2000 the Council entered into a disciplinary process against the Project Director and in 2001 dismissed him. He appealed and applied to the Industrial Tribunal.

This process led eventually to the then Minister for Health, Social Services and Public Safety in Northern Ireland commissioning a review of the Northern Ireland Hospice in December 2002. The report of this review indicated that when the Council was taking its action against the Project Director large numbers of people began to be enrolled as members of the Hospice and the total number of members grew from under 400 to nearly 2000. Some of these new members were active in support of the Project Director while others supported the Council. However, at the Hospice's 2001 AGM, the members elected a new Council. The new Council reached agreement with the Project Director, which ended the proceedings of the Industrial Tribunal, and referred the matter to an independent panel. The panel concluded that the Project Director had been unfairly dismissed but that he should not be reinstated although he was awarded compensation. The new Council, following its own review, decided to appoint a Chief Executive for the Hospice. The former Project Director applied for this position and was appointed to it. That decision got a mixed reaction and a TV programme about it brought the controversy into the public view. Following that, at the request of the Council, the Minister commissioned his review.

Source: www.dhsspsni.gov.uk/publications/2003/hospice_report.pdf, accessed 19 May 2007.

Comment

The case of the Northern Ireland Hospice illustrates the potential problems of community participation in the control of third sector organisations. The increase in the Hospice's membership at the time of the action against the Project Director was thought by some to be the result of a reaction by his supporters who set out to recruit new members who would support his case.

> **CASE 5.2 (cont'd)**
>
> As a result, by signing up many like-minded people, his supporters were able to secure the appointment of a new Council and thus to some extent dictate the policy of the organisation. Depending on the point of view taken, this outcome could be considered to be either representative of the community's reaction and wishes, or to be a form of coup perpetrated on the community by a particular faction. To reduce the possibility of such a coup in their affairs, there has been a tendency by some other third sector organisations to specify, in their constitutions, that there should be a limit to the number of their members and/or that new members must be acceptable to the controlling body. In that way the organisations concerned hope to be able to remain true to their founders' intentions, but such approaches might be viewed as limiting community involvement and therefore to be undemocratic.

There is also a range of organisations in which the owners are not only the members but are also the beneficiaries. In other words, the extent of mutuality varies. Many third sector organisations, charities for example, are run for the benefit of non-members, but credit unions and some community businesses, co-operatives and community enterprises are run primarily for the benefit of the members themselves. Moreover, the degree of democratic participation by members varies enormously also.

As noted in the previous section, French SCICs (unlike CICs in the UK) embody the concept of democratic ownership, one of the criteria proposed by EMES, the European research network, in its definition of social enterprise. It sees a participatory approach as important, whereby not only the users of the social enterprise's services but also its employees, owners, public authorities, volunteers and other representatives contribute to decision-making. Some see democratic ownership as a key factor in sustainability as it may help to maintain closer links with stakeholders and their needs as well as keeping the organisation grounded in its community. On the other hand, given the proposed increasing role of social enterprise in public procurement, consideration should be given to potential conflicts of interest if stakeholder relationships become too close and varied.

Undoubtedly, a strong view exists that the ethos of the social enterprise requires ownership to be shared across stakeholder groups, particularly users (consumers) and deliverers (employees) – despite the obvious tensions that may be exacerbated as the drive for greater commerciality is pursued by some.

Organisation and management

The best approach to leading and managing people, and to structuring an organisation and its processes, will be influenced by many factors, not least the external environment and the organisational purpose. While no two organisations are alike, it is possible to discern some general organisation and management characteristics often associated with the social enterprise sector.

Bull and Crampton[8] highlight, from their project on social enterprises, a number of issues common to the sector as a whole. Those relating to organisation and management are summarised below as typical of the responses received from interviewees.[9]

Business, planning and plans

- One of the difficulties faced was that many people did not see themselves as 'being in business' or their organisations as 'businesses'
- Because of the insecurity and short-term nature of much funding, many social enterprises felt they were not in control of their own destiny – or of where their businesses were heading. Business plans were commonly deemed irrelevant.
- Business courses tend to be aimed at market exploitation, maximising human and capital resources, and are judged not to cater for more philanthropic aims.
- Business planning was something that many felt was either informal or out of date, yet visioning led by mission strategies was more appropriate.
- Social enterprises create a range of social and environmental impacts beyond their financial return. They experience tension and conflicts between these priorities that mainstream businesses do not face.

Management structures and systems

- Social enterprise organisations tend to have less hierarchal organisational structures, more informal communications systems, but a participatory culture with a strong sense of social mission and community.
- Informal communication processes were stifling growth past micro stage or organic growth phases.
- Social enterprises were slow to update structures, systems and procedures.

Role of the board

- In many cases the Board of Directors was a key feature in decision-making giving direction and passing on expertise within social enterprises. Whilst many reported that their Board's involvement was critical to the success of the organisation, there were a few exceptions:

  The Board met once every two months, they came in here when everyone's gone home, they never see the business operating. They get sent information the week before – but they don't read it – so how can they make decisions? ... their suggestions are not very good either.[10]

- Boards of Directors were key attributes in organisational knowledge, bringing in higher level management skills – some, but not all, totally appropriate to the small social enterprise.

Other management and organisational issues

- Issues were raised about aligning skills bases with organisational structures (management functions and roles and responsibilities).
- Social enterprises were constantly wrestling with insufficient resources and meeting immediate impact needs and service delivery levels.
- Short-term funding adversely affected sustained employment in social enterprises where contracts were tied to short-term funding periods.
- Inclusive decision-making was highly regarded.
- Organisational structure was a key issue to the management and participation of social enterprises.
- Informality and flexibility were key attributes of social enterprises.

As can be deduced from some of the above comments, a significant issue for those involved in decision-making in social enterprises is dealing with the multiple bottom line. Reconciling social and environmental objectives with financial objectives poses real problems for many. In a private business, the objective is reasonably straightforward to express – to maximise profit over the medium to long term – although not all owners choose to maximise, but instead 'to satisfice' (i.e. to balance the earning of a satisfactory and sustainable return with the expense of a reasonable amount of effort).

When one is seeking to meet the needs of poorer households with services such as housework, shopping, childcare, elderly care, help with schoolwork or gardening, it is difficult to decide on the emphasis to be placed on maximising profit, even if it is retained in the business to subsidise services in the future. How management prioritises and balances these sometimes conflicting goals is a major challenge. Should it be about purely social aims or purely commercial aims or is there a defensible and rational middle ground, especially in the absence of readily available measures of social impact (see Illustrations 5.2 and 5.3)?

There is no doubt that maintaining stakeholder satisfaction is a constant trade-off between financial constraints and service needs for many enterprises. It can be argued that democratic participation and inclusive decision-making processes can make the resolution of the challenge simpler. But equally, it can produce more complex and slower decisions based on 'the least unacceptable' option.

A move towards private sector practices?

The issue of the organisation and management of third sector organisations is closely linked to their 'ownership' and, within the social enterprise segment in particular, it has been the subject of much debate in recent times. This has been generated in part by the greater emphasis in some quarters on the sustainability of these organisations, not least in times of tightened public funding.

Illustration 5.2   Choosing Amongst Alternatives: The Multiple Bottom Line

Organisations which are trying to survive financially while also achieving their primary purpose are often faced with awkward choices such as the following:

- To raise prices or to cut services?
- To employ disabled people or to put productivity first?
- To purchase 'green' products at higher prices or to select cheaper but less 'ethical' products?
- To recruit the most suitable person for a job or to recruit someone who can most benefit from it for their future employment?
- To rely on external funding and donations to support the work of meeting the needs of the disadvantaged, or to seek financial autonomy at the expense of the range of services and quality?

Illustration 5.3   Ethics or Profits – an Example of Conflicting Values

One of the authors asked a colleague if he would like to facilitate a strategy formulation session for a newly formed social enterprise. The colleague, however, found it to be a very frustrating experience and his subsequent report was brief but informative:

> I no longer wish to be with people who devote more time to arguing whether it is unethical to price products at £9.99 instead of £10 than to considering how and where they could generate additional sales income.

Increasingly in the UK, for example, public services which are not delivered directly by the public sector are being subjected to market forces by being put out to competitive tendering. As a consequence, third sector organisations, which had formerly relied on grant income from government or philanthropic organisations to support the delivery their services, are now having to change to a business-based 'contract culture' in which, in order to survive, they must compete with other social or private enterprises to secure contracts (and perhaps forming socially responsible partnerships with the business sector in order to do this) (see Illustration 5.4).

Bull and Crampton[11] state that 'competition, scarce resources and the push towards sustainability through non-profit commercialisation has led to an emphasis on competitive strategies' and 'models or tools imported or copied from the

> ### Illustration 5.4   A Disadvantage of Separation from the Market?
>
> The disadvantage of creating temporary work schemes which are prohibited from trading in the market is that their employees are prevented from building links with the mainstream economy and hence prevented from integrating. A more promising approach is to award a wage subsidy to individuals who suffer some disadvantage in the labour market, and then allow the enterprise that employs him or her to trade freely.
>
> *Source*: GHK, 'Social Enterprise: An International Literature Review', a report submitted to SBS/SEnU (March 2006), para 143, p. 35.

business world'. In addition, there are demands for even greater accountability to funders and for transparency and public accountability.

The UK's Department of Trade and Industry asserted that 'the ability to show that a social enterprise is meeting both its financial and its social bottom lines – reconciling its mission and its money – will be increasingly important . . .' and '. . . to help achieve this, it may be helpful to develop . . . minimum standards of behaviour or an accreditation system . . .'.[12] It further stated that it wanted to 'make social enterprises better businesses'.[13]

Thus it is evident that in many instances the dividing line between commercial and social enterprises is blurring, at least in the US/UK model of the latter. This convergence has not met with universal approval. Because the non-profit organisation has multiple bottom lines, Anheier sees it as a conglomerate of multiple organisations. He states, 'the notion of non-profit organisations as multiple organisations and as complex, internal federations or coalitions requires a multi-faceted, flexible approach, and not the use of ready-made management models carried over from the business world or public management. This is the true challenge non-profit management theory and practice face: how to manage organisations that are multiples and therefore intrinsically complex.'[14]

With the emphasis on performance measurement, the adoption of tools developed in the business world remains controversial. Bull and Crampton[15] quote the Social Enterprise Partnership as reporting that 'many social enterprises see impact measurement as a burden, rather than . . . a useful management tool' and 'little work has been done at a sector wide level to see how existing tools work for social enterprises'.

Or a move towards public sector practices?

At the same time as some people are detecting a move towards private sector practices in some parts of the third sector, others are highlighting the danger of importing aspects of public sector culture. This, they suggest, can arise when the public sector is closely involved in controlling how its contracts are performed

---

CASE 5.3

The Public Sector by Another Name

The UK Government has stated that it wishes to see the third sector win more contracts to deliver public services. However, 'charity leaders are alarmed that public bodies are setting up social enterprises to bid for contracts against smaller, local voluntary organisations.'

The Department of Health has given a number of public sector organisations 'pathfinder' status, which provides funding to set up social enterprises to 'lead the way in delivering innovative community services in health and social care.'

With the majority of the pathfinders coming from outside the voluntary sector (e.g. from Primary Care Trusts), it would appear that government is content to see public bodies spin-off their service-providing arms and become established in the third sector as social enterprises, some as Community Interest Companies (CICs). However, some have reservations about 'a new breed of voluntary sector behemoths with their roots in the health sector' and 'being dominated by quasi-governmental, monolithic bodies that are rife with a public sector culture'.

While the Department of Health argues that Primary Care Trusts (PCTs) should divest themselves of their provider arms to ensure that commissioning and service provision are clearly divided (to demonstrate the fairness and transparency of the commissioning process), others contend that such state-created new organisations are 'no substitute for the genuine engagement with the local community, choice, innovation and wider wellbeing that the third sector can deliver.'

Source: http://www.thirdsector.co.uk/news, accessed 14 August 2007.

---

or, even more, when it is involved in the establishment of third sector organisations to deliver those contracts (see Case 5.3).

Overall

The competing pulls of the public and private sectors on at least the social economy part of the third sector arise because the social economy exists at that part of the private returns/social returns continuum in which activities undertaken to create social value can also create financial returns. While third sector organisations can in turn re-apply financial returns for social purpose, those managing them, with other stakeholders, need to be clear about the ways in which their enterprises contribute to the creation of social value and articulate it in a balanced way alongside the financial returns they generate (see section 'Measures of Success' later in this chapter).

One commentator has sought to draw comparisons between the managerial and the organisational characteristics of market-led or private sector organisations

Illustration 5.5   Comparison of Market Sector and Social Economy Characteristics

Issue	Market sector characteristic	Social economy characteristic
Responds to	Demand (which generates profit)	Need (which generates sympathy and appreciation)
Objectives	Profit	Financial and social return
Strategy	Product/market led	Need/competence/value driven
Organisation structure	Hierarchical	Flat
Pricing	What the market will bear	What client can afford
Decision-making	Quick, one boss, single bottom line	Slow, participative, based on trade offs, multiple bottom lines
Culture	Stand alone, viability	Dependency, grant driven
Ethos	Autocratic, effective	Democratic, caring, laid back
Approach to risk	Managed	Mainly averse
Managerial attitude	(Get out of) my way	All together, communal, shared approach, shared vision
Business model	Production (emphasising efficiency and results)	Administrative/strategic (emphasising process and people)

Source: Based on a presentation by P. Quinn to a joint INCORE and Cresco Trust seminar the Magee Campus of the University of Ulster on 5 May 2006.

and those in the social economy which are value led with social objectives as shown in Illustration 5.5.

Employment

The issue of employment can often provide particular challenges, as well as benefits, in the third sector. To date in the UK there has not been an adequate empirical base upon which to form solid conclusions on employment characteristics. Nevertheless, there is an area which continues to be topical and is worthy of consideration and that is the quality of jobs in the sector.

Job quality

The third sector is often faced with the assertion that the jobs it generates are of 'low quality'. The meaning of 'low quality' in this context often seems to lack precision but it generally appears to reflect a perception that many jobs in the

---

CASE 5.4

Should an Issue of Supply and Demand Lead to Low Wages?

'Don't let charities bid for services' – Amicus

In November 2006 trade union Amicus urged the Treasury to bar voluntary and private sector organisations from bidding for public sector contracts.

The union met Stephen Timms, the chief secretary to the Treasury, to try to persuade him to abandon procurement processes that allow charities to bid. It claims the competition leads to a deterioration in services for users and in conditions for staff.

'The most cost-effective bid wins the contract,' Rachael Maskell, national officer at Amicus, told Third Sector. 'Organisations cut back on terms and conditions to shave off margins.'

She said some of its voluntary sector members had complained about a decline in their working conditions because charities were cutting corners to produce competitive bids. The union wanted a more collaborative approach.

'If all stakeholders met to decide what the service is, what the cost is and how they are going to deliver it, that gives greater consideration to the actual service rather than placing the emphasis on the procurement process,' Maskell said.

Stephen Bubb, Chief executive of Acevo, said: 'Amicus is living in cloud-cuckoo-land. We should focus on what public services are there for – providing a service to communities.'

He refuted Maskell's claim that staff working for charities delivering public services saw any decline in their working conditions.

Source: http://www.thirdsector.co.uk/Channels/Fundraising/Article/621812, accessed 14 August 2007.

---

third sector have low remuneration and are relatively unskilled, temporary and/ or part-time. There is, however, a lack of reliable data upon which to substantiate or refute such assertions. The (then) DTI's Small Business Service survey[16] has looked at part-time working and found that 85 per cent of all social enterprises have some part-time staff with just over one-third (38%) of all staff working part-time (i.e. less than 30 hours a week). It did not report on their remuneration.

The factors which contribute to a prevalence of low remuneration, temporary and/or part-time employment, if that is the case, are seen to be not only a consequence of the market factors of supply and demand (see Case 5.4) but also in many ways intrinsic to the sector.

If the remuneration is low some of the causes may be the following:

- The task content of many social economy jobs is often quite basic requiring limited skills and consequently earning low levels of remuneration.

- Social economy organisations may often themselves be operating at the margins of sustainability and therefore only able to afford to pay low wages and/or they may recruit, as a matter of policy, those who find it difficult to get into the labour market and who do not expect a higher wage.

- The third sector is not yet perceived as a valid career or employment option by many people and so it attracts less-well-qualified and less-capable people for whom higher levels of remuneration would not be justified.

- As social objectives of third sector organisation may have primacy, it may be assumed that in some ways employees are attracted by the mission and values and are less concerned about the financial rewards of their employment.

- As social non-profit organisations, or charities, are dependent often upon donations and grants, it might be assumed that there should be a strict, if not parsimonious, attitude to remuneration levels.

- As the recipients of the sector's services are often the disadvantaged, marginalised and excluded, this should be reflected in restraint, or even sacrifice, by the providers of those services in order to deliver as much service as possible from limited budgets. Thus it might be perceived that high levels of remuneration would be inappropriate or even unethical.

- There can be a blurring of the distinction between employees and volunteers, inducing an attitude that employees are 'paid volunteers'.

Similarly, the temporary nature of jobs may be attributed to the following factors:

- The unpredictability of the funding base of organisations, which means that their ability to offer 'permanent' or continuous employment is limited.

- There can be a lack of a clear distinction between the role of volunteers (including Board Members) and that of professional staff in meeting the needs of the community.

- There is an almost unconscious mindset which perceives that this is 'how the sector does things'.

- In the absence of a strong business culture amongst the directors and senior staff, there can be a dilettante approach to the commercial necessities of organisational life.

It can also be relevant to ask what a 'quality' job is in this context. Many people might feel that a quality job would be one which requires high skills/qualifications, is well remunerated, has status and stability, is full-time and permanent, and includes regular training and opportunity for professional advancement. However, an indication of a high-quality job might also be a low employee turnover rate. A low turnover rate might indicate that the people concerned like their jobs, or at least prefer them to alternatives available, and that preference might not only depend on the set of criteria just listed.

Quality can also be interpreted as meaning 'fitness for purpose', instead of just 'degree of excellence' and, in the context of employment, there can be more than one purpose for a job. If, for instance, a job is seen as contributing to economic development then it might be hoped that it would be high-value-adding, export-producing, new technology and/or knowledge-based, full-time and long-lasting. From the point of view of a job seeker, on the other hand, the purpose of a job might be to support a lifestyle and, in that case, issues such as convenience of working hours and accessibility of location, prospects for career progression and learning opportunities, an acceptable working environment, flexibility allowing for other tasks such as child-rearing, and making a 'useful' contribution to society might all be very relevant.[17] On that basis many third sector jobs, even if not very well remunerated, may offer other compensating features and provide some people with what are, for them, better quality jobs than the alternatives. In short, quality jobs may be interpreted as those which support, or at least are compatible with, the sort of life people want to live. Many would argue that many third sector employment opportunities are of this sort.

Indeed Borzaga and Defourny[18] note that a telling feature of Italian social co-operatives is the measure of job satisfaction reported by workers. By comparison with their counterparts in the public sector, workers in social co-operatives

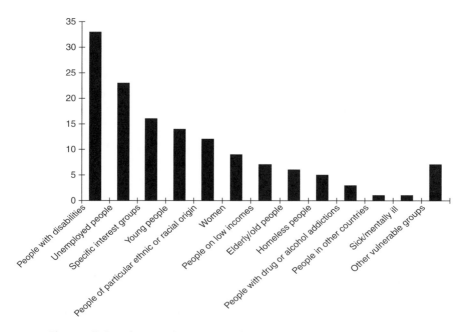

Figure 5.1   Groups of people helped through employment (in thousands)

Source: IFF Research, *A Survey of Social Enterprises Across the UK*, research report prepared for the Small Business Service, July 2005, p. 30.

are more satisfied with job quality and the overall employment environment, including their perception of their work as a key source of self-fulfilment. This sense of job satisfaction is directly related to the perception that they work in an environment of shared values, and their status as decision-makers in the design and delivery of the co-operative's services.

It is interesting to note that one specific job purpose which is relevant to a number of social economy organisations is helping unemployed people back into work, and the employment which those organisations offer is often designed and supported to do that. The (then) DTI's Small Business Service survey found that about 25 per cent of the total number of social enterprises surveyed targeted specific groups of people for employment and helped a wide range of people into work. Figure 5.1 shows the breakdown.

Volunteers

> The Welfare Society is that which delivers welfare beyond the State. At the heart of the Welfare Society is the army of people who, for love of neighbour and community, shoulder the massive burden of care. I think of the daughter caring for a sick mother, the volunteer in a children's hospice, the ex-addict helping others escape drugs. Within Britain's welfare society nearly all forms of need are being overcome by somebody, somewhere. The Welfare Society remains the largest deliverer of care in Britain today, dwarfing the State; without it the State would be overwhelmed.
>
> *Source*: Conservative Party Social Justice Policy Group 'Breakthrough Britain: Third Sector' 27 (www.volunteering.org.uk).
>
> The Social Justice Policy Group's interim report on the third sector highlighted the damagingly low levels of volunteering in general in the UK. Less than half of all adults formally volunteer even once a year, and only 25 per cent volunteer once a month. These levels are thought to be even lower in key poverty-fighting areas.
>
> *Source*: http://povertydebate.typepad.com/voluntary_sector/.

One characteristic of many third sector organisations is that they rely, at least in part, on volunteer labour. Indeed, as Chapter 3 notes, the sector is sometimes referred to as the voluntary sector. It could be said that the nature of the sector makes the use of volunteers both necessary and possible. It is necessary because many third sector organisations do not have enough resources to pay for all the labour needed to run them and it is possible because some of the labour is only required part-time, so those providing it can earn a living from other full-time jobs, and because those providing the labour want to contribute in that way to the organisations' activities. Indeed sometimes people establish third sector organisations to provide a vehicle for their volunteer contributions.

Volunteers can help third sector organisations at all levels. At the strategic level the directors or trustees of companies limited by guarantee, trusts and similar organisations are often not paid for their input, and the constitutions of many of those organisations actually preclude such remuneration. At the operational level many organisations rely on volunteers to carry out much, if not all, of their service delivery work. In between, some third sector organisations have management or specialist staff who are paid because they need them full-time or because they could not otherwise obtain their services on a reliable and consistent basis. Often a lack of volunteers can result in a greater dependence on external funding sources, a weakened human resource potential as well as reduced monitoring and quality control in organisations.

Yet volunteering can be seen as the extreme of low pay. Indeed, it very often involves the supply of services that neither the public sector nor the private individuals are willing to pay for. However, just because it is not paid, volunteering is not without value. It can be beneficial both to the volunteers and to the recipient organisation, which is why it continues. The benefit to the recipient organisation is that it is provided with the labour it needs. The benefits to the volunteers can include not just a sense of making a contribution to the organisation and its work but also help with their personal development. Some volunteer work is even promoted for this benefit because it can help unemployed people to re-enter the labour market by means such as

- giving them training and work-related skills
- giving them the experience of regular work
- helping them to acquire, and to show that they have acquired, work disciplines such as regular time-keeping
- enabling them to apply for jobs from a position of regular employment.

The existence of volunteers can nevertheless make the management of an organisation more difficult. Traditional management approaches to rewards and punishment are often related to financial remuneration which does not apply to volunteers. They have to be motivated by a different set of incentives.

That volunteering underpins so much of the work of the third sector is recognised in various ways (see Illustration 5.6) and, in the UK and elsewhere, has led to the formation of voluntary associations promoting the concept. The UK government estimates the contribution that volunteers make 'to service provision and support' is 'equivalent to over 1 million full-time workers'.[19] It further states that over 20 million people in England volunteered formally or informally, equating to half the adult population and that almost one quarter of employees work for an employer with a scheme for volunteering.[20]

Illustration 5.6   Volunteering Websites

www.vinspired.com

This website was set up by the charity V, which was founded in 2006 to develop the recommendations of the government's Russell Commission on volunteering. The website was launched to encourage young people to take up volunteering opportunities and it allows people to search for volunteering opportunities near them by category of charity. Categories such as 'drugs and addiction', 'homeless and housing' and 'education and literacy' hope to encourage greater volunteering.

www.queensawardvoluntary.gov.uk

To celebrate her Golden Jubilee, the Queen announced a new annual award to recognise and reward excellence in voluntary activities carried out by groups in the community. The Queen's Award for Voluntary Service (formerly known as The Queen's Golden Jubilee Award) is given for outstanding achievement by groups of volunteers who regularly devote their time to help others in the community, improve the quality of life and opportunity for others, and provide an outstanding service.

www.VolunteeringEngland.co.uk

Volunteering England is an independent voluntary agency committed to supporting, enabling and celebrating volunteering in all its diversity. Its work links research, policy innovation, good practice and grant making in the involvement of volunteers and it tries to raise the profile of volunteering on the public policy agenda. Volunteering England is home to the Institute for Volunteering Research.

Rewards

Employees in the third sector, including volunteer employees, seek some reward for their efforts. Except for the volunteers, the rewards sought and expected by employees include money, and that is common across all three sectors of an economy. There is little doubt, however, that in terms of financial remuneration, the rewards at least for senior staff in the third sector fall, on average, significantly below that of their counterparts in the private and even public sectors.

That private sector rewards can be relatively very large is very apparent. The media regularly expresses its concern, if not outrage, at the latest announcement of salary/bonus awards for directors and CEOs of large corporations. Indeed even owners of small and medium-sized businesses can earn substantial sums if their businesses are successful. Many such people, when questioned, will contend that money is not pursued for money's sake (nor even for what it can buy), but that it is their way of measuring their success. It is a form of scorecard that reflects the result of their efforts and many strive consistently to improve that score. Satisfaction derives from such improvement and provides the motivation to continue to strive.

While senior public sector employees do not typically reap the same level of financial rewards at the top end of the scale as their private sector counterparts, they can receive other forms of reward which provide a motivation for them. Recognition through the award of honours, for example, is common for senior civil servants and presumably compensates in some way for the shortfall in earnings compared to the private sector. Honours are clearly not the preserve of those employed in the public sector but they receive disproportionately more of them than those in the private sector who in turn rely on senior public sector support for their endorsements. Similarly, it can be argued that security of employment is greater in the public sector to which can be attached a monetary equivalent. Senior staff in the third sector, however, receive on average less than their counterparts in either of the other two sectors (see illustration 5.7).

Some of the reasons why this situation prevails have been highlighted already (see section 'Job quality' above). That it has existed for so long and shows little signs of changing in the foreseeable future suggests that senior staff are motivated by something more than the level of the financial remuneration. It is reasonable to deduce that such motivation derives from fulfilling the mission and sharing the values of the organisation employing them. Such emotional, even spiritual, rewards are likely to count substantially for the sense of well-being of leaders of value-driven organisations. Whether someone is acting to reduce the number of road deaths, heart attacks, cancer patients or ill-treated animals, he/she is often totally committed to the central *raison d'être* of their organisation. As in Maslow's hierarchy of needs/wants, once one's basic material needs are met, individuals strive for emotional fulfilment and ultimately 'self-actualisation'.

Market economics would suggest that rewards, whatever form they take, should equate across sectors assuming that the competences sought in senior staff are similar and transferable. That financial rewards vary significantly is due,

---

Illustration 5.7   Charity Chief Executives' Pay Breaks the Six-Figure Barrier

The typical salary for chief executives of large charities has broken the £100,000-a-year mark for the first time, according to research carried out by Acevo.

The View From Here, a remuneration survey by the chief executives body ... shows that the median pay for heads of charities in England with more than 1000 staff rose to £103,000 in 2006/07, up by 3.9 per cent on the previous year.

By Andy Ricketts, Third Sector

Source: www.thirdsector.co.uk, accessed 31 October 2007.

inter alia, to the non-monetary 'rewards' inherent in certain occupations. Undoubtedly, job satisfaction deriving from the desire to generate social, ethical, environmental, cultural or sporting benefit constitutes a significant non-monetary reward for many in the third sector.

Measures of success

It is generally perceived that 'business' is about profit and making money for the business's owner(s). This view is reinforced, at least in countries such as the UK, by legal requirements that companies should prepare and submit annual financial accounts and by the traditional format of company annual reports which always include the financial accounts showing, on the 'bottom line', the financial profit or loss made by the business during the year. Most 'business' is private sector business and is generally thought to have a single objective and so a single bottom line, or measure of success, which is the level of its financial profit.

As already noted, third sector organisations can have more than one objective. Their objectives can be social, but they also need to maintain their financial viability if they are to survive. Without that, nothing else is possible, and the more financial profit they make the more they have available to put back into their operations. Financial profitability is of interest therefore to third sector organisations, but as a means to an end, rather than as the end itself or as a measure of business success. Thus the success of a social enterprise is measured not only, or even mainly, by its financial profit (or surplus) but also by its social, environmental, cultural and/or ethical impact, and this has given rise to the concept of the double, triple or even quadruple bottom line, depending on how many kinds of key objective the organisation has.

The existence of a double (or multiple) bottom line suggests forms of measure expressed in terms wider than just financial profitability. It may be in terms of one or more of a wide range of social, environmental or other impacts such as the number of people helped into employment, the number of hungry people fed, the number of lives saved, the number of persons reached by an artistic venture, the scale of CO_2 emissions eliminated or other impacts.

Thus, in the late 1990s, the concepts of 'social accounting' and 'social auditing' emerged in their latest manifestation, along with various related measurement tools, to help the social enterprise to develop the monitoring, documentation and reporting systems for recording its impacts across all its objectives. Through a social accounting and audit process, the social enterprise, it is argued, can both understand and account for its social, environmental and economic impacts on its beneficiaries in the surrounding community. It may also be hoped that, in so doing, the enterprise will be more accountable and will engage more with its key stakeholders because it can measure and demonstrate its value in both quantitative and qualitative ways, and also possibly see where its performance might be improved. Ultimately, the communities served should be better able to evaluate its contribution and investors to assess whether their investment in the enterprise has achieved the added value intended.

While the term 'social auditing' has been used to cover the process of both recording and checking social achievement, there is now a tendency to differentiate the activities. Social accounting refers to the process of gathering and using data to report to stakeholder groups in the accounts. Social auditing seeks to verify (vouch and check) the performance claims made in those accounts. While the terms are also observed to be used interchangeably, strictly the distinction is like that between financial accounting and financial auditing.

There is no single method of social accounting for use by third sector organisations (and others[21]), not least because there is no one single social objective shared by all third sector organisations. Advocates of social accounting would also stress that, in this sense, it is not like an external evaluation. Rather, it is for 'social and community enterprises themselves to identify their values and their social, environmental and economic objectives and take responsibility for fully reporting on them, including consulting with the stakeholders'.[22]

Overall, it has been said that what the social auditing process, or really the whole social accounting, auditing, reporting and feedback process, 'boils down to' is stated below:

- Do you know what is important to you and to your stakeholders?
- Do you know what your impact is and what your stakeholders think of it?
- Are you responding to this?[23]

Undoubtedly, there is in the UK an increasing pressure, especially for those servicing government-funded contracts, to demonstrate in measurable form their impacts as a basis for continued funding. The emphasis on assessing social enterprises in a holistic way is likely to grow and represents an additional challenge to managers in this sector. To date there is little evidence to suggest that many social enterprises are measuring their social and environmental impacts. While recognising the pressure to become more proactive in recording and marketing their social values, most social enterprises limit themselves to mission statements incorporating values and aspirations or to responding merely to the requirements of funders for measures. There are, however, now a number of bodies which will advise on social accounting and/or perform an independent social audit of the results of a social accounting process.

Accounting and audit tools

There is a range of accounting and audit tools from which to choose and these are complemented by strategy and performance/quality improvement systems. By no means all of these concepts or tools are new or innovative. Many are adapted from the traditional business world. Table 5.2 offers a sample of the tools which are currently available to help the enterprise to focus, measure, control and ultimately publicise its impacts. The 'proliferation of organisations that produce social accounts and the diversity of social accounting techniques'[24] available have led to increased efforts to establish international standards for the practice of social and ethical accounting, auditing and reporting.

Table 5.2   Examples of social accounting management tools

Focus	Tools
Holistic accounting and reporting	Social Accounting and Audit AA1000 Assurance Standard Social Return on Investment
Measuring impact and performance	Eco-mapping GRI (Global Reporting Initiative) KSCPI (Key Social and Co-operative Performance Indicators) LM3 (Local Multipliers 3) Prove It
Quality/performance improvement systems	DTA (Development Trust Association) Healthcheck EFQM (European Foundation for Quality Management) PQASSO (Practical Quality Assurance for Small Organisations) IIP (Investors in People)
Strategic management	Social Enterprise Balanced Scorecard Social Firms Performance Dashboard

Source: Adaptation of powerpoint slides of Martin Cooper, *New Economics Foundation*, presented at University of Cambridge, April 2006.

Note: For fuller explanations regarding 'Tools' see box titled 'Sources of Social Accounting Guidance and Tools' in 'Suggestions for further reading' at the end of this chapter.

Measuring outputs and outcomes

There is a further aspect of performance measurement that is particularly relevant to those organisations, whether in the third sector or sometimes in the private sector, which receive grants for aspects of their activity. It is the need sometimes to distinguish outputs from outcomes and to ensure that both are measured. In this terminology outputs are the things that an organisation undertakes to provide, such as a car manufacturing business undertaking to produce cars. The outcomes are then the benefits which it is hoped that having the outputs will lead to, such as the social status which having a particular type of car might be thought to indicate. Understanding this distinction can be important because it is the outputs which are contractual whereas it is the anticipated outcomes which are usually the reason for the grants being given.

For instance, a third sector organisation might undertake to provide training courses for unemployed people in the expectation that the recipients of the training would more readily find employment. The delivery of the training courses would be the output and the subsequent employment would be the anticipated outcome. Sometimes outcomes are separated into shorter-term results and longer-term impacts and, in the training case, the qualifications obtained would be a result and the employment obtained through the possession of those qualifications an impact. This distinction between outputs and outcomes, between what is contracted and what is desired, is relevant to the measurement process and

---

CASE 5.5

An Example of Outputs and Outcomes

This analysis of a project from a remote farming community illustrates the difference between outputs and outcomes.

In this community, farm incomes were low and, as a result, young people were leaving the area. To encourage them to stay and to keep the community alive, the local community enterprise devised a scheme to improve farm incomes by improving the quality of the cattle the farms produced.

The output of the scheme therefore was better quality cattle, and the outcomes hoped from that were that farm incomes would increase and that more young people would stay in the area to take over the farms. In this case the increase in farm incomes was the anticipated result and the retention of young people was the impact this was hoped to have.

The community enterprise was successful in obtaining a rural development grant to help it to implement the scheme which involved introducing better AI to provide better genetic stock and better silage-making and better byres to provide better over-wintering feed and care for the cattle. What actually happened as a result of the scheme was that the farms involved did produce better quality cattle, which was demonstrated by veterinary inspections and the fact that they sold in better quality markets. So the scheme delivered what it was contracted to deliver. However, farm incomes did not increase as a result because, in the meantime, the BSE problem had arisen and depressed the price for all cattle. The scheme could not be blamed for this but it did mean that the hoped-for result was not achieved. In this case, however, there was some evidence that more young people were staying on the farms, possibly because they saw that some attention was now being given to the area. Thus the desired impact, to some extent, was happening.

Without that distinction between outputs and outcomes and, within outcomes, between results and impacts, and without some measurement of each aspect separately, it would not have been possible to analyse properly the effectiveness of the project.

---

can be helpful in determining why things work well or in identifying where the problem lies when they go badly (as Case 5.5 describes).

Problems/dangers

Reasons for the slow uptake of these relatively new forms of measurement, and also some dangers, are highlighted as follows:

- A lack of resources, typically time and money, to prepare for and carry out the measurement.

- Lack of knowledge on how to get commitment (or 'buy-in') within the organisation and to effectively embed the processes.
- Being too ambitious in scope when implementing the accounting/audit process for the first time. It is deemed useful to prioritise objectives and take each in turn to allow the processes to evolve in manageable 'chunks'.
- The process can become dysfunctional if there is too strong a desire to produce results to meet unreasonable expectations from key stakeholders. In such a situation the learning and improving dimension of the accounting process may be lost. Moreover, the 'quality of social performance verification has been severely criticised'.[25]

Benefits

While there are problems and dangers as noted above, three distinct sets of benefits from measuring social achievements are frequently articulated. They are as follows:

- business credibility is supported, productivity increased and corporate reputation enhanced;
- relations with stakeholders are improved; and
- marketing performance is improved from listening to customer demands.[26]

Summary

Third sector organisations are not completely different from private or public sector organisations. They all involve groups of people supposedly trying to achieve a common purpose. Third sector businesses, such as social enterprise, are, in many respects, like private sector business, especially in their need to earn sufficient income to maintain their existence. There is a significant difference, however. For a profit-seeking private sector business, having raised income and/or reduced costs enough to be 'in the black', making the profit sought then involves doing more of the same. For a third sector business, while being 'in the black' is essential for survival, achieving the organisation's purpose then involves not only delivering more financial surplus, but also delivering social, environmental, cultural and/or ethical outcomes on top of that. This might suggest that, size for size, managing a third sector organisation can be more challenging than managing a private business.

Such might not be the public perception, and sometimes private sector managers might seem to be under greater pressure to get results than third sector managers. That perception might reflect a lack of understanding of the third sector. In their aims, legal structures, ownership, organisation and measures of success third sector organisations face many similarities with organisations in the other sectors, but also some significant differences. This chapter has tried to describe some of them.

Key Points of Chapter 5

- Third sector organisations share some characteristics with organisations in other sectors but have other characteristics which are unique to this sector.
- Consideration of the particular characteristics of third sector organisations throws light on aspects of their uniqueness. They include

  - the founders and their motivations
  - the variety of aims of the sector's organisations
  - the possible legal structures and their suitability and flexibility
  - the concept of ownership and its complications
  - their organisation and how they are affected by, for example, culture, values, style, staffing and multiple bottom lines
  - employment profiles and perceptions of job quality
  - the role, and management, of volunteers.

- With a wide range of aims, third sector organisations often have a complex task in reporting to stakeholders on their effectiveness and on the success, or otherwise, of their efforts. There is now a proliferation of accounting and audit tools with the potential to help with this.
- It is useful to distinguish, in performance terms, between outputs and outcomes, and between results and impacts.

Questions, Exercises, Essay and Discussion Topics

1. Of the issues considered in this chapter, what are the characteristics revealed which are shared by many third sector organisations, but not by most public of private sector organisations?
2. Of the organisations listed in table 3.1, which ones share those characteristics?
3. Is it possible, in a moral rather than a legal sense, to be an investor in a CIC (see Illustration 5.1) taking a dividend from the investment while also being a benefactor of the community by virtue of the same investment?
4. In Case 5.2, who were the 'owners' of the Northern Ireland Hospice who should have had the final say in directing its affairs: the founders of the Hospice, the original membership of just under 400, the new membership which grew to nearly 2000 or the Council of the Hospice?
5. In what ways does management of a social enterprise tend to differ from that of a private sector organisation?
6. When is it likely to be worth the investment of time and money to prepare social accounts?

SUGGESTIONS FOR FURTHER READING

G. Dees, J. Emerson and P. Economy, *Strategic Tools for Social Entrepreneurs*, New York, Wiley (2002).

I. Foka, The FSM: A Holistic Approach to Measuring Social and Ethical Performance, *Business Ethics: A European Review*, 12(4), pp. 314–24.

J. Pearce, *Social Audit and Accounting: Manual, Workbook and CD-Rom*, West Calder: Community Business Scotland Network and Liverpool, Social Enterprise Network (2001).

SEPGB Quality and Impact Project – Social Accounting Manual and Quality Impact Tool Kit.

www.proveandimprove.org.

Social Audit Network (SAN).

www.social_audit_network.org.uk.

Institute of Social and Ethical Accountability (ISEA) – AA100.

Sources of Social Accounting Guidance and Tools

Social Accounting and Audit – www.socialauditnetwork.org.uk

AA 1000 Assurance Standard – reporting standards propagated by AccountAbility, an international not-for-profit organisation: www.accountability21.net/default.aspx?id=54

Social Return in Investment (SROI) – a calculation methodology that monetises impacts to demonstrate to social investors the value creation for society of projects and programmes: www.neweconomics.org/gen/newways_socialreturn.aspx (and www.sroi.london.eu)

Eco-mapping – a tool to analyse and manage a small enterprise's environmental behaviour: www.proveandimprove.org/new/tools/ecomapping.php

GRI (Global Reporting Initiative) – another form of reporting framework (called G3): www.globalreporting.org/ReportingFramework/ReportingFrameworkoverview

KSCPIs (Key Social and Co-operative Performance Indicators) – an alternative way to assess impact: www.co-operatives-UK.coop/live/dynamic/login2.asp?component

LM 3 (Local Multiplier 3) – a tool to assess how a business or initiative impacts on the local economy. Based on the Keynesian multiplier, it measures three rounds of spending: www.neweconomics.org/gen/tools_lm3.aspx

Prove It! – a method for measuring the effect of community regeneration projects on the quality of life of local people: www.proveandimprove.org/new/tools/proveit.php

DTA (Development Trust Association) Healthcheck – a diagnostic tool for reviewing performance and facilitating best practice: www.dta.org.uk/activities/services/healthcheck/

(cont'd)

EFQM (European Foundation for Quality Management) – a framework for self-assessment, benchmarking and improvement: www.efqm.org/default.aspx?tabid + 35

PQASSO (Practical Quality Assurance for Small Organisations) – a quality system designed for voluntary sector organisations facilitating setting of priorities and improved performance: www.ces-vol.org.uk/index.cfm?pg = 42

IIP (Investors in People) – a framework to help improve performance through the effective management and development of an organisation's people: www.investorsinpeople.co.uk/Pages/NewCustomersHomePage.aspx

Social Enterprise Balanced Scorecard – a mechanism to track quantitative and qualitative data simultaneously allowing an organisation to measure and communicate its social impacts: www.sel.org.uk/balanced_scorecard.html

Social Firms Performance Dashboard – a tool developed for emerging and established social forms which seeks to offer a simplified version of the Social Enterprise Balanced Scorecard (see above): www.proveandimprove.org/new/tools/socialfirm.php

References

1. J. Pearce (1999), Epose Regional Report – UK, Community Business Scotland Networks (p. 2), www.cbsnetwork.org.uk/EPOSErep.html.
2. 'Rethinking the Social Economy'. An unpublished paper based on a forum sponsored by the Belfast Local Strategy Partnership and The Queen's University of Belfast (January 2006).
3. GHK, *Review of the Social Enterprise Strategy*, A Final Report submitted to the Small Business Service (2005), p. 1.
4. 'Rethinking the Social Economy', An unpublished paper based on a forum sponsored by the Belfast Local Strategy Partnership and The Queen's University of Belfast (January 2006).
5. GHK, *Social Enterprise: An International Literature Review*, A report submitted to the Small Business Service/Social Enterprise Unit, March 2006, Executive Summary, p. 8.
6. Ibid., p. 26.
7. Ibid., p. 26
8. M. Bull and H. Crampton, *Business Practice in Social Enterprise* (Manchester Metropolitan University Business School, June 2005).
9. Ibid., pp. 21–38.
10. Ibid., p. 33.
11. Ibid., p. 12.
12. DTI, *Social Enterprise: a strategy for success* (July 2002), Pub6058/5K/07/02.NP. URNO2/1054, p. 9.
13. Ibid., p. 77.
14. H.K. Anheier (2000), Managing Non-Profit Organisations: Towards a New Approach, Civil Service working paper 1. www.ise.ac.uk/collections/CCS/publications/CSWP/cswp1-abstract.html.
15. M. Bull and H. Crampton, *Business Practice in Social Enterprise* (Manchester Metropolitan University Business School, June 2005), p. 14.

16. Howarth, R. and Sear, L. 'A Policy Overview of "Enterprise for Social Profit": Understanding and Supporting Social Enterprise', Foundation for SME Development (University of Durham) (October 2001), p. 5.

17. Based on S. Bridge, *Quality Jobs*, report to Department of Agriculture and Rural Development for Northern Ireland (2001).

18. Based on C. Borzaga and J. Defourny, *The Emergence of Social Enterprise* (London: Routledge, 2001).

19. HM Treasury Cabinet Office, *The Future Role of the Third Sector in Social Regeneration: Final Reports*, CM 7189 July 2007, p. 35.

20. Ibid., p. 45.

21. Some primarily private sector businesses have used social auditing to help them to demonstrate non-financial impacts which are increasingly of interest to their shareholders and the wider public.

22. Social Audit Network, CD2 '*Social Accounting and Audit*: A Framework for Social, Environmental and Economic (SEE) reporting'. Undated (p. 1).

23. Said by Simon Zadek at *Improve it: Social Auditing to Win Business*, a seminar organised by The Cat's Pyjamas and Social Enterprise Magazine and held in London on 29 April 2003.

24. M. O'Carroll, 'Social Enterprise Performance Verification: An analysis of three social audit tools'. Paper presented at Annual Conference of the Institute for Small Business and Entrepreneurship, Cardiff (October/November 2006), p. 2.

25. Ibid., p. 3.

26. Ibid., p. 8.

Financing the Third Sector

6

Key Concepts

This chapter covers

- the distinctive financial environment of the social economy and how it differs from private and public markets;
- the type and range of financial supports available to the sector;

(cont'd)

- how the financial market operates within the social economy in both the demand and the supply of resources;
- the distinctive financial obstacles to capitalising the social economy;
- the importance of community development – based financing and whole-sale models of support for the social economy; and
- how to make the financial supports for the sector work more effectively in growing and developing the social economy.

Learning Objectives

By the end of this chapter the reader should

- understand the importance of financial resources for the development of the social economy;
- appreciate the range of financial supports and products and how they are used to support social enterprises with different development needs;
- be able to identify the strategic and operational obstacles to financing the sector and capitalising social enterprises;
- evaluate the importance of community development finance for investment in the social economy; and
- appreciate the importance of business support and skills development for strengthening financial management in the social economy.

Introduction

Animals cannot survive without food, and businesses and other organisations cannot survive without money. And just as an animal needs food to provide both the energy it needs to survive and the building materials it needs to grow, so too an organisation needs money both to cover the costs of its operations and to provide the resources needed for growth.

There are many sources of food available to animals but not all sources will be appropriate to all animals. So too there are many different sources of finance for organisations but they are not all appropriate for every organisation. Financial sustainability is crucial to the creation of a viable social economy and knowing what type of finance is required is a crucial skill in the management of social enterprises.

This chapter considers the sources of finance used by third sector organisations, and in particular those sources which are either used mainly, or exclusively, by third sector organisations or have been developed especially for them. Interest has also grown in the whole idea of community banking as a real alternative to private financial institutions, which is creating new pressures on the sector:

The third sector, as it grows in importance, will need access to finance to expand its activities and to adapt to meet the ever changing demands of communities it serves.

> At the same time, the people managing these organisations will have to accept that borrowing and a certain degree of financial risk will enable them to achieve far more than if they take a more restricted viewed of their capacities.[1]

As indicated above, organisations generally need finance for two things: to pay for the 'capital' costs associated with the start-up, expansion or redevelopment of the organisations, and to pay for all the organisations' day-to-day operating expenses. A sustainable organisation is one which attracts enough income to cover its operating costs but all organisations, at least at the start-up stage, need some external capital finance, although some of them can and do fund later expansion from retained operating surpluses.

A recent Bank of England[2] review of finance for social economy organisations highlighted the range of ways in which they raise money and the often complex financial mix required to maintain their financial sustainability. One of the most important and traditional areas of support for the third sector has been grant aid. Grants are still important for many social enterprises, especially during their start-up phase, as they may otherwise lack the finance needed to create a viable business. The Bank of England review highlighted the difficulties of grant funding including the problems associated with creating surpluses, the restrictions on what agencies can do with the aid and the potential of 'mission drift' whereby organisations adapt their plans to meet the funders' priorities. Therefore, there has been an emphasis on diversifying the funding streams for social enterprises, especially in encouraging innovation and reducing dependency from non-tradable activities. Non-grant sources have a number of benefits including their longer-term nature, which can facilitate more effective planning, strengthening organisational efficiencies and enabling greater flexibility in the activities the organisation can engage in to support service delivery.

The Bank of England report also shows that lack of access to finance is one of the major obstacles to growth, and so this chapter reviews the issues in funding for the social economy and social enterprises in particular. It looks first at the range of financial sources open to social enterprises before describing specific schemes, especially in a UK context. The chapter then examines the diverse needs of organisations in the sector and the mix of supply dealing with enterprises of different size, scale and stage of development. The final part of the analysis highlights the implications for skills development in finance and fiscal initiatives tailored to the sector.

Finance for third sector organisations

Third sector organisations have access to many of the same commercial sources of funding as private sector businesses, limited only by their ability to offer sufficient return on investment. They also have access to private sources of funding and, like private sector businesses, they can earn income through their operations. In addition, they have access to a number of other sources which in either kind or degree are not normally available to the private sector.[3]

Sources of funding for third sector organisations can typically be divided into four types:

1. Commercial sources of funding.
2. Private sources of funding.
3. Earned income.
4. Special sources of funding.

Commercial sources of funding

Commercial sources of funding include the banks, venture capital, the stock market, offering overdrafts, loans and various forms of equity finance. However, most third sector organisations are limited in their ability to avail of such sources. Often, because they have a constitution which prevents them from distributing profits to investors, they are unable to attract commercial investments from sources which are specifically seeking a significant financial return. Also, because their focus is on their social purpose as well as on sustainability, they may not generate enough income to cover the interest on, and eventual repayment of, significant loans, although they may avail of an occasional overdraft facility.

Private sources of funding

Private sources of funding are often summarised as the three F's: founders, friends and foolish strangers. However, these categories of funders also often hope for some return from their investment, or at least expect eventually to get their money back, so it can be harder for third sector organisations to attract their support, unless it is in the form of a donation to support the purposes of the organisation, and in that case it might be considered to come under the special sources category.

One UK initiative to allow social enterprises to return some of their earnings to shareholders and thus to facilitate some private investment finance, albeit with a social purpose, was the legislation which provides for the creation and operation of CICs. In effect, a CIC is a bespoke company limited by shares, which allows some payments to be made to directors and/or investors (see also fuller description in Illustration 5.1).

Earned income

Third sector businesses which trade by selling goods or services do earn income through their operations. Because they do this in order to cover operating costs and seek to reapply any surplus to support their social purpose, they may be less able than comparable private sector businesses to fund the development of the business from retained earnings.

Special sources of funding

While third sector organisations do use commercial methods of funding such as overdrafts they are generally less able to avail of those sources which are the main financers of private sector businesses. Many third sector organisations engage in their own fund-raising, often soliciting charitable donations in various forms. This form of funding can be sustainable provided the organisation can continue successfully to solicit donations. Some churches, for instance, have sustained themselves for many hundreds of years on this basis. Endowments, it might be argued, are just a form of donation but, if big enough, can contribute to sustainability because the recipient organisation can cover at least part of its operating costs from the interest the endowment can earn. Donations, often in the form of grants, might be sought from those trusts and foundations which give money to third sector organisations. Grants might also be sought from a number of public sector sources which have budgets to use for supporting specific activities.

No one, it has been suggested, has ever parted with money without expecting to get something in return. The traditional highwayman was supposed to have offered the victim his or her life in exchange for the victim's money, and charity flag sellers offer a clearer conscience to those who donate something. Therefore it is suggested that what donations, endowments and grants (see Illustration 6.1) have in common is that they are two-way transactions because, even if it is not obvious, the source of the money nevertheless wants something in return for that money. In this sense those sources are customers and the potential 'suppliers' are more likely to secure a deal if they can identify what those 'customers' are looking for and show how their service will offer it. Appreciating that the donor will want to know 'what's in it for me?', even if the question is not framed in that way, can indicate how to phrase a request for funding.

Illustration 6.1   Grant Programmes

In the UK there is a wide variety of grant programmes and they do not all apply just to the third sector. Nevertheless, although some private sector businesses can and do use the programmes to which they can apply, grants are, on the whole, more important to the third sector, and especially to the social economy. While some grants are given out by third sector organisations, such as foundations, they are normally considered in the context of public sector grants, whether awarded directly by government departments and their agencies or by other public sector bodies such as the lottery funding bodies.

When they are available, grants are normally requested using a dedicated application form, and then, after a decision process which may or may not include further negotiations with the applicant, they are awarded by the issue of a letter of offer. The letter of offer usually states the amount of grant offered together with some indication of how it is to be used (although this may only be a reference to the original application and a set of conditions).

Grants are used by third sector organisations, if and when they can get them, both to provide the funding needed for capital investments and to cover operating costs. For a number of third sector organisations grant finance has been crucial both for their start-up or expansion and for their day-to-day operation.

Grant schemes for third sector organisations have sometimes been criticised when they are made available to cover operating costs because there is generally no

Illustration 6.1   (cont'd)

guarantee, and often little possibility, of further grant support for the same activity, which means that the activity may not be sustainable. Public sector grant givers however, while wanting to support certain activities, do not want to commit their budgets for long periods into the future. This encourages organisations to engage in certain activities with a one-off grant, often of up to 100 per cent of the funding required, but with no guarantee that they can or will be repeated. Grants have therefore been said to encourage dependency while not being able to deliver continuing support.

An alternative view of grant schemes

Although grant letters of offer, once accepted, become legally binding contracts, grant schemes are not often seen by either the grant givers or the grant recipients as two-way transactions. Instead they are often viewed, at least by the grant recipients, as some form of entitlement, rather like unemployment or other statutory benefits. Thus grant recipients may often resent the monitoring requirement which the grant givers then seek to impose. That, however, is not a helpful attitude. Morrissey and Bridge,[4] for instance, have argued that the grant system is essentially a customer–supplier relationship and that the grant giver is, in essence, trying to buy something with its money, the delivery of which it should seek to monitor. But both the lack of a clear indication that the system is a two-way process and the absence in many grant letters of offer of a clear statement of what is to be delivered in exchange for the grant contribute to a lack of clear communication.

The sort of issues that cause confusion about the real nature of grants can include the following:

- Third sector organisations often fail to view grant givers as potential one-off customers and to decide whether or not to engage with them on that basis. Many private sector businesses would be pleased to sell to one-off customers – although they might prefer to get customers who might come back – and do not have customers lined up for years ahead.

- What the grant giver may actually want is the potential benefits (or 'outcomes') of the process, not the process itself and its direct deliverables (which are sometimes referred to as the 'outputs'). For instance, training courses for unemployed people might be funded in the expectation that the unemployed people would then find employment with their enhanced skills, but it is only the delivery of the training, not the subsequent employment, which should be made contractual, as the delivery of the training is within the suppliers control, whereas the subsequent employment of the people trained is subject to other external factors such as the availability of suitable jobs.

- Grant applicants might consider the desirability of investing in making a good sales pitch if they want to have a reasonable chance of securing an order though the availability of grants may have led some third sector organisations to become better at writing successful grant applications than at the subsequent delivery of their projects.

Third sector finance schemes

The need for special third sector finance schemes

The demand for social finance varies from small grants and loans to more sophisticated financial products including equity capital. The New Economics Foundation has argued that the rising number, size and complexity of social enterprises has created demand for social equity capital in which issuing shares in the company through an equity listing is a route to raise significant capital. This builds the number of stakeholders, offers an exit for early-stage investors and provides a basis for future investment.[5] Its study calls for developing a social equity capital prototype, stronger links with ethical investors, developing market intermediaries, building awareness and supporting businesses to attract social equity investment.

While most small business owners probably feel that they have faced difficulties in finding the finance needed to start or develop their businesses, commentators have pointed out that many third sector organisations face additional barriers specific to that sector. For instance, according to the (then) DTI,

> At present many social enterprises are under-capitalised and struggle to access external finance, particularly when starting up, growing or moving away from grant dependency. Whilst this is often to do with a lack of financial skills, in many social enterprises it is also a result of an understandable reluctance to take on debt. In addition, it is some-times that investors do not understand the social enterprises' market and this situation is exacerbated for those social enterprises located in disadvantaged areas where the transaction costs associated with such investments can be extremely high.[6]

According to Mayo et al., in an extensive review of community investment in the UK, the demand and supply barriers which limit access to capital for community businesses are as follows:

1. Lack of viable proposals:

   - Voluntary organisations are resistant to using private capital.
   - There is a lack of skills for putting a business case together.
   - There is a lack of credit history to satisfy banks.

2. Return:

   - The risk means that interest rates are set too high.

3. Information asymmetries:

   - Lenders are unable to assess the risk of repayment from voluntary agencies.
   - There is a lack of understanding of the sector among bankers.

4. Transaction costs:

   - The financial costs of administering small loans to micro enterprises are high.

5. Risk:

- Bank underwriting criteria are inappropriate for certain voluntary/
community markets.
- Bankers may reject viable projects.[7]

The 2000 report of the Social Investment Task Force (SITF) and the research
papers that underpinned its conclusion have provided an important and comprehensive series of recommendations on the development of the social economy in
the UK.[8] A core concern of the Task Force was the barriers that stood in the way of
enterprise and wealth creation in under-invested communities which it identified as

- a systematic failure between government, banks and sources of capital;
- public sector grants and charitable funding which create over-dependence
and stifle enterprise;
- weak incentives for private investment in communities;
- low levels of entrepreneurship, indicated by a low rate of small business creation;
- a lack of information about bank lending activities and the potential markets
in under-invested communities;
- the UK has an under-developed community finance sector compared to
the US;
- the interpretation of UK charity law lacks clarity as it relates to community
development finance;
- the lack of a coherent approach by different tiers and departments of
government;
- entrepreneurial behaviour in the voluntary sector tends to be fettered by its
traditions, laws and established practices;
- the existence of public policy obstacles (such as the benefits system) to entrepreneurship.

As a result of this investigation the core recommendations of the Task Force
were that there should be

- a Community Investment Tax Credit to encourage private investment in
under-invested communities, via Community Development Finance Institutions
(CDFIs);
- a Community Development Venture Fund – a matched funding partnership
between the government on the one hand and the venture capital industry,
entrepreneurs, institutional investors and banks on the other;
- disclosure by banks of their commitments to business finance in deprived areas;
- greater latitude for charitable trusts and foundations to invest in community
development initiatives;
- technical support for CDFIs.

The Chancellor of the Exchequer in the UK announced in June 2000 that the government would be willing in principle to support this recommendation by matching community development venture funding. As noted above, the Task Force also recommended a programme of disclosure by banks of the level of investment in deprived areas. This follows the broad approach of the Community Reinvestment Act 1977 in the US, which has produced profitable and safe returns in some of the most under-invested areas of the country. The Task Force also highlighted the need to review Charity Law to clarify when and under what circumstances programme-related investments by charitable organisations comply with legal requirements. Table 6.1 lists the types of third sector finance schemes.

Figure 6.1 summarises the Task Force's view on the need for a mixed community development finance sector comprising Community Development Banks, Community Loan Fund, Micro-loan Funds standing between government, banks and other investors on the one side and businesses and social community

Table 6.1   Types of third sector finance schemes

- Ethical share issues using the plc. rules
- Withdrawable share capital
- Community finance loans
- Mutual guarantee mechanisms by a federation of mutuals
- Non-profit licensing of new technology
- Mezzanine finance
- Social business angels

Source: Finance for Social Enterprises, www.renewal.net, accessed 2004.

Government agency accredits

1. CDFIs for CITC allocation to be passed on to lenders and equity investors in CDFIs

2. CDVFs for matching Govt funding

CDFIs attract loans and equity capital from banks, companies, institutional investors, individuals and charities by passing on their allocated tax credits to them

CDFI	CDFI	CDFI	CDFI
Micro-loan funds	Community loan funds	Community development banks	Community development venture funds

Self employed + micro businesses

Growth & other business as well as non-profit social and community enterprises

Growth businesses

KEY: CITC= Community Investment Tax Credit; KEY: CITC= Community Investment Tax Credit; CDVF= Community Development Venture Fund; CDFI= Community Development Finance Institution

Figure 6.1   The Social Investment Task Force vision of a community investment finance sector

Source: Based on Social Investment Task Force, *The Report of the Social Investment Task Force* (2000), p. 9.

enterprises on the other. The proposed Community Investment Tax Credit is designed to help to increase the scale and capacity of CDFIs by increasing private investment flows. But other actions were also suggested to bolster this process:

- Organisations that wish to become national (or regional) intermediaries should equip themselves with the business expertise and skills in this arena.
- CDFIs should work closely with Regional Development Agencies and Local Strategy Partnerships.
- Government should help by supporting CDFI development through the Phoenix Fund and banks and large corporate organisations and entrepreneurs should also be encouraged to help.

The range of third sector capital finance schemes

Satter and Fisher[9] highlighted some examples of these sources such as *Triodos,* which operates as a social bank in Britain, the Netherlands and Belgium. They also cite the Ashton Reinvestment Trust as an example of a community loan fund as the organisation attracts and recycles investment funds for housing and business development in inner-city Birmingham. Similarly, the Prince's Trust offers a good example of a micro-loan fund aimed at business start-up in the UK.

Mayo et al.,[10] described the functions of community finance as providing the catalytic capital resources or means of risk reduction to secure the interest of mainstream finance in enterprise development and to provide the means for widening economic opportunities for marginalised individuals, business and communities. Table 6.2 describes different community development finance initiatives and how they can be used in different circumstances (also see Illustration 6.2).

Community Development Finance Institutions

The New Economics Foundation (NEF) recently conducted a wide-ranging review of CDFIs which showed, using its definition, that approximately 80 have been established across the UK and that the sector has achieved a high degree of diversity, ranging from the provision of small personal loans of £50 to social enterprise loans of £1 million. The study also showed that they have been effective in getting funding into under-invested areas but that most are small, growing slowly, and that there is over-optimism about their economic impact. NEF argues that government needs to have a longer-term and better-resourced vision for the sector in which funding is more secure to allow CDFIs to sustain their portfolios in the longer term.

> Overall, we found that CDFIs are at a critical juncture. Without renewed support the sector will become increasingly fragmented and weak. CDFIs could wither and many may disappear, providing another set-back to disadvantaged communities. With the right support from government, regional agencies, funders and banks, however, CDFIs could play a major role in addressing issues of access to finance in the UK.[11]

Table 6.2   Community development initiatives

Circumstances	Action	Reason
If a community needs fewer financial services and in smaller amounts (including cheque and savings accounts to consumers); needs an institution that is less expensive to form or adapt than a commercial development bank; wants to focus on low-income consumers; has little or no other access to savings and credit facilities.	Community Credit Union	Sustainable at a much smaller scale of activities than other initiatives, community credit unions have volunteer support and lower overheads. They can service more small accounts, are competitive on loan interest rates and are well suited to encourage members to increase savings. *But* many community credit unions have lower asset sizes than is ideal for sustainability.
If a community or sector needs flexible, high-risk business financing or potentially equity capital; needs specialist or locally responsive and knowledge-able regeneration finance for housing, charities, social enterprise or small business.	Community Loan Fund	Such loan funds can operate at a smaller scale than commercial banks and can be formed by a skilled group of committed people. They have significantly more leeway in the kinds, sizes and terms of loans they make. They have the potential to develop relationships with mainstream banks as a local partner or agent. *But* this is an evolving model, which to date has required significant development time and still faces the dilemma of how to provide high-risk loans with capital from social investors that may be intended as low-risk.
If a community needs credit for micro-enterprises, including disadvantaged borrowers; needs other micro-level financial services.	Micro-Finance Fund	These are attractive for the innovations they make, such as peer and group lending, for managing risk and for reducing operating costs through outsourcing costs to group borrowers. *But*, while highly effective in poor countries, schemes in industrialised countries rarely achieve the same scale of operation and financial sustainability.

If small businesses need access to development finance or better terms from banks, have capital they are willing to pool as a guarantee fund.	Mutual Guarantee Society	This is a creative, self-help way of responding to finance needs among small businesses, encouraging better terms from banks and developing mutual support.
		But, these are relatively new in the UK and it will not always make sense for entrepreneurs to tie up liquidity in guarantee funds. Credit unions that offer finance for micro-entrepreneur members may be more suitable for small loans.
If a community or sector can support a dedicated finance institution with assets of £5 million or more; needs a variety of services; can attract the necessary organisers, banking experience and capital.	For-profit Social Bank or subsidiary/ initiative of a commercial bank	A for-profit bank is viewed as a credible and solid institution. They provide a range of services including deposits. If profitable they can produce income sufficient to attract mainstream equity investors.
		But, large organising costs, substantial initial capitalisation and regulatory demands are major hurdles. Some argue that EU Banking Directives make it too difficult for new social banks to emerge. Some community loan funds aspire to become banks in due course.

Source: Based on E. Mayo, T. Fisher, P. Conaty, J. Doling and A. Mullineux, *Small is Bankable: Community Reinvestment in the UK* (York: Joseph Rowntree Foundation, 1998).

Illustration 6.2   Community Development Finance Initiatives and Institutions

In this chapter, reference is made to both community development finance initiatives and community development finance institutions with the latter being a specific organisational form of the former. Both of the initiatives and the institutions are, however, sometimes referred to as CDFIs, which can be confusing.

To try to reduce that confusion this books has tried to spell out community development finance initiatives in full, and to use the initials CDFIs only to refer to a community development finance institutions.

NEF outlined a particular approach to Community Banking Partnerships, which brings together both credit union(s) and a Community Reinvestment Trust whose members jointly form a Charitable Trust. A Community Reinvestment Trust is a non-profit organisation providing loans and other financial services to small businesses, community enterprises and individuals in under-served communities. The approach aims to open credit to non-bankable residents and to attract clients from local high-cost moneylenders in particular. The Partnership combines access to credit with money and debt advice, bill payment services and energy advice, especially given high levels of fuel poverty in disadvantaged areas. Some examples of social venture capital include the following international schemes:

- The first specific law in Europe for social enterprises helped establish the Banca Populare Etica in Italy in 1998. The bank provides innovative financing for social and ecological ventures in particular.

- In France, Club Cigales is encouraged by a national tax credit to target micro-social business (fewer than 10 employees). It operates a business angel approach to provide risk capital along with management and marketing expertise.

- The CREDO fund in Ireland, capitalised initially by several religious orders, has been deploying social venture capital for growth projects in the social economy.

- In the US, CANDO offers a rolling 10-year loan facility automatically extended each year as a loan product but in the form of long-term patient capital.

The Bank of England Review

In 2003 the Bank of England produced one of the most comprehensive and authoritative accounts of the financing of social enterprises in England.[12] The key findings of this research were as follows:

- 'Demand for debt finance among social enterprises is limited both by the availability of other, cheaper forms of funding such as grants, and by a cultural aversion to the risks associated with borrowing'.

- Larger, more established organisations use a range of financial instruments to address cash flow difficulties or to purchase or develop assets.

- Social enterprises are more likely to be rejected for finance than SMEs with possible explanations being lack of available security and personal financial stake; use of organisational structures and grant-funding streams with which lenders may be unfamiliar; some element of credit and behaviour scoring; reputational risk to the lender and low levels of investment readiness among some social enterprises.

- There is little evidence of demand for or supply of conventional venture capital or business angel finance to the social enterprise sector.

One area where the Bank of England research showed evidence of demand was for some form of patient capital:

The term is variously defined to range from 'investment' grants to products that are structured as debt or equity, where investors are willing to accept lower, and in some cases uncertain, financial returns in exchange for social outputs.

According to the Bank a key issue in tapping into the social investment market is the ability of the social enterprise to describe and account for social costs and benefits, and in this context the methodology of social auditing is encouraged for social enterprises.

In order to stimulate demand the Bank of England recommended the following:

- Advertising and transferring best practice models of lending across the social economy.

- The devolved administrations could ensure that mainstream business support arrangements recognise the particular needs of social enterprises.

- Public sector agencies should expand their funding for researching on the feasibility of a business idea.

- Building on existing financial awareness programmes could increase the level of investment readiness of social enterprises.

- A greater emphasis on providing more information and guidance on access to social finance sources.

On the supply side, the Bank of England recommended the following:

- Increasing the amount of money available to CDFIs specialising in the social enterprise from regional authorities, the private sector and through take-up of the Community Investment Tax Relief (see also Illustration 6.3).

- Developing joint lending (e.g. between banks and CDFIs) and encouraging co-financing where possible.

- Encouraging CDFIs that lend to social enterprises to become approved lenders under the Small Firms Loan Guarantee Scheme.

- As important, the development of clearer means of distinguishing social enterprises from other borrowers especially by identifying financial indicators specific to the sector.

- The development of a brokerage service at a local level by an expert in the range of finance services available to the sector.

- The reviewing by banks of their procedures for ensuring that broad policy intentions at head office level related to lending to social enterprises are implemented effectively at branch level.

- The British Bankers' Association could usefully act as a source of information for banks on social enterprises via their website and other communications channels.

- Grant providers, including government, could review the administration of grants so as not to impede the ability of social enterprises to leverage in other forms of finance.

Illustration 6.3   Community Investment Tax Relief

Community Investment Tax Relief (CITR) is available to individuals and corporate bodies investing in accredited Community Development Finance Institutions (CDFIs), which then in turn provide finance to qualifying profit-distributing enterprises, social enterprises or community projects. CITR will enable an accredited CDFI to offer tax relief as an incentive to investors willing to provide it with patient capital for at least five years. These funds can then be on-lent by the CDFI to borrowers within its target market. The design of CITR draws a distinction between loans made by CDFIs to profit-distributing small and medium-sized enterprises (SMEs) and those to 'community projects'. The latter category includes both non-commercial activity as well as commercial activity that is small-scale and purely local in nature. Many social enterprises will therefore be included within the scope of that description and thus benefit from the greater flexibility permitted in CDFI transactions with community projects. In particular, when using funds raised under CITR, an accredited CDFI:

- May make a loan of up £250,000 to a community project, compared with a limit of £100,000 for loans to profit-distributing SMEs;

- Is not required to apply the European Commission Hurdle Rate as a minimum interest rate when making loans to community projects, which it must do when lending to profit-distributing SMEs;

- May make an equity investment of up to £250,000 in a community project, but may not make equity investments in profit-distributing SMEs.

Source: Bank of England, *The Financing of Social Enterprises: A Special Report by the Bank of England* (London: Bank of England, 2003).

Micro-finance initiatives

In the UK, micro-finance initiatives aim 'to widen the access of disadvantaged people and neighbourhoods to capital and other financial services. Such services include micro-financial services provided, for example, by credit unions; neighbourhood regeneration initiatives, such as community loan funds; and loan funds and social banks targeted at relevant sectors, such as small businesses, community and social enterprises, or charities'.[13] Moseley and Steel highlighted their value in disadvantaged areas of the UK by offering loans, advice and business support to self-employed people and micro-enterprises that were viewed as un-bankable by the mainstream commercial sector.[14]

A number of writers and commentators have been concerned about the lack of a coordinated approach to the support of these interventions over time and across countries. Parker and Lyons, for instance, were critical of government and policy support for the development of CDFIs in Australia but suggest that as well as a clearer policy framework and investment the sector also needs to support itself via effective networking and cross learning between the active organisations.[15] Parker and Lyons highlighted the need for greater spatial integration of services and access to money, and NEF also pointed out that both domestic and business finance were needed in under-invested communities:

> Over a quarter of British households aren't able to use mainstream financial services and have no savings to meet future needs. These are the poorest households. This 'financial exclusion' means that they are often charged excessive rates and penalties. A high percentage of them must pay a typical charge of 8–10 per cent commission to cash cheques at 'money shops'. And the sky is the limit on interest for small loans. Over three million households use doorstep lenders with charges from 160 per cent to 1,500 per cent APR. There is no statutory ceiling on interest rates, and profitability is high for these lenders. New lenders from abroad are now entering this lucrative market. There is an urgent need for alternative and affordable sources of credit.[16]

Street UK is a midlands-based organisation set up in 2000 to offer loans, advice and business support to self-employed people and micro-enterprises that were viewed as un-bankable by the mainstream commercial sector. The scheme has supported more than 200 clients with bespoke business support and credit finance, especially in assisting businesses in the transition from the undeclared to the declared economy. Williams[17] evaluated the initiative and highlighted the multiple, business, economic and social benefits and improvements from small amounts of credit released via not-for-profit finance. These included

- moving from part-time to full-time work;
- moving from home to business premises;
- keeping basic level records;
- keeping higher level accounts;
- purchasing public liability and employers' liability insurance;
- hiring employees on a PAYE basis;
- using a bank account for their business transactions;
- obtaining the required licences and permits to operate the business such as health and safety inspection certificates;
- graduating off all non-work state benefits;
- graduating from majority cash revenues to majority invoiced revenues;
- incurring a formal business tax liability; and
- becoming VAT registered.[18]

Experience in the United States

Much of the development of the social economy in the US originated from the implicit and explicit exclusion of some ethnic neighbourhoods where banks, building societies and insurance companies would not invest. The Community Reinvestment

Act (1997) states that financial institutions have an affirmative obligation to meet the credit needs of communities where they are based. The 1993 Community Development Finance Institutions Fund Act provides public support through a development fund for community finance initiatives and for bank subsidiaries promoting community reinvestment. Since the Community Reinvestment Act was passed almost $400 billion has been advanced to community lending by mainstream banks who have, for the most part, found this to be profitable business.[19] Mayo et al. point out that there are typically five models of community finance in the US:

1. Community Development Banks (more than 10).
2. Community Development Credit Unions (130 +).
3. Community Development Loans Funds (46).
4. Micro-finance Funds (50 +).
5. Neighbourhood Equity Funds

Some initiatives have emphasised their 'community capitalisation' by helping to stabilise or prevent the collapse of the local economy. They often seek to work with other specialist non-profit parties, multi-purpose development agencies or coalitions providing advice or technical support. CANDO was formed in Chicago in 1979 in response to the Community Reinvestment Act. It is the largest local urban partnership coalition in the US with 100 non-profit neighbourhood development organisations as members and more than 130 private affiliate members. CANDO's programmes include lobbying, developing publicly owned land especially for local housing projects, organising local business groups to revive brown field land and helping to revive local retailing.

Financial instruments

Demand and supply of finance for the social economy

As with any financial market, maintaining a satisfactory relationship between the demand for and the supply of capital is essential for sustained growth and business development. A key issue for the third sector as a sector within the wider macro economy is the asymmetry between the supply of and the demand for investment. In an extensive review of 'patient capital' (see Illustration 6.4) in Scotland, CEIS[20] showed that there was a strong undercurrent of investor interest as a result of the desire of the public sector to shift from grants to more commercial arrangements and to the more straightforward profit motive of the private sector. It makes the point that traditionally the private sector has invested in social enterprises for philanthropic or promotional reasons but that they are being increasingly attracted by returns available in growth areas of the sector. Picking up on this pattern, the Bank of England report in social enterprise finance[21] showed that this emerging investment lay in commercial businesses concerned with ethical issues (recycling or ethical trading) rather than in social economy businesses *per se*.

Illustration 6.4   Patient Capital

The main characteristics of patient finance are as follows:

- It is long-term in nature, enabling it to be used for both start-up and subsequent development funding.
- If structured as debt, it could have capital and interest payment holidays, perhaps to the extent of deferring all capital repayments until the end of the loan. Alternatively, it could be structured as a zero-interest loan, analogous to a recoverable grant.
- If structured as equity or quasi-equity, it would involve little ceding of control and would not require an explicit exit strategy.
- However structured, the financial returns would be sub-market, in return for social gains.

In suggesting an extension of patient capital the Bank of England recommended that

- Government may need to extend the availability of support, such as subordinated matched funding or tax relief.
- The Social Enterprise Coalition could investigate the possibility of establishing a 'social angels' network to match social investors with social enterprises needing investment.
- The results of pilot projects such as the Adventure Capital Fund and Futurebuilders would provide more information on how innovative approaches might be applied across government.
- Patient finance could be stimulated by sharing best practice and by encouraging larger social enterprises to invest in start-up projects.
- In view of the regulatory and cost burden on social enterprises wishing to make a public share offering, the government and the Financial Services Authority could review current regulatory exemptions relating to share issues in the light of the particular characteristics of social enterprises.
- Social auditing techniques should ensure that they meet the needs of investors and provide a means of benchmarking performance.

Source: Based on Bank of England, *The Financing of Social Enterprises: A Special Report by the Bank of England* (London: Bank of England, 2003).

The CEIS review argued that there was no technical bar to linking supply and demand but identified a number of dimensions to market failure including the following:

- Information and knowledge is the primary obstacle to efficient market operation in terms of both those seeking resources and those attempting to make investments.

- A sustainable deal flow has two dimensions in that the size of investment and availability of a commercial return will dissuade private investors especially on a comparative basis with other sectors.

- Exit strategies are not clear for investors in social enterprises. It might be clear how they put money into the organisation but it is less clear how they get it out easily and efficiently.

- Transaction costs on equity deals tend to be high given the technical competencies and systems required to maintain the investment.

- Culture and skills gap especially in moving the community and voluntary sector from a grant-based funding arrangement to a loan-based one is a significant short-term obstacle. The CEIS highlighted the contradictory value base of the public sector and its concern for accountability and the private sector with its acceptance of risk and flexibility in investment decisions.

The CEIS report[22] also highlighted the need to harness the skills of the private investment community in mainstreaming social economy equity investment. In particular, it stressed

- the need to educate the market place in both demand and supply sides;
- the need for action to create and retain surpluses in social economy organisations;
- the need to unblock constraints to developing an effective lending market which includes

  - the absence of exit mechanisms for investors
  - the limited size of the market and its effects on transaction costs
  - the relatively high cost of development support
  - the lack of appropriate investment skills in the social economy
  - the need to foster demand that is latent, via education, marketing and demonstration projects.

In *Revaluing the Social Economy in Scotland*, McGregor, Glass and Clark[23] pointed out that 54 per cent of all organisations surveyed identified difficulty in obtaining appropriate or sufficient funding as the main obstacles to sustaining or developing their organisation. The research showed that

> the lending as opposed to granting agenda will be difficult to deliver, on the assumption we are talking about loans that must be repaid notwithstanding the patience of the lender in terms of when this happens. However, one of the key constraints is revenue out of which to pay off debt, and the evidence of the survey is that revenues from charges has grown only modestly with even the largest social economy organisations still looking to grant funding in the first instance.[24]

McGregor et al. also point to the contradiction in funding regimes whereby organisations that make surpluses are penalised by a progressive withdrawal of mainstream grant income. They are simultaneously being told to 'be entrepreneurial but don't make surpluses'.[25] However, the report also showed that the bigger organisations attract more mainstream funding and that the larger they become the less likely they are to locate in or employ people from areas of high disadvantage. Dayson also made the point that

> there has been a systematic failure with a 'grant culture' that has led to over-dependence and there was no incentives for private sector investment. Additionally a risk adverse culture was limiting business start-ups and entrepreneurship.[26]

Supply of finance

Metcalf et al.,[27] referred to the current supply of community finance as a 'jumble' while Collin et al.[28] argued that even soft loans raise issues about their sustainability, community involvement and accountability. Here, Coparisow[29] argues that micro-finance needs to be targeted on ethnic minorities, and women specifically to improve self-confidence, business survival rates and access to finance. Dayson usefully identified the reasons for the patchy development of community development finance initiatives in a UK context:

- Problematic definition of a charity.
- Failure to provide the right mix of grant and loan funding.
- Cultural inability to understanding that 'not for profit' is not charity or 'for loss'.
- It is difficult for banks to support CDFIs undertaking the same activity as themselves in areas they rejected and by using different methodologies.
- There is a lack of integrated welfare to work incentives.
- There is a lack of appropriate legislation and regulation.
- Credit Unions also have difficulties with bespoke lending, while the requirement to save before borrowing can exclude or delay clients.
- Soft loan schemes are too focused on the most deprived and often provide no opportunity for second loans.[30]

In a separate report that helps to address these structural and cultural obstacles, Westall et al. identified the key characteristics of Europe-wide community development finance activities and these are shown in Table 6.3.[31]

Collin et al. state that soft loans are short-term, supported by a government agency or a programme, which cover part of the operating costs, are less concerned and are usually life limited.[32] Soft loans were, in particular, regarded as a method to help shift organisations from grant to lending. Collin et al. were highly critical of soft loans because a high proportion were un-lent and default rates were also comparatively high, and because of their poor disclosure practices.[33] Coparisow argues that most CDFIs have started small which has made them reliant on public subsidy for longer and at a higher cost.

Table 6.3   Good practice in community development finance lending
in Europe

- Lending to groups or individuals often based on peer lending where collateral is based on mutuality and social ties;

- Providing pure credit with business support;

- Financing of start-ups or existing businesses;

- Funding is targeted at specific groups such as women or ethnic minorities;

- Unlike Credit Unions, most CDFIs only offers loans due to local banking regulations;

- They provide 'free loans' or charge a commercial rate which imposes financial discipline on the borrower and helps the CDFI become sustainable.

Source: A. Westall, P. Ramsden and J. Foley, *Micro-entrepreneurs: Creating Enterprise Communities* (London, IPPR and NEF, 2000).

For Dayson[34] the agenda for development consists of a number of interconnected stages:

- A cultural shift in both the operation of schemes including realistic interest rates and the debt collection.

- Improvements in structures and the quality of governance, management and management information systems is needed to transfer soft funds into sustainable CDFIs.

- There is a crucial need to achieve cost minimisation by streamlining services through a technologically driven back-office service with revenue maximisation (i.e. issuing many loans), which overcomes the danger of limited growth enhancement in lost minimisation approaches.

The economic environment

Despite the more attractive taxation environment for social finance funding, the Scottish Council for Voluntary Organisations (SCVO) has identified important limitations to the impact of fiscal instruments in the community and voluntary sector. They showed[35] that 70 per cent of the UK population give to charity in a typical year but less than 10 per cent use the tax breaks available. Lack of awareness and assumptions that it would be technically difficult to operate seem to lie behind the low tax relief take-up rates. The Gift Aid scheme rewarded donations to charity through tax relief at the basic rate of income tax (22%) and the scheme has been progressively widened and simplified since the March 2000 budget. SCVO highlights the opportunity to pursue payroll giving, deeds of covenant and gifts of quoted shares and securities as ways of responding to the uncertain financial climate faced by charities and voluntary sector groups.

Financial 'wholesaling' for the third sector

Ainger et al.[36] researched the possibility of a wholesale intermediary for community finance and found that a fully commercial wholesaler, even partly capitalised by government, would not be viable in the short term. However, they found that some form of interim or transitional central funding organisation could provide a valuable catalyst towards a more commercially sustainable future for the community development finance initiative sector. The aim of the wholesaler would be to raise private and public sector financing to on-lend to CDFIs to support their development and growth and increase their scale and impact. Ainger et al. set out seven functions for intermediaries.

1. An intermediary with specialist experience in raising private finance could bring a measure of coherence to the scramble for funds amongst CDFIs and give greater coherence to potential investors.

2. An intermediary could also contribute to quality control among CDFIs.

3. The wholesaler might jointly finance larger loans to community groups, where such loans are too large to be taken into the CDFIs' books for reasons of prudence.

4. The wholesaler could play an important role in the syndication of tax incentives for investment in CDFIs under the CITC scheme.

5. The wholesaler could reduce the costs of fund-raising both for funders as well as for the recipients.

6. An intermediary might help to keep resources to the sector flowing.

7. An intermediary could provide a more secure source of funds then grants or subsidised funds, which are neither secure nor likely to be sustained over the long term.[37]

The Ainger et al. research is particularly useful for estimating the size of and behaviour within the community development finance initiative market. Table 6.4 shows that the estimated total community development finance initiative assets in Britain were nearly £700 million with a high proportion of assets located in credit unions.

Table 6.4   Community development finance initiative breakdown by type and size

Type	Number	Estimated total assets(£)
Social banks	Not known	122m
Credit unions	700	215m
Community development loans	25–30	110m
Finance organisations: local (soft) loan funds	100	210m
Community development: venture capital funds		40m
Total		697m

Source: Based on B. Ainger, R. Brocklehurst and S. Forster, Feasibility Study into a Wholesale Intermediary for Community Development Finance (London, Housing Finance Corporation, 2002), pp. 11–12.

The key findings of the research were as follows:

- Community development finance initiatives all demonstrated a strong commitment to serving 'unbankable' clients and achieving a community level impact.
- Many community development finance initiatives were small and young but growing rapidly.
- Performance and risk profiles varied widely for different community development finance initiatives but on average they had a loan fund size of £1.5 million and a portfolio outstanding of £680,000.
- Community development finance initiatives surveyed did not have a sufficiently developed capital structure or revenue basis for a wholesaler to present a robust credit story to commercial banks for commercial on-lending to the sector.
- Community development finance initiative credit worthiness was expected to increase over the next two to three years.
- There was interest in the concept of a specialised wholesaler, especially in the skills, time and cost advantages it could bring to the sector.
- In the short term there was limited demand or capacity for fully commercial borrowing.
- Community development finance initiatives were focused, in the short term, on increasing access to concessional borrowing if rates were less than 1–2 per cent over base.
- The study concluded that even in the short term a wholesale arrangement could be a useful mechanism to channel funding to CDFIs and start to build a financing source that could be there for the long term.
- The study estimated that the demand for wholesale financing for the next 3–5 years would not exceed £15–20 million.[38]

In recent years the UK government has been trying to diversify the supply of capital to at least parts of the third sector, as Cases 6.1 and 6.2 indicate.

CASE 6.1

Aston Reinvestment Trust

Aston Reinvestment Trust (ART) is one of the best-known CDFIs and it operates in Birmingham as a mutual society providing loans to the voluntary organisations and SMEs which have viable projects that cannot obtain funding from mainstream banks. Its overall aim is to create local jobs for local people. ART's main features, as an Industrial and Provident Society, are 'one member, one vote'; maximum shareholding of £20,000 (individual or corporate), withdrawal of shares with three months' notice; no prospectus or opening and closing dates required to issue shares; regulations of IPS similar to that of

CASE 6.1 (cont'd)

Credit Unions; ART raises money from private companies, personal investors, housing associations, charitable foundations and the public sector. They have raised some £2.4 million including £417,000 in share capital from 172 members, £460,000 as subsidised long-term social investment loans and £170,000 from public sector area regeneration initiatives. Loans range from £20,000 to £40,000 and repayments can be made from six months to ten years, secured or unsecured, with capital repayment holidays if required. ART highlights the importance of scale economies in terms of geographical coverage, referral flow and loan portfolio. Ideally it would like to have a portfolio of £3 million out on loan instead of £1.1m as at present.

Source: www.reinvest.co.uk (accessed 2004).

CASE 6.2

Futurebuilders: An investment fund for voluntary and community sector public service delivery

The Futurebuilders initiative was an attempt to develop the capacity of community and voluntary sector organisations to access public sector contracts and services. In the 2002 Spending Review,[39] the UK Government announced the £125 million, one-off, Futurebuilders investment, spread over three years to March 2006, to assist the voluntary and community sector in its public service work. Futurebuilders was intended to showcase the best of voluntary and community service delivery; to transform the capacity of some individual organisations, or groups or organisations, working together, to engage in service delivery; and to capitalise on the sector's distinctive contribution to service delivery and ability to be creative. It was meant, therefore, to reinforce the independence of the sector, highlight its potential and lead to a better understanding of its role in service delivery.

The principal test for schemes resourced by Futurebuilders would be whether the investment enabled an organisation, or group of organisations, to expand or improve their service delivery. Investments were intended to help remove obstacles and enable organisations to modernise to achieve this. It would help tackle the lack of capital investment and development funding in the sector. It would aim to fund the best ideas, wherever they may be, to create exemplars that inspire and lead public delivery service.

Target Organisations. Futurebuilders was aimed at:

- Existing service delivery organisations that want to do more;
- Organisations new to service delivery; or
- Existing and new service providers that want to deliver services in a different way.

CASE 6.2 (cont'd)

Principles. Futurebuilders would assist schemes that are underpinned by six guiding principles:

Improving service for users;

Investing in sustainable schemes;

Promoting greater collaborative working;

Making the money go further;

Stretching and challenging organisations;

Inclusiveness.

Priority Service Areas. Futurebuilders would be directed at those organisations working in, or across the fields of:

• Health and social care;

• Crime;

• Community cohesion;

• Education and learning; and

• Support for children and young people.

Assets. The overall funding could be used to buy a wide variety of assets within three broad categories:

1. Physical assets (e.g. for buildings);

2. Intangible assets (for knowledge and skills; an evidence base; and research); and

3. Development funding (e.g. one off resource spend).

There would be no fixed allocations between the different forms of assets. The fund manager(s) would have flexibility to apportion the fund to best effect, within an overall annual investment plan, approved by government ministers.

Finance. Futurebuilders would offer grants and different forms of loans, and there would be no fixed allocation between the different types of finance. The emphasis would be on maximum flexibility, so that the specific type of finance could be tailored to suit the needs of individual organisations. The loans culture was new to many in the voluntary and community sector and, while suitable for some, would not be right for all. The loans element of Futurebuilders would be tailored to meet the needs of the sector. There would be no minimum or maximum levels of investment. The fund manager(s) would have the flexibility to invest small as well as large amounts in individual schemes.

Source: Bank of England, *The Financing of Social Enterprises: A Special Report by the Bank of England* (London: Bank of England, 2003).

CASE 6.2 (cont'd)

Delivery. After an open competitive tendering process the winning consortium set up Futurebuilders England Ltd in 2004 to run the Futurebuilders programme until March 2008. An additional £65 million was allocated for phase two of Futurebuilders, which was re-tendered. The Adventure Capital Fund won this contract to manage the Futurebuilders programme from 2008 until 2011.

Source: www.futurebuilders-england.org.uk, accessed 21 April 2008.

CASE 6.3

Adventure capital fund

The Adventure Capital Fund was established in 2002 in order to pilot a range of approaches to investing directly in independent community based organisations working in disadvantaged areas.

- A £360,000 Bursary Fund to invest in approximately 20 revenue bursaries to staff, each up to £15,000. The bursaries are intended to strengthen and assist in the development of its investment readiness.
- A £2 million Patient Capital Fund to invest in 10 capital investments with a ceiling of £400,000. The Patient Capital Investments are designed to establish/strengthen the asset base and increase the scale of operations of the selected community enterprise.

The Adventure Capital Fund is delivered by a community sector partnership comprising the Local Investment Fund, the Development Trust Association, the Scarman Trust and the New Economics Foundation, with the active participation of the Active Community Unit of the Home Office. The designers of the Adventure Capital Fund programme have incorporated a number of process elements designed to strengthen the delivery process. The introduction of the Supporters Programme, the use of balanced score cards, the exploration of measures of social impact, the development of strong interlocking partnership arrangements and an innovative approach to the evaluation process invest the Adventure Capital Fund with a structure that has the potential of being both robust and supportive.

Thake[40] later evaluated the performance of the Adventure Capital Fund and his analysis showed that significant progress was made in the key areas of the programme but that more needed to be done to ensure that it was financially robust:

Nevertheless, the future is not risk free. Many of the Patient Capital investees are still operating with the benefit of capital and interest payment

> **CASE 6.3 (cont'd)**
>
> holidays: they have yet to make any substantial repayments on their loans. In addition, further work needs to be undertaken to establish the depth of the market for Bursaries/ Business Development Grants and Patient Capital investment as well as how to develop the capacity of community-based organisations in neighbourhoods and communities where the local infrastructure has been severely eroded.[41]
>
> *Source*: S. Thake, *Sustainable Futures: Investing In Community-Based Organizations* (London: NEF, 2004).

A summary

Table 6.5 indicates the range of instruments which, according to the (then) DTI, are now available to grow the social economy in general and social enterprises in particular.

Table 6.5   The supply side funding regime

Source	Details
Cooperative action	New foundation established to support the development of new forms of co-operative and mutual enterprise by giving grants and making loans of between £5000 and £200,000 in developing or supporting new or existing co-operative enterprises, organisational structures and research.
Community Investment Tax Relief	Encourage up to £1 billion investment in start up businesses and social enterprises in deprived areas.
Community Development Finance Institutions (CDFIs)	Independent financial institutions providing capital and other financial support to enterprises in disadvantaged areas.
Industrial Common Ownership Finance (ICOF)	ICOF was set up in 1973 and is a loan fund for employee-owned cooperatives and social enterprises. It is supported by pubic shares and is fully self-sustaining.
Local Investment Fund	The Fund was established with support from government, Business in the Community and the private sector and Natwest. Since it was established it has offered 25 loans totalling £29 million and has leveraged £15 million into community regeneration.
Bridges Community Development Venture Fund (CDVF)	CDVF is a 50/50 partnership between government and the venture capital industry aimed at supplying venture capital, which was launched in 2002 by the Chancellor. It supplies capital finance to firms operating in some of the most disadvantaged areas in England. More details of the fund can be found at www.bridgesventures.com.
Charity Bank	The Bank has attracted £10 million in exempt deposits and gifts to provide finance and related support to help charities and other organisations develop sustainable charitable ideas.

Business Angels	Business angels can provide total finance at a key stage and often business advice. Social enterprises are potentially a prime recipient of attention from business angels who want to put something back into society.
Community Asset Transfer	The Active Community Unit has been exploring the potential to transfer physical assets such as community centres, parks and redundant building to social enterprise management.

Source: Based on Department of Trade and Industry, *Access to Finance for Social Enterprise* (London: DTI, 2003).

Financial skills for the third sector

The East of England Development Agency (EEDA)[42] has highlighted the importance of preparatory assessment work before selecting from the range of financial products that are on offer. In particular, it suggests that there needs to be a stronger assessment of what social enterprises need, of the skills and staff they need to access and manage non-grant finance income, and of how to set prices and understand markets in developing sustainable services and products. It is not, therefore, enough just to create additional sources of finance for third sector organisations. If that finance is to be applied successfully, those sources need to be made readily available and third sector organisations need to know how to access and use that finance.

It has been suggested that there is, in particular, a shortage of professional finance staff working in social enterprise organisations. Many social enterprises need funders to provide the financial skills they lack and often

---

CASE 6.4

East End Micro Credit

East End Micro Credit started in East London in 1998 as a network to help increase access to finance for the self-employed. The group recognised the need for two types of partners: technical aid providers to support business mentoring, loan support, outreach and capacity building; and a loan fund to provide the finance and administration. Many of the loans involve peer group lending whereby groups of between four and six people train together and learn business basics for two months. Individual loan applications are sanctioned by the rest of the group and assisted by a facilitator but failure to repay means that no further loans can be made. Since 2000, 50 peer groups have been formed involving over 250 people and by that time about 150 loans have been made. As a result 130 new self-employed micro businesses have been established with only two defaults to date.

Source: Based on Bristol City Council, *Bristol City Council Community Finance Initiative: Report of the Learning Group* (Bristol: Bristol City Council, 2003), p. 45.

lack information about the range of types and sources of finance available, meaning that it is difficult to assemble the mixed finance packages that are often required. This is because finance organisations operate in isolation and there is a lack of intermediaries able to broker deals on behalf of social enterprises.[43]

Sourcing financial support and advice

Smallbone et al. showed how many successful social economy businesses started on shoestring budgets with soft loans providing valuable start-up resources. However, their research also showed that

> Even social enterprises that are committed to commercial viability for at least part of their operations often show little tendency to access business advice from commercial or other formal mainstream channels, particularly at or close to start up.[44]

The Smallbone Review was especially critical of Business Link services and their understanding of social enterprises and the distinctive services that social enterprises require. Only 25 per cent of surveyed Business Links claimed to have a specific policy towards social enterprises while only 9 per cent had a social enterprise database. Business Link has carried out its own review of services to the social economy which highlighted the need for an integrated programme to support the sector that include the following:

- Outreach services concentrating on rural drop-in facilities, presentations in schools, contact with other agencies and publicity; Gateway Services for handling enquiries that focus on initial referrals and systems for tracking external referrals. Pre-start services are required which are tailor-made to new organisations and which can help to build network relationships between groups in the sector.
- Specialist services and skills bespoke to social economy enterprises.
- Inter-agency referrals on a planned and integrated basis.[45]

However, the Smallbone review also highlighted the need for a wider range of services in

- accessing finances;
- preparing funding bids;
- developing knowledge and expertise to access funding sources;
- new forms of grant finance designed to assist start-up or growth of social enterprises;
- the need for loan finance to aid start up;
- the need for local delivery mechanisms to ensure that loan finance is effectively used within communities where it is needed.

Conclusions

Micro-finance initiatives have proved critical in communities where the absence or withdrawal of the banking sector has left many poor communities at the mercy of predatory lenders. Grants and endowments are still important, especially in supporting incubation or fledging organisations, and the tension between tradable and charitable aims of community sector organisation is a distinctive pressure facing new entrants to the social economy. There are also structural barriers to finance including the technical proficiency of enterprises as well as awareness and understanding of financial suppliers. New 'products' have emerged to support the sector, especially to sustain itself on a commercial basis, and initiatives such as Adventure Capital Fund has proved important in diversifying the supply of finances to the sector.

Key Points of Chapter 6

- Social enterprises, like other enterprises, need access to finance to start, develop and grow.
- There are various ways in which social enterprises can access financial support including grants, endowments and commercial loans.
- More recently, there has been a growth in the sophistication of financial supports for the sector, reflecting its diverse needs. This includes the availability of patient capital and soft loans and even the use of social equity finance.
- Fiscal measures, in the form of Community Investment Tax Relief, are attempting to incentivise investment into the community and voluntary sector, whilst growing interest for ethical investment is also attracting commercial resources to the social economy.
- There are important obstacles to more effective assembly and use of funding cocktails including the capacities and preparedness of organisations to manage investment and the lack of awareness of risk-sensitive commercial lenders.
- There is growing importance attached to making the financial market work better for the social economy, with intermediates attempting to connect supply and demand more efficiently across businesses.

Questions, Exercises, Essay and Discussion Topics

1. What do you understand by the term 'patient capital'?
2. Why are there different types of financial support for the social economy?

(cont'd)

3. Are the financial support needs of the social economy different to those of the private economy?

4. What sort of organisation might need social venture capital?

5. What are the obstacles to the effective financing of social enterprises?

6. What knowledge set and skills do social enterprises need among their staff to manage their finances effectively and efficiently?

7. Describe the different forms of finance available to social economy enterprises?

8. When might a social enterprise need social equity finance and how might this be used?

9. How might fiscal initiatives such as Community Investment Tax Relief aid the development of social enterprises?

SUGGESTIONS FOR FURTHER READING

Bank of England, *The Financing of Social Enterprises: A Special Report by the Bank of England* (London: Bank of England, 2003).

S. Collin, T. Fisher, E. Mayo, A. Mullineaux and D. Satter, *The State of Community Development Finance* (London: NEF, 2001).

Task Force, The Report of the Social Investment Task Force (SITF) (London, SITF, 2000).

References

1. A. Cadbury, 'A vision of community finance', In INAISE *Up-scaling Social Investment: Fifty Case Studies* (Paris: INAISE, 2000), pp. 8–9.

2. Bank of England, *The Financing of Social Enterprises: A Special Report by the Bank of England* (London: Bank of England, 2003).

3. For instance, see F. Capber, 'A greater space for social banking', In INAISE *Up-scaling Social Investment: Fifty Case Studies* (Paris: INAISE, 2000).

4. M. Morrissey and S. Bridge, *Lessons of Peace II: A Review for Proteus* (Belfast: Proteus, 2006), especially pp. 30–2.

5. New Economics Foundation (NEF), *Developing a Social Equity Capital Market* (London: NEF, 2006), p. 11.

6. Department of Trade and Industry (DTI), *Social Enterprise: a strategy for success* (London: DTI, 2003), p. 64.

7. E. Mayo, T. Fisher, P. Conaty, J. Doling and A. Mullineux, *Small is Bankable: Community Reinvestment in the UK* (York: Joseph Rowntree Foundation, 1998).

8. Task Force, *The Report of the Social Investment Task Force* (London: SITF, 2000).

9. D. Sattar and T. Fisher, *The Scope and Opportunity for Social Investment in the UK, Social Investment Taskforce Papers* (London: NEF, 2002).

10. E. Mayo, T. Fisher, P. Conaty, J. Doling and A. Mullineux, *Small is Bankable: Community Reinvestment in the UK* (York: Joseph Rowntree Foundation, 1998).

11. New Economics Foundation (NEF), *Reconsidering UK Community Development Finance* (London: NEF, 2007).

12. Bank of England, *The Financing of Social Enterprises: A Special Report by the Bank of England* (London: Bank of England, 2003), (direct quotes p. 1).

13. B. Rogaly, T. Fisher and E. Mayo, *Poverty, Social Exclusion and Microfinance in Britain* (Oxford: Oxfam, in association with the New Economics Foundation, 1999), p. 3.

14. P. Moseley and L. Steel, 'Microfinance, the labour market and social inclusion: a tale of three cities', *Social Policy and Administration*, Vol. 38, No. 7 (2006), pp. 721–743.

15. K. Parker and M. Lyons, *Community Development Finance Institutions, Evidence from Oversees and Australia* (Sydney: University of Technology, 2004).

16. New Economics Foundation (NEF), *Community Banking Partnership: A joined Up Solution for Financial inclusion* (London: NEF, 2004).

17. C. Williams, 'Harnessing the hidden enterprise culture; the Street UK Community Development Finance Initiative', *Local Economy*, Vol. 21, No.1 (2006), pp.13–24.

18. Ibid., p. 19.

19. E. Mayo, T. Fisher, P. Conaty, J. Doling and A. Mullineunx, *Small is Bankable: Community Reinvestment in the UK* (York: Joseph Rowntree Foundation, 1998), p. 40.

20. CEIS, *Sharing in Success Patient Capital for the Social Economy in Scotland* (Glasgow: CEIS, 2002).

21. Bank of England, *The Financing of Social Enterprises: A Special Report by the Bank of England* (London: Bank of England, 2003).

22. CEIS, *Sharing in Success Patient Capital for the Social Economy in Scotland* (Glasgow: CEIS, 2002), p. 4.

23. A. McGregor, A. Glass and S. Clark, *Revaluing the Social Economy* (Glasgow: University of Glasgow, 2003).

24. Ibid., p. 34.

25. Ibid., p. 35.

26. L. Dayson, *Community Finance Solutions* (Bristol: Bristol City Council, 2003), p. 9.

27. H. Metcalf, H. Crowley, T. Anderson and C. Bainton, *From Unemployment to Self-employment: The Role of Micro Finance* (London: ILO, 2000).

28. S. Collin, T. Fisher, E. Mayo, A. Mullineaux and D. Satter, *The State of Community Development Finance* (London: NEF, 2001).

29. R. Copisarow, The application of micro credit technology to the UK: key commercial policy issues, *Journal of Micro Finance*, Vol. 2, No. 1 (2000), pp.13–42.

30. L. Dayson, 2003; ibid., p. 13.

31. A. Westall, P. Ramsden and J. Foley, *Micro-entrepreneurs: Creating Enterprise Communities* (London: IPPR and NEF, 2000).

32. S. Collin, T. Fisher, E. Mayo, A. Mullineaux and D. Satter, *The State of Community Development Finance* (London: NEF, 2001).

33. Ibid.

34. L. Dayson, *Community Finance Solutions* (Bristol: Bristol City Council, 2003).

35. Scottish Council for Voluntary Organisations (SCVO), *Tax Effective Giving to Charity* (Edinburgh: SCVO, 2002b).

36. B. Ainger, R. Brocklehurst and S. Forster, *Feasibility Study into a Wholesale Intermediary for Community Development Finance* (London: Housing Finance Corporation, 2002).

37. Ainger et al., 2002, pp. 8–9.

38. Ibid., p. 16.

39. HM Treasury, *2002 Spending Review – Opportunity and security for all: Investing in an Enterprising, Fairer Britain*, Chapter 1, Cm. 5570. Available on the HM Treasury website at www.hmt-treasury.gov.uk (July 2002), accessed February 2008.

40. S. Thake, *Sustainable Futures: Investing In Community-Based Organisations* (London: NEF, 2004).

41. Ibid., p. 8.

42. East of England Development Agency (EEDA), *Finance Think Tank: Issues for Social Enterprise Finance* (Norwich: EDDA, 2005).

43. DTI, *Access to Finance for Social Enterprises* (London: DTI, 2003).

44. D. Smallbone, M. Evans, I. Ekanem and S. Butlers, *Researching Social Enterprise* (Sheffield: Small Business Service, Research Report RR004/01, July 2001), p. 38.

45. Business Link, *Business Support for Social Enterprise Final Report* (London: Business Link, 2001) (www.businesslink.org), p. 23–4.

Social Capital

Key Concepts

This chapter aims

- to explore the origins of social capital across a range of different intellectual and policy traditions;

- to cover the relationship between social capital and other forms of capital relevant to development;

- to determine the role of social capital in economic, enterprise and area-based development;

- to examine negative effects of social capital, especially linked to the delivery of broad-based economic development practice;

- to explore some of the issues in measuring social capital.

(cont'd)

Learning Objectives
By the end of this chapter the reader should

- understand origins of social capital as a conceptual and applied policy concept;
- appreciate the necessary connection between social capital and other forms of capital resources essential for local development;
- understand the connection between the concept of social capital and the performance of the economy and the social economy in particular;
- recognise the connection between the social economy and regeneration;
- identify the limits of social capital, especially as it is applied to the social economy; and
- understand the problems in measuring social capital across time and place.

Introduction

This chapter looks at social capital, its relationship to the social economy and the third sector, and its role in addressing deprivation. Some academics and policy makers consider social capital to be a necessary prerequisite for effective economic growth,[1] whilst for others it is a by-product of community-inspired responses to economic disinvestment.[2] However, critics suggest that social capital and notions of community cohesion are weak alternatives to the provision of hard economic resources such as jobs, cash, skills and opportunity.[3] Concepts such as empowerment and capacity building ring hollow in places and communities which economic capital has abandoned or ignored.

Nevertheless, the connection between social capital and the necessary means for community advancement is a potentially attractive one for programme managers and policy makers concerned with the improvement of disadvantaged neighbourhoods across the developed world.[4] A viable stock of social capital in the form of organisations, networks, trust and norms can, it is suggested, be an important foundation for local economic mobilisation and for the creation of a virtuous circle of economic and social growth and sustainable community development.

Baron et al.[5] argue that the current interest in social capital reflects a growing recognition of the excesses of individualism and a concern that, in the market orientation politics of the 1980s, valuable social assets and morals were eroded, which in turn had deteriorating effects on communitarianism and the quality of life. Francis Fukuyama[6] also argued that the success of the strongest and most advanced capitalist societies has been based on a relatively high level of trust in business and politics. In countries such as Japan and Germany, social capital is the defining factor that explains the strength of their political economy as well as their cultural vitality. Capitalism has proved to be a more successful and enduring system than the failed communist order and, within capitalism, trust facilitates friction-free economic development and political maturity.

Not surprisingly, the potential capacity of social capital to enrich or even rescue civic society has a powerful appeal to politicians, not least in the UK, where notions of a stakeholding society and third way politics focuses attention on the erosion of civility and social cohesion.[7] The decline of civic society is 'real and visible...it is seen in the weakening sense of solidarity in some communities and urban neighbourhoods, high levels of crime and the break up of marriages and families'.[8] For Giddens the repair process involves government and civil society working in partnership, community renewal through harnessing local initiative and involvement of the third sector in service delivery. He is especially attracted to the notion of social investment whereby the state works with multiple actors, especially in the community and voluntary sectors, in the production of a broader and more shared sense of a welfare society not a welfare state:

> Since the revival of civic culture is a basic ambition of third way politics, the active involvement of government in the social economy makes sense. Indeed some have presented the choice before us in stark terms, given the problematic status of full employment: either greater participation in the social economy or facing the growth of 'outlaw cultures'.[9]

This chapter therefore presents the concept of social capital in relation to other forms of capital, and aims to show the relationship between civic society, social capital and the social economy in practical ways. It begins with a brief review of the concept of social capital before looking in more detail at its application to the economy, enterprise and entrepreneurship. The analysis also considers whether social capital has specific contributions to make to, or a specific dependence upon, the social economy, which are distinct from its relationship to business performance in private markets and the added value it contributes to economic development generally.

The concept of social capital

The concept of social capital is not new. Its intellectual roots in the social sciences rest with a concern for communitarianism, pluralist associated life and both representative and participative forms of democracy.[10] Pierre Bourdieu re-energised the study of social capital by connecting it to both cultural and material economic assets. The capital that individuals are able to accumulate defines their position in the social class order but there are important distinctions in the way in which these forms of capital work in practice. For Bourdieu social capital is not reducible to economic or cultural capital but it is not independent of it either, and economic capital is the most efficient form of capital in shaping class and society in advanced countries. The reproduction of economic capital, on its own, creates wealth and power disparities but, in Bourdieu's model, individuals have 'the capacity to exercise control over one's own future and that of others'.[11] Social capital is thus the aggregate of real and potential resources which are linked to durable relational networks between individuals and institutions.[12] This suggests that it has two dimensions:

- First, it is a resource that is connected with group membership and social networks and the volume of social capital possessed by an individual depends on the size of the network created.
- Second, it is about the quality of these relationships and especially the capacity of the groups to mobilise resources in their own interests.[13]

Bourdieu used the term 'narrowly' being primarily interested in explaining how some people gained access to power and resources via their social connections. Coleman's analysis shared some of these ideas but he viewed social capital as a functional concept that could also be employed neutrally or in non-political ways. Coleman saw social capital consisting of two components that reflect some aspects of social structure and facilitate the actions of actors within that structure. This structure is passive and can be used in positive or negative ways, which in each case is determined by the motivation and objectives of actors within any given network. Thus, it simultaneously reproduces greater connection between the actors and imposes obligations and sanctions on the membership.

Portes in particular criticised Coleman's version of social capital, especially for its definitional vagueness.[14] Here, he stressed the distinction between the membership of social structures and the resources gained via such membership. Coleman's work drew heavily on 'dense networks' such as kinship and neighbourhood links, which understates the importance of weak or informal ties in securing economic advantage. Like Putnam, Portes criticised Coleman's understanding of social capital as functionalist and organic which places particular value on the family. This has left the approach open to criticism from feminists and by those who identified the exploitative labour practices sometimes associated with familial business commitments.

Few writers have done more to boost the status of social capital, in the West at least, than Robert Putman. His early definition referred to social capital as 'the networks, norms and trust that enable participants to act together to effectively pursue shared objectives'.[15] In his later work he shifted the emphasis from trust to reciprocity and an acknowledgement that social capital has a dark side, especially in multi-ethnic societies.[16,17] His approach is examined in greater detail later in the chapter but it has attracted particular criticism from those who argue that it is a neo-liberal concept urging conformity with, not resistance to, the pervasive power of public and private markets. Law and Mooney[18] in particular argued that Putnam's work represents a constructivist, simplistic and descriptive account of social capital that fails to theorise power relations and the dominant role of economic capital in creating social exclusion.

Definitions and different forms of social capital

Social capital, like the social economy, has a multitude of definitions. These reflect different emphases such as the strength of networks, the quality of structures and institutions or the intended outcomes or beneficiaries from its activation in particular settings. For example, Kay's interpretation of social capital is especially interesting as he makes the connection between resources generated by its presence and a vibrant social economy. For Kay social capital is 'that tangible "something" that exists amongst individuals and organisations within a community; the connections and trusting contacts that people make while going about their daily business. These contacts can be used on a mutual and reciprocal basis both to further their own ends and/or for the development of the community'.[19] Table 7.1 is based on a *Discussion Paper* by the UK Cabinet Office and lists a few of the definitions and the different emphases they place on social capital and its economic, political and social purposes.[20]

Table 7.1   Definitions of social capital

- features of social life – networks, norms, and trust – that enable participants to act together more effectively to pursue shared objectives...Social capital, in short, refers to social connections and the attendant norms and trust.[21]

- Social capital is seen as the foundation on which social stability and a community's ability to help itself are built; and its absence is thought to be a key factor in neighbourhood decline.[22]

- the institutions, relationships and norms that shape the quality and quantity of a society's social interactions[23]

- networks together with shared norms, values and understandings that facilitate co-operation within or among groups[24]

- The term 'social capital' is increasingly used by policy makers as another way of describing 'community', but it is important to recognise that a traditional community is just one of many forms of social capital. Work-based networks, diffuse friendships and shared or mutually acknowledged social values can all be seen as forms of social capital.[25]

The DFID model

The UK Department for International Development (DFID) developed an international approach to understanding vulnerability and how it can be managed more effectively in different situations and settings. This 'sustainable livelihoods' approach sees peoples' poverty connected to a range of factors, each of which needs to be addressed to achieve sustainable routes out of exclusion and deprivation:

> The livelihoods approach is concerned first and foremost with people. It seeks to gain an accurate and realistic understanding of people's strengths (assets or capital endowments) and how they endeavour to convert these into positive livelihood outcomes. The approach is founded on a belief that people require a range of assets to achieve positive livelihood outcomes; no single category of assets on its own is sufficient to yield all the many and varied livelihood outcomes that people seek.[26]

The 'sustainable livelihoods' model (see Figure 7.1) includes five types of 'capital' asset which have limited substitution potential and all of which are considered to be important in building a strong community. The five-capital pentagon lies at the core of the livelihoods framework as it highlights the important interrelationships between the various assets affecting people's quality of life.

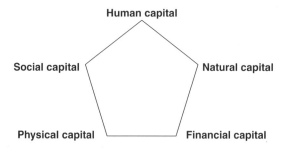

Human Capital: Human capital represents the skills, knowledge, ability to labour and good health that together enable people to pursue different livelihood strategies and achieve their livelihood objectives. At a household level human capital is a factor of the amount and quality of labour available; this varies according to household size, skill levels, leadership potential and health status. Human capital appears in the generic framework as a livelihood asset, that is, as a building block or means of achieving livelihood outcomes.

Social Capital: Social capital is the resources upon which people draw in improving their quality of life and are developed by:

- networks and connectedness, either vertical (patron/client) or horizontal (between individuals with shared interests) that increase people's trust and ability to work together and expand their access to wider institutions, such as political or civic bodies;

- membership of more formalised groups which often entails adherence to mutually-agreed or commonly accepted rules, norms and sanctions; and

- relationships of trust, reciprocity and exchanges that facilitate co-operation, reduce transaction costs and may provide the basis for informal safety nets amongst the poor.

Natural Capital: Natural capital is the term used for the natural resource stocks from which resource flows and services (e.g. nutrient cycling, erosion protection) useful for livelihoods are derived. There is a wide variation in the resources that make up natural capital, from intangible public goods such as the atmosphere and biodiversity to divisible assets used directly for production (trees, land, etc.).

Physical Capital: Physical capital comprises the basic infrastructure and producer goods needed to support livelihoods. It includes:

- infrastructure which consists of changes to the physical environment that he people to meet their basic needs and to be more productive; and

- producer goods which are the tools and equipment that people use to funct more productively.

Financial Capital: Financial capital denotes the money resources that people use to achieve their livelihood objectives. The definition used here is not economically robust in that it includes flows as well as stocks and it can contribute to consumption as well as production.

Figure 7.1   Forms of capital

Source: Department for International Development (DFID) (1999), *Sustainable Development Guidance Sheets*, London, DFID, p. 5.

DFID pays particular attention to the relationship between social capital and other assets that even the poorest communities can secure to improve their chances. Government policy can provide some assets such as the provision of essential infrastructure and determine access to assets and influence their ownership and control through, for instance, the operation of the taxation system. Transforming structures and processes within the livelihoods framework are the institutions, organisations, policies and legislation that shape livelihoods. They operate at all levels, from the household to the international arena and across both public and private markets in order to determine

- access (to various types of capital and to decision-making bodies and sources of influence);
- the terms of exchange between different types of capital; and
- returns (economic and otherwise) to any given livelihood strategy.

Other views on social capital

The DFID model has been described here to provide a framework with which other views can be compared and contrasted. Hirschman, for instance, helpfully unpacks the concept of social energy into interpersonal or human friendship, ideals or a shared sense of values, and ideas which underscore the value of intellectual capital in the formation of valuable communal structures and networks.[27] Putnam points out that 'whereas physical capital refers to physical objects and human capital refers to properties of individuals, social capital refers to connections among individuals – social networks and the norms of reciprocity and trustworthiness that arise form them'.[28] This distinction is important and highlights the reinforcing value of social capital with other assets that places and communities possess or need to acquire in order to secure long-term development.

Bowey and Easton also argue that it is necessary to understand the interdependences, both traded and un-traded, between the various 'capitals' rather than seeing them as independent or exclusive phenomenon. They see entrepreneurship as 'actors with interests' who are involved with 'resources' such as social capital through a range of activities. In their analysis social capital is a method of accessing other resources and that access to resources such as finance, technology or market information also conditions social capital. Thus, social capital is transformational with activities both economic and social being the flows that maintain, build or even deplete resourceful social relationships. It is also driven by the ideology of participants such as their commitment to fraternalism, openness and trust as well as the quality of relationships and reciprocation involved in business transactions. Further, they argue that net social capital such as the reputation or credibility of a network and the compatibility of the actor's interests also determine the durability of social capital.

The advantages of social capital

Table 7.2 describes some of the advantages attributed to social capital in the exercise of public participation, in engaging the private sector and in service provision. These include specifically the following:

- By improving the efficiency of economic relations social capital can help increase people's incomes and rates of saving (financial capital). (Isolated studies have shown that communities with 'higher levels' of social capital are wealthier, but questions remain about measuring social capital.)
- Social capital can help to reduce the 'free rider' problems associated with public goods. This means that it can be effective in improving the management of common resources (natural capital) and the maintenance of shared infrastructure (physical capital).
- Social networks facilitate innovation, the development of knowledge and sharing of that knowledge. There is, therefore, a close relationship between social and human capital.
- Social capital, like other types of capital, can also be valued as a good in itself. It can make a particularly important contribution to people's sense of well-being (through identity, honour and belonging).

Governments and policy makers are naturally attracted to the wider economic benefits of social capital.[29] The Performance and Innovation Unit (PIU) in the UK Cabinet Office in 2002 concluded that

Social capital may contribute to a range of beneficial economic and social outcomes including: high levels of and growth in GDP; more efficiently functioning labour

Table 7.2   Social capital and building an inclusive transformational structure

Building structures that represent the poor: Membership organisations can help people to draw down services, increase local information flows and innovation, exert influence on higher-level structures and processes and perform numerous other functions.

Promoting reform within structures that make policy and provide services to the poor: Increasing the responsiveness of various organisations to the poor is an important objective. Sometimes this can be achieved through helping organisations to extend the scope of their activity.

Providing support to the establishment or expansion of scope of private sector organisations: Competitive markets are valued for their economic efficiency and 'built in' responsiveness to clients. But they will not function in the absence of traders (individuals and organisations).

Supporting joint forums for decision-making and action: There are many dangers associated with the creation of entirely new organisations. However, it can be important to support the establishment and operation of new forums that bring together existing interests and organisations. Such forums may be problem-oriented and temporary (e.g. if they are formed to resolve a particular conflict) or more lasting (e.g. if they oversee common resource management).

Source: Department for International Development (DFID) (1999), *Sustainable Development Guidance Sheets*, London, DFID, p. 20.

markets; higher educational attainment; lower levels of crime; better health; and more effective institutions of government.[30]

The Unit also highlighted the factors that lead to a healthy stock of social capital including history and culture; whether social structures are flat or hierarchical; the family; education; the built environment; residential mobility; economic inequalities and social class; the strength and characteristics of civil society; and patterns of individual consumption and personal values. The accumulation of social capital, it argues, should be prioritised as an outcome of government policy, which intellectually draws on Putnam's wider interpretation of the relationship between capital and changing familial and social structures. Table 7.3 suggests that intervention should be concerned with support for families and parents as well as employing area-based and national fiscal measures to lever competitive advantage from social assets and resources.

According to PIU, social capital has multiple social, political and economic effects. It can enhance economic performance by strengthening the levels of trust in business to business relationships. Fukuyama suggests that global enterprise requires a high degree of trust in order to grow, trade across cultural and fiscal boundaries, and secure markets and strategic partnerships; and where it is not present business models remain muted and vulnerable.[31] Social capital can create information symmetries between businesses and between producers and consumers and helps, in part, to explain the localised strength of business clusters, especially in high growth sectors of the economy evidenced by the dynamism of Silicon Valley in California. Social capital can help labour markets to work more effectively as it can increase knowledge and awareness of job opportunities and identify supplies of the skills required by growing industrial sectors. Education can benefit by tapping into physical and intellectual resources and crime is reduced as a stronger sense of local identity strengthens community

Table 7.3   Illustrations of the UK government support for social capital

At the individual level
- greater support for families and parenting;
- mentoring;
- new approaches to dealing with offenders; and
- volunteering.

At the community level
- promoting institutions that foster community;
- community IT networks;
- new approaches to the planning and design of the built environment;
- dispersing social housing; and
- using personal networks to pull individuals and communities out of poverty.

At the national level, the available levers include
- service learning in schools;
- community service credit schemes; and
- measures to facilitate mutual trust.

Source: Based on Performance and Innovation Unit, 2002, *Social Capital A Discussion Paper*, London, Cabinet Office.

values as well as offering sanctions against deviant behaviour. Finally, the PIU argues that social capital improves health by bolstering community support systems and strengthens government institutions by developing citizens as more sophisticated political consumers.

Social capital and economic performance

Kay has argued that the best way to see the value of social capital is to look at communities where it is absent or where there are few social networks, a lack of trust or limited shared commitment to place, cohesiveness and development.

> Social enterprises generate social capital in their area, mostly by using social capital. Explicit, shared values create solidarity between like-minded social enterprises. Trust and reciprocity build up into cooperation and collaboration. Informal and formal social networks are actively built upon – bonding the social enterprises together and also bridging to other social enterprise organisations outside the immediate group.[32]

Crucially, he draws on the DFID analysis to suggest that social capital alone cannot build the social economy and that financial, human and physical resources need to be present in sufficient quantities, and linked together to create sustainable development. In a local community the market, public sector and community activity exist together and effective social capital helps to reduce transaction costs, provide services and facilitate synergy between the three sectors in any given place. Social capital provides a framework for integrating the *third sector* putting it to work, providing strategic guidance and helping to clarify how the social economy needs to work in concert with both private and public markets.

More recently, the idea of social capital as a theoretical concept, relevant to policy and politics, was given particular impetus by the work of Robert Putnam. In his study of Italy he argued that cooperation for mutual benefit is at the heart of the differential economic performance between the north and the south of the country:

> Success in overcoming dilemmas of collective action and self-defeating opportunism that they spawn depends on the broader social context within which any particular game is played. Voluntary cooperation is easier in a community that has inherited a substantial stock of social capital in the forms of norms, reciprocity and networks of civic engagement.[33]

Here, social capital therefore refers to features of social organisations including trust, norms and networks that can improve the efficiency of society by facilitating coordinated actions. Putnam's analysis of the regions of Italy suggests that social trust has been a key ingredient sustaining economic dynamism and government performance in the north compared with Naples and the wider south. Similarly, Fukuyama[34] argued that relationships form a virtuous circle of growth in which trust encourages co-operation, and co-operation breeds trust in the steady accumulation of social capital. Social trust in modern societies arises from norms of reciprocity and networks of civic engagement. Norms of reciprocity evolve because they lower transaction costs between people, groups or interests and because they facilitate mutual cooperation. In turn reciprocity can be of two types:

- Balanced reciprocity refers to a simultaneous exchange of items of equivalent value; and
- Generalised reciprocity refers to a continuing relationship of exchange that involves mutual expectations that the benefit granted should be repaid in the future.

Generalised reciprocity is likely to be associated with a dense or *thick* network of social exchange. Formal or informal communication and exchange can be either horizontal, which bring together interests with equivalent status and power; or vertical, which connects with unequal agents in a hierarchical relationship.

For Putnam it is the quality and durability of personal and business networks that are critical in explaining the difference between competing and declining economies. Table 7.4 shows that rational benefits result from belonging to, and maintaining, relational webs that might have a vertical or horizontal character. Putnam argues that vertical networks cannot sustain social trust and co-operation as those lower down the hierarchy may have less influence and control in these types of relationships. Yet for others who refer to this relationship as linking Social capital it is connections that provide those outside public or private markets with access to decision-making arenas, although dependent relationships based on patron–client exchanges are more likely to be characterised by opportunism than by mutuality.[35]

Table 7.4   The strengths of relational webs

Strength	Description
Transaction	Networks of civic engagement increase the potential costs to a defector in any individual transaction; in other words, he/she will lose in other and future transactions by not being involved.
Norms	Networks of civic engagement foster robust forms of reciprocity, help to understand the rules and expectations governing relationships and reinforce reputation and trust between actors.
Communications	Networks build civic engagement, facilitate communication and improve the information flow about the trustworthiness of individuals.
Collaboration	Networks build on past successes of collaboration and build informal routines and continuity between actors.

Source: Based on Putnam, R. (1993) *Making Democracy Work: Civic Traditions in Modern Italy*, Princeton, Princeton University Press. pp, 173–174.

Horizontal relationships, he contends, have a more robust quality but Putnam makes an important distinction between internal and external relationships in group dynamics:

> Dense but segregated horizontal networks sustain cooperation within each group, but networks of civic engagement that cut across social cleavages nourish wider cooperation. This is another reason why networks of civic engagement are such an important part of the community's stock of social capital.[36]

Putnam's most recent work also acknowledges the multiple forms and purposes of social capital (see Table 7.5) and the crucial distinction between bonding (exclusive) and bridging (inclusive) social capital. Bonding social capital is good for mobilising solidarity and cohesion and can provide important socio-psychological networks for mutual support among groups that share a common set of interests as varied as ethnic minorities or entrepreneurs. Bridging networks, on the other hand, are better for linking to external assets and resources and for both spreading and exchanging knowledge and ideas. Bonding social capital forms what Putnam refers to as 'sociological superglue'[37] which might have negative side effects in the exclusion of the out-group and negative consequences of *otherisation*. The relationship between the two is complex. In some instance it might be linear with effective bonding providing a departure point for more collaborative forms of bridging; or they can occur simultaneously and both can have independent positive and negative effects. They are also clearly dynamic and change across both time and place.

For Putnam, atomising technology, rampant sub urbanisation, changes in the labour market and the decline of the family and participatory religion have eroded the stock of social capital in the USA over the last 50 years:

> The ebbing of community over the last several decades has been silent and deceptive. We notice its effects in the strained interstices of our private lives and in the degradation of our public life but the most serious consequences are reminiscent of the old parlor puzzle: 'What's missing from this picture?' Weakened social capital is manifest in the things that have vanished almost unnoticed – neighbourhood parties and get together with friends, the unreflective kindness of strangers, the shared pursuit of the public good rather than a solitary quest for private goods.[38]

Table 7.5   Types of social capital

- Bonding social capital – characterised by strong bonds (or 'social glue'), for example, among family members or among members of an ethnic group.

- Bridging social capital – characterised by weaker, less dense but more cross-cutting ties ('social oil'), for example, with business associates, acquaintances, friends from different ethnic groups, friends of friends and so on.

- Linking social capital – characterised by connections between those with differing levels of power or social status, for example, links between the political elite and the general public or between individuals from different social classes.

Source: Based on Performance and Innovation Unit, 2002, *Social Capital A Discussion Paper*, London, Cabinet Office, pp. 11–12.

In *Better Together: Restoring the American Community*, Putnam et al.[39] built on the experiences of the *Saguaro Seminar: Civic Engagement in America*, which brought together a range of expert academics and practitioners to unpack and develop the concept of social capital. The seminar series and the book aimed to build a knowledge bank of ideas and innovation to prevent the erosion of social capital and to reconstruct it in different places, economic sectors and across civic society. In particular it highlights the need to address racial and religious fracturing, post 9/11, and to acknowledge the diverse methodologies and material benefits in the maintenance of community solidarity in a less certain world. His strategy for addressing these structural societal weaknesses and imbalances is to develop civic engagement in order to grow and secure crucial bridging social capital reflected in increased rates of political participation, grass-roots social movements and team sports. The strategy had a number of interlocking elements including the following:

- developing extra-curricular programmes and civics education programmes that engage pupils in the social capital project in their formative years;
- developing family-friendly and community-congenial policies to support kinship and friendship ties both inside and outside the work place;
- redesigning the built environment to reduce commuting and increase personal interaction in the public realm;
- developing the spiritual community and tolerance of multiple faiths and practices across the state;
- using technology to develop active connections with other citizens rather than the personalised and insular ways employed in contemporary America; and
- growing participation in diverse cultural activities and community events that respect difference and value citizenship.

Social capital, networks and entrepreneurship

In 2007, the *International Small Business Journal* dedicated an entire edition (25: 3) to the connection between social capital and entrepreneurship. In particular, the contributions to the Journal valued the quality of networks and relationships as a resource which could help to explain the performance of entrepreneurs:

> Relationships clearly matter to entrepreneurs, but understanding how they function requires an appreciation of social capital. The presence or absence of social capital is likely to influence the very nature of the entrepreneurial venture. Social capital involves social interaction and would appear to reside in and between connections to others. It could even be regarded as representing 'networking capital' since in essence it is really a relational phenomenon and a term that actually refers to the social connections entrepreneurs use to obtain resources they would otherwise acquire through expending the human or financial capital.[40]

Anderson et al. saw social capital as 'a relational artefact, produced in interactions but that resides within a network. Individuals may have a high or low propensity to develop social capital, but they can only do so within social interactions'.[41] Thus it is not a capital asset in any conventional sense but is a condition that adheres to and is determined by the number, range and quality of social interactions. As a result, the literature on the economic and entrepreneurial value of social capital places a particular emphasis on business networks and interpersonal trust in the development and maintenance of efficient production chains.[42]

Casson and Della-Giusta argued that different types of networks are needed to support entrepreneurship at different stages of development. The network literature suggests that social capital can be defined as the creation of high-trust social networks, and to Casson and Della-Giusta these are evident at local, regional, national or the global level. Given the emphasis on interpersonal contact much research has concentrated on the local level, but in regional and national interests shaped around sectors such as tourism or mining more mobile and adaptive networks can be identified. Place, in short, does not restrict the scope or quality of networks.

Casson and Della-Giusta also further stratify the definition to look at local business networks, social networks and physical networks (such as a common transport spine or rail hub) which are all important to entrepreneurial performance. These networks can vary therefore in their shape and in the way communications and trust flows between actors. A web-based network is more informal and based on shared mutual pursuits whilst a hub-based network is centred on a point where large number of concentrations converge or where a dominant agent drives the relationships. Both rely on ease of communications and trust. Ease of communications is clearly facilitated by a shared language, customs, cultures and efficient technologies. Trust is based on the obligations between parties and the rational interest they have in reciprocal exchange of these obligations in business transactions.

Casson and Della-Giusta also distinguish between vertical networks in the chain of production and horizontal connections between people engaged in the same stage of production such as suppliers or manufactures or retailers. The latter improve economic performance, competitiveness or simply yield scale economies that would be missed by individuals working on their own. Interestingly, they are critical of network approaches with exclusively social concerns where the dispossessed are brought together in relationships that often accentuate their victim mentality and marginalisation. This social exclusion rationale has limits and bridging to those with entrepreneurial expertise and values may stimulate new thinking and financial resources to tackle exclusion.

In their review of leadership in the social economy Chambers and Edwards-Stuart[43] identified the common features of successful social entrepreneurs, which include

- integrative, speculative thinkers;
- high drive and persistence;
- strong value base;
- strong focus;

- developed sense of self;
- good reading of others;
- strong networking;
- sense of responsibility for others and for outcomes; and
- creating a sense of excitement, vibrancy and progress.

They argued that entrepreneurs need support throughout the cycle of business development including incubation, start-up, building a sustainable organisation and growth or replication of the organisation. They further argued that there are common success traits in successful social entrepreneurs who have been pivotal in the establishment of their businesses: they have had strong relationships with their supporters based on a common value or belief system; they were active and inquisitive learners; and they tended to be self-sufficient and less reliant on procedures and system to manage their organisations.

Murray et al.[44] highlighted the need for distinctive support for social entrepreneurs and point to the School for Social Entrepreneurs (SSE) as important in developing and deepening the competencies of leaders in the sector in the UK. Their review of the School showed that there needs to be a more flexible and less rigorous curriculum reflecting the distinctive needs and style of entrepreneurs working in community business in particular; a need for more practice-based learning; and a stronger understanding of attribution and accounting for the distinctive value added, of their role within the sector and of the sector in local development. Similarly, Farr[45] argues that education and skills development are essential for the development of strong social capital and the SSE illustrates how this is applied specifically to the development of social economy (see Case 7.1).

CASE 7.1

School for Social Entrepreneurs

The School for Social Entrepreneurs (SSE) was established in 1997 to develop and support the talents of leaders in the social economy in the UK. There are six members of the SSE Network based in London, Belfast, East Midlands, Aston and Liverpool. The overall aim of the SSE is to support sustainable, effective solutions to community problems by enabling individuals to learn and experience for themselves the skills needed to deliver social change. The organisation offers a unique form of business support and learning programme centred on the individual needs of entrepreneurs and stimulates their educational development via high quality reflective methods. This has emphasised the importance of learning from practice, from peers and from the failure of social enterprises in a range of live settings. The School works to build a *cycle of growth* by extending the knowledge, contacts and experiences to form a new infrastructure to support education and training on social economics and entrepreneurship. An independent evaluation of the project carried out by Murray et al. demonstrated that

CASE 7.1 (cont'd)

the SSE has helped to support business survival, create full and part time jobs in the participant's organisations and assisted in the growth of annual turnover.

Source: Murray, R., Cooper, M. and Sanfilippo, M. (2007) *Evaluation of the School for Social Entrepreneurs 1997–2007*, London, New Economics Foundation.

Social capital and social enterprise

A number of writers have critically examined the relationship between social capital, social economy and social enterprise. Chell[46] highlighted the value of research into enterprise that drew upon social constructionism in which attention is paid to the social embeddedness of entrepreneurial practices. She has indicated the social as well as the material value of entrepreneurs as agents of change. Entrepreneurs garner a range of resources and use various forms of human, financial and social capital in order to create wealth and add social value.

Johnstone and Lionais[47] also highlighted a central contradiction in community business initiatives which expected part of the market to fix what capitalism has used up or abandoned in de-industrialised or depleted communities. It might be expected that a different type of entrepreneur would emerge, but it raises important issues about the deployment of locally based social capital networks as a resource for redevelopment. Thus, Birch and Whittam[48] highlighted an important contradiction in the social capital functioning of entrepreneurs which questions the logic of regional and local development policy. They draw upon Dees,[49] to define the characteristics of the *public entrepreneur*:

- adopting a mission;
- pursuing new opportunities to achieve that mission;
- continually innovating, adapting and learning;
- avoiding limitations of current resources; and
- being concerned with accountability to their clients and that community.

Fulfilling these functions creates a central paradox in that the social entrepreneur needs to collaborate with many disparate groups, maintain that network and develop and use it in the pursuit of the social objective. These weak ties outside the strong bonding ties with the local community are critical for success and the two may not be reconcilable:

> Social entrepreneurship can therefore be positioned as a response to the exclusivity and closed structure within community networks. It operates as a linking capacity between groups, bringing together agendas and resources in the pursuit of particular projects; such as 'gate-keepers' draw on a range of different capacities within the community. It is therefore a version of weak networks that connect disparate groups and enables social cohesion through stopping fragmentation. Because social entrepreneurs pursue

projects, it is a temporary process that provides links dependent upon the individual capabilities of the entrepreneur or entrepreneurial organisation involved. The social capital inherent within social entrepreneurship can be characterised in contrast to that inherent within communities, which implies that the proposition of the former will be detrimental to the retention of the latter.[50]

Linked to this, there are a range of criticisms about the policy rationale for promoting social entrepreneurship:

- First, the development of a strong trading ethos within a social enterprise inevitably reduces the rationale of a community link in order to sustain development or provide a cost service.
- Second, the emphasis on the market reoriented activities to business activities that improve the management, and cognitive and environmental environment within which they operate with significantly less attention paid to the value base of the organisation.
- Finally, there are inevitable displacement effects with institutionally thick communities receiving the benefits of social capital whereas others are left with either none or the remnants of entrepreneurial activity.

Pearce (2003) and Howarth[51] (2006) also questioned the market-led values and assumptions underpinning the enterprise shift within community development policy and programme delivery. Howarth in particular traced the adoption of social entrepreneurship in Western policy discoursers to the established tradition of community economic development, to a concern for civic emancipation and neighbourhood self-reliance and to a response to top-down market economics of the 1980s and early 1990s. However, uncritically interlocking social capital and entrepreneurship has not been without theoretical and practical or operational difficulties. Her study showed that many social entrepreneurs rejected this conceptualisation and had a stronger sense of communal and kinship values directing the value base of their work. Whilst they exhibit characteristics associated with private entrepreneurs, including being proactive, opportunity seeking and risk taking, these were part of a wider process of community change rather than the preserve of individual 'leaders'.

Social capital and regeneration

Illustration 7.1 shows that some commentators have identified a connection between deficiencies in social capital and the spirals of decline experienced by communities and even countries. Among others, Miles and Tully made the connection between social capital and urban and regional degeneration:

> In a national economy an absence of social capital is often seen as a feature of market failure, in which co-operation, collective action, risk sharing, innovation and entrepreneurship are lacking or severely constrained. This form of market failure can also characterize regional economies and disadvantaged local communities.[52]

Illustration 7.1   Social Capital and Disadvantage: Two Views

We still don't have a good word to describe what is missing in Cameroon, indeed in poor countries across the world. But we are starting to understand what it is. Some people call it 'social capital', or maybe 'trust'. Others call it 'the rule of law', or 'institutions'. But these are just labels. The problem is that Cameroon, like other poor countries, is a topsy-turvy world in which it's in most people's interest to take action that directly or indirectly damages everyone else.

Source: T. Harford, *The Undercover Economist* (London: Little Brown, 2006) p. 201

In terms of social capital, deprived neighbourhoods with relatively stable populations may have levels of intra-community 'bonding' social capital that are equal to, or above, that of more affluent districts. The downside of heavily bonded communities is an insular and exclusionary local culture which limits connections to external networks. There is often an absence of extra-community 'bridging' social capital, which connects different gro.ups and individuals to a wider range of social networks that extend beyond their community.

Source: D. North and S. Syrett (2006) *The Dynamics of Local Economies,* London, Department for Communities and Local Government, p. 9.

They suggested that there are a number of reasons why social capital might assist in area-based regeneration including improving the ability of an area to recover from a shock such as a factory closure, to rebuild itself by enabling access to decision-makers and politicians and to open access to the labour market via formal and informal networks. However, their review, based on the Northeast of England, again emphasised the need for local social capital to connect more formally with tangible economic assets capable of providing work, income and investment to a neighbourhood:

> A combination of traditional support programmes (e.g. area-based integrated labour markets (ILMs), education and training, enterprise development) with social capital building (e.g. promoting community/business co-operatives, support networks, labour and cultural exchanges etc.) is perhaps required.[53]

Forrest and Kearns[54] and Callois and Aubert[55] also highlighted the fundamental point that internal social capital aimed at social cohesiveness has limits, especially when the economic sustainability of a place is increasingly dependent on globalisation and regional economic performance. Looking at the problems of peripheral rural areas in France, Callas and Auburt noted that sociological factors are vital in helping communities organise themselves but that business, personal and political networks that link outside the region are becoming more important in determining the pace of economic and agricultural restructuring the area.

Thus, Moulaert and Nussbaumer[56] made the point that the study of social capital at the neighbourhood level needs to acknowledge that

- Social capital is not held by individuals and groups but is part of the social relationship between agents.
- There is a link between social and other forms of capital and whilst these are variously intertwined economic capital or its absence can negatively affect the effectiveness of social capital.
- Development trajectories of areas are important (as noted in Chapter 4) so that long-lasting economic decline can deplete and even paralyse social capital.
- The interaction between various types of capital (human, ecological, business, social or institutional) can have both destructive and creative effects.

Kleinhans et al.[57] noted that policy makers and practitioners have acknowledged the diverse and interconnected quality of various forms of localised capital, especially in the presence and depth of relationship building around area-based and housing redevelopment programmes. Forrest and Kearns set out the domains of social capital exhibited at a neighbourhood level and how and where policy makers should support them (see Table 7.6). Their work moves beyond abstraction, unpacking social capital in a spatial context and describing an area-based agenda that connects social capital and community cohesion.

A criticism of highly localised approaches is that they concentrate on micro-variables such as the performance of housing management systems, street parties or localised actors such as wardens, but that, at least in part, they fail to address the deeper structural problems facing disadvantaged neighbourhoods.[58] Woolcock argued that micro and macro forms of social capital are essential, especially if local communities are to influence or work with governments, corporate

Table 7.6   Domains of social capital and supporting policies

Domain	Description	Local policies
Empowerment	The people feel they have a voice which is listened to; are involved in processes that affect them; can themselves take action to initiate changes.	Providing support to community groups; giving local people 'voice'; helping to provide solutions to problems; giving local people a role in policy processes.
Participation	That people take part in social and community activities; local events occur and are well attended.	Establishing and/or supporting local activities and local organisations; publicising local events.

Table 7.6   (Continued)

Domain	Description	Local policies
Associational activity and common purpose	That people co-operate with one another through the formation of formal and informal groups to further their interests. Developing and supporting networks between organisations in the area.	Developing and supporting networks between organisations in the area.
Supporting networks and reciprocity	The individuals and organisations co-operate to support one another for either mutual or one-sided gain; an expectation that help would be given to or received from others when needed.	Creating, developing and/or supporting an ethos of co-operation between individuals and organisations which develop ideas of community support; good neighbour award schemes.
Collective norms and values	That people share common values and norms of behaviour.	Developing and promulgating an ethos which residents recognise and accept; securing harmonious social relations; promoting community interests.
Trust	The people feel they can trust their co-residents and local organisations responsible for governing or servicing their area.	Encouraging trust in residents in their relationships with each other; delivering on policy promises; bringing.
Safety	That people feel safe in their neigh-bourhood and are not restricted in their use of public space by fear.	Encouraging a sense of safety in residents; involvement in local crime prevention; providing visible evidence of security measures.
Belonging	That people feel connected to their co-residents, their home area, have a sense of belonging to the place and its people.	Creating, developing and or supporting a sense of belonging in residents; boosting the identity of a place via design, street furnishings, naming.

Source: Forrest, R. and Kearns, A. (2001) Social cohesion, social capital and the neighbourhood, *Urban Studies*, Vol. 38, pp. 2125–2143, p. 2140.

institutions and wider civic society.[59] Thus, Amin et al. suggested that we have overemphasised the importance of place and that the most successful examples of social enterprises are those which connect to external circuits of capital, knowledge, supply and demand in the formation of a sustainable business model. They made the point that the spatial 'context matters in how the social economy is locally instantiated rather than as a social context reduced to particular types of place (e.g. low- or high trust environments, spaces of face-to-face familiarity, powers of community, circuits of local need). Places, in our study, have mattered as social formations with varying geographies of connectivity, not as spatial formations.'[60] Table 7.7 is drawn from their work, which identifies the factors

Table 7.7   Elements of a successful local social economy

1. The presence of voiced minority cultures expressing non-mainstreamed needs and values.
2. The presence of a market for welfare intermediaries in between the state and the private sector, such as contracted out services.
3. An open, willing and supportive local state such as a local authority.
4. A strong political culture of protest and values.
5. Connectivity with other communities, the local authority and other areas and linkages to the wider economy and labour markets.
6. The extent of local socio-economic disadvantage as those areas with large scale structural unemployment, depleted social capital and limited demographic heterogeneity have restricted resources on which to base a thriving social economy.

Source: Based on Amin, A., Cameron, A. and Hudson, R. (2002) *Placing the Social Economy*, London, Routledge.

that can create a sustainable social economy premised on strong internal and external networks of social capital.

Amin et al. argued that it is the capacity of the social economy to be different from private or public markets that gives it its reformist potential. The social economy can

> never become a growth machine or an engine of job generation, or a substitute for the welfare state, but it can stand as a small symbol of another kind of economy, one based on meeting social needs and enhancing social citizenship. For this, the characterisation of the social economy as a 'localised' solution to the problem of social exclusion must be broken.[61]

This requires the sector to be seen as a way of organising alternative economic models and ideas, fostering social solidarity and developing human capabilities not as a local substitute for welfare or work. In sum, they identified the influences on effective performance of the social economy in the UK, which include

*   the quality and inspiration of visionary leaders of social entrepreneurs and intermediaries;
*   clarity of purpose and an ability to retain focus on a clearly expressed and agreed set of aims and goals;
*   systematic and careful market research that explores the sustainability of businesses, products and services beyond local areas and needs;
*   risk intermediation and patient support for emerging enterprises, which acknowledges market obstacles and realties is an essential quality often unrecognised in short-term, audit-led and risk-adverse government programmes;
*   the strength of the wider economy and its capacity to generate employment needs, surplus capital and intellectual or technical resources.

The dark side of social capital

> Those excluded from power, consequently, often do not see their goal as *solidifying* the existing status quo, but *challenging* the very foundations upon which the 'community', including its boundaries, membership and norms, is constituted.[62]

Even the most enthusiastic supporters of social capital as an instrument of social and economic reform acknowledge that it has a dark side.[63] Putman highlights the intellectual and empirical connection between social capital and the historic debate, in the USA at least, with community and communitarianism. Without doubt the existence of community groups which have failed to legitimise their activities among community residents can dilute the rationale and potential for capacity building. Instead of acting as the 'glue that holds a community together'[64] or as a 'moral resource'[65] such groups can be viewed by residents as self-serving, irrelevant, remote and hierarchical. In addition, there is no universal law that communities must be guided by natural and shared values or by communal tastes for collective action. In addition, many communities are composed of diverse groups that compete among themselves both for resources and for influence. As his own exploration of social capital developed, Putman revealed a concern for the role that race, religion and organised ethnic groups played in reproducing segregation in American society, arguing that 'in the short to medium run, immigration and ethnic diversity challenge social solidarity and inhibit social capital'.[66] Constructing durable bridging social capital networks is, he argues, the great challenge in redrawing the lines of social identity around a respect for diversity.

The social turn in local development policy produced a broad debate on the nature of discursive flows within area-based strategies, the inclusive capacity of new governance forms and the knowledge infrastructure and competencies of local activists.[67] However, much of this literature treats 'community' uncritically and as a distinctive, and for the most part, unitary concept.[68] Edwards argued that 'more rhetorical fluff attaches to "community" than most other words in the social science lexicon (with the possible exception of "empowerment"). We still seem to have a romantic conception of community; all unitary values and communitarianism.'[69] Capacity building and the formation of social capital have attracted both theoretical and policy interest as developing 'the features of social organisation, such as trust, norms and networks that can improve the efficiency of society by facilitating co-ordinated actions'[70] was vital to the efficient and effective delivery of a whole range of programmes. However, for Levitas, this debate has more dangerous overtones:

> My first worry about 'capacity building', as about 'community development', is that it often seems to be a way of expecting groups of people who are poorly resourced to pull themselves up by their collective boot straps. So-called social capital is expected

to take the place of economic capital. The imputed absence of social capital is potentially stigmatising and laid at the door of (mainly) poor people themselves. 'Capacity building' may be an alternative to economic regeneration. A large part of the effective resourcing therefore takes the form of unpaid work.[71]

Law and Mooney[72] argued that social capital is about political and social conformism and that New Labour have emphasised the neo-liberal attributes of the concept at the expense of social inclusion and alternative economics. In order to avoid this sort of conservatism they suggest a more politically active 'recalcitrant voluntarism'. This involves resisting capital accumulation projects which dictate and direct social relations, and not seeing social capital in isolation from the political economy (in the way, they argue, that Putnam does). Leonard[73] also made the point that bonding social capital in Belfast enabled the communities to counter discrimination, provide economic and welfare services and mobilise in the context of violence and conflict. The conditions for bridging social capital, she argues, requires excluding some, especially the more vulnerable, from networks designed to build new economic and political relationships outside the neighbourhood. There are also displacement effects with efficient and well-resourced middle-class communities successfully organising to resist unwanted building developments (not-in-my-back-yard) that disorganised working-class communities would find it difficult to counter.[74]

However, Bridgen argues that this merely illustrates the multiple interpretations of social capital and of what it is and how it is said to work. He makes a distinction between Putnam's concern over social capital as a public good and Bourdieu's conceptualisation of social capital as a weapon: a resource to be used by those who possess it to wield power and influence. Bourdieu defines social capital as

> The aggregate of the actual or potential resources which are linked to the possession of a durable network of more or less institutionalized relationships of mutual acquaintance and recognition – or in other words to membership in a group – which provides each of its members with the backing of the collectively owned capital.[75]

Taylor[76] advocated a more radical agenda to develop social capital and community empowerment less reliant on state resources and patronage. She argued that despite the rhetoric of governance-beyond-the-state, new governance spaces are still inscribed with a state agenda. However, her research shows that there is potential for communities to become 'active subjects' and manipulate prevailing discourses to their own advantage, and to identify the opportunities that new governance spaces have opened up. This necessitates a clearer understanding of the skills and techniques involved in acting politically, which in turn requires a level of community sophistication simply not present in the most disadvantaged neighbourhoods. Additionally, successful community governance requires the building of a movement, on all scales, that will be both political and social:

- the building of a political alliance dedicated to the principles and practice of participatory democracy; members of this alliance can work within a number of different political parties but with common objectives with regard to the transformation of UK political institutions and beyond;

- programmes for making UK institutions, both public and private, more democratically controlled and accountable to the people, for example, through processes of mutualisation.[77]

Measuring social capital

It is difficult to talk about social capital as a real and meaningful concept, and as something that policies might be designed to create, without considering how it can be measured. However, as Pearce admits, 'the measurement of social capital is not easy. This is because the definition remains rather woolly and because each of the elements is qualitative and open to subjective interpretation.'[78] Nevertheless attempts have been made to measure levels of social capital using proxy indicators. Pearce cites one occasion, the Conscise Project, in which this was attempted and which, although it 'was inconclusive due to the small size of the sample and other biases, did demonstrate that the measurement of social capital may not be impossible'.[79] Illustration 7.2 provides a summary of the Conscise Project and its proxy indicators.

Illustration 7.2   The Conscise Project

The Contribution of Social Capital in the Social Economy to Local Economic Development in Western Europe (Conscise) project's first report looked, among other things, at definitions, measures and indicators of social capital. For this it encapsulated the key parts of definitions of social capital under the six headings of:

Trust.

Reciprocity and mutuality.

Shared norms and behaviour.

Shared commitment and belonging.

Both formal and informal social networks.

Effective information channels.

To try to measure social capital in a local area, the project then used proxy indicators in the form of statements about which local people were asked to indicate the extent of their agreement. For example:

Two examples of statements on Trust:

- When everything is taken into account, this locality is a safe place to live.

- If I were looking after a child and in an emergency I needed to go out for a while, I would trust my neighbours to look after the child.

Illustration 7.2   (cont'd)

Two examples of statements on Reciprocity and Mutuality:

- By helping other people you help yourself in the long run.
- If I see litter in the neighbourhood, I normally pick it up even if I have not dropped it there.

Sources: J. Pearce (2003) *Social Enterprise in Anytown*, London, Calouste Gulbenkian Foundation, p. 76; and www.malcolmread.co.uk/conscise, accessed 9 October 2007.

Community Evaluation Northern Ireland (CENI) developed a model based on measuring, through questionnaires, the output of community and voluntary sector organisations on bonding, bridging and linking social capital.[80] Linking social capital relates to the impact an organisation has had on decision-takers or politicians beyond its own sphere of activity by, say, being members of networks or decision-making forums or having a detectible influence on the way in which programmes are delivered. This in part draws on Putnam's suggested approach to measurement which concentrated on measuring community activism, volunteering and sociability.[81] The measure of trust and engagement in public issues is also identified via a range of attitudinal and numeric counts of a range of activities (see Illustration 7.3).

Illustration 7.3   Measuring Engagement and Trust

1. Measures of community organisational life:

    - Percentage served on committee of some local organisations in last year;
    - Percentage served as officer of some club or organisation in last year;
    - Civic and social organisations per 1000 population;
    - Number of club meetings attended in last year; and
    - Mean number of group membership.

2. Measures of engagement in public affairs

    - Turnout in presidential elections in 1992 and 1998; and
    - Percentage attended public meeting on town or school affairs in last year.

3. Measures of community volunteerism:

    - Number of non-profit organisations per 1000 population;

Illustration 7.3 (cont'd)

- Mean number of times worked on community project last year; and
- Mean number of times did volunteer work last year.

4. Measures of informal sociability

  - Agree that 'I spend a lot of time visiting friends'; and
  - Mean number of times entertained at home last year.

5. Measures of social trust

  - Agree that 'Most people can be trusted'; and
  - Agree that 'Most people are honest'.

Source: R. Putnam (2000) *Bowling Alone: The Collapse and Revival of American Community*, New York, Simon Schuster, chapter 16.

In the UK, the Office of National Statistics introduced a social capital set of questions into the General Household Survey (GHS) in 2000/01 (see Illustration 7.4). This takes the key dimensions of social capital, especially as offered by Putnam, and operationalises them as a series of attitudinal and behavioural questions.

Illustration 7.4 GHS Measurement of Social Capital

Theme	Description
View of local area	This topic looks at the physical environment in which people live, the facilities in their area and whether they feel safe in the area. People's feelings about their physical environment can relate to each of the other aspects of social capital.
Civic engagement	This looks at people's role in their community, and whether they feel they can influence events within the community. Indicators of civic engagement and trust of civil institutions and processes are central to Putnam's understanding of social capital. It is measuring the amount of self-empowerment and control that people think they have and their involvement with the community.

<table>
<tr><th colspan="2">Illustration 7.4   (cont'd)</th></tr>
</table>

Reciprocity and local trust	This section looks at how many local people respondents know and trust, and whether people would do favours for them, or vice versa. Trust of the stranger is a central dimension of Putnam's concept of social capital.
Social networks	This section looks at how often respondents see or speak to relatives, friends or neighbours, and how many close friends or relatives live nearby. Social networks are seen as an important aspect of social capital, as the number and types of exchanges amongst people within the network, and shared identities that develop, can influence the amount of support an individual has, as well as giving access to other sources of help.
Social support	This section looks at how many people the respondent could turn to if they needed help ranging from practical to financial to emotional support. This section also asks to whom they would turn for help. The degree of individual support a person has can influence health outcomes and health behaviour.

Source: Office of National Statistics (2002) *Assessing People's Perceptions of their Neighbourhood and Community Involvement*, London, ONS.

Onyx and Bullen used survey-based techniques to audit and plot social capital in localised communities and showed how these can be aggregated across time and different spatial scales.[82] Also working in Australia, Stone[83] offered a different perspective on measurement by concentrating on the range and strength of networks rather than on attitude and behaviour. These include

- network size and capacity;
- local and global networks;
- open and closed networks;
- dense and sparse networks;
- homogenous and heterogenous networks; and
- vertical and horizontal network relations.

Measurement is clearly a problematic area, especially in the way in which social capital is quantified with a battery of statistics and quantitative techniques that gives the illusion that it can be determined with precise point measures. This methodological reductionism is especially shaky when it comes to large-scale comparative and international studies, where different social, cultural and developmental conditions determine the type and depth of social capital.[84] There are also temporal issues, as social capital changes across both space and time slowly and in response to different pressures and opportunities. Disaggregating the deadweight influences on the reproduction of social capital over time becomes particularly challenging in complex economic systems. Linked to this is a scalar argument which assumes that social capital can be aggregated, in measurement terms, from the individual, community, regional, national and even global levels.

Baron et al. also raised the issue of circularity in that it can be difficult to distinguish between social capital as a characteristic of a flourishing society and the social capital that achieves or helps to achieve growth in the first place. Often, indicator approaches fail to distinguish between the cause and effect dimensions of social capital and, crucially, how it accumulates (or depletes) in measurement terms. Finally, there is the issue of what Baron et al. call normative control, by which they mean the application of norms that produce negative as well as positive forms of social capital. An emphasis on measuring what social capital is *for* needs to acknowledge that it has multiple effects and relationships that have both advantageous and disadvantageous effects.

Does the social economy create social capital?

As a final comment on social capital it is noted that there have been suggestions that the social economy has a particular potential to help disadvantaged communities through the mechanism of social capital. Such claims are, for instance, summarised by Birch and Whittam, who report that

> The lack of social networks, usually referred to as social capital, has been highlighted within both policy and academia as the main method to empower communities. The social economy is supposed to be a means to encourage the development of social capital by encouraging mutualism amongst communities through grass-roots empowerment based on 'active participation' and a 'stakeholder society'. In a somewhat circular conceptualisation, social entrepreneurship is supposed to provide the means to achieve this mutualism through the social economy.[85]

This claim, in effect, reduces to the two assumptions that for disadvantaged communities the key lack is often social capital and that the social economy creates social capital. From these two assumptions the conclusion is drawn that the social economy will therefore help disadvantaged communities.

However, as the earlier part of this chapter showed, the relationship between social capital and disadvantaged communities depends on just what is meant by social capital because it is a very diverse concept. There are nevertheless grounds for saying that there is something which is often referred to as social capital which is often lacking in disadvantaged communities and which is probably an essential component for improvement. Whether it alone can effect improvement is much less certain and whether the social economy creates social capital is also debatable. Again, depending on which meaning of social capital is used, it might be argued that all enterprises can create social capital, just as all businesses can create financial capital, but they can also lose it and generally they only create it when the conditions are particularly favourable. Examined in this way, therefore, the 'social economy helps disadvantage' claim does not seem to be particularly strong. Indeed a counter argument is that just as financial capital is needed to start businesses, so too is social capital needed to start enterprises, including social enterprises and, as disadvantaged communities often lack social capital, they are not good places in which to start social enterprises. As Amin et al. conclude,

> We find, against the dominant communitarian and Third Way thought (that local community mobilisation for local provision can help resolve local social exclusion), that rarely is the social economy genuinely rooted in the resources of local communities. Indeed, areas of marked social exclusion are precisely those that lack the composite skills and resources necessary to sustain a vibrant social economy, resulting in either highly precarious and short-lived ventures that fail to meet local needs, or ventures reliant on public sector leadership, peripatetic professionals and social entrepreneurs, dedicated organisations such as religious or minority ethnic bodies, or market links that stretch well beyond the modest offerings available locally.[86]

The Key Points in Chapter 7

- Social capital is not a new concept, but is a contested one.

- Some writers argue that the current interest in social capital is about governments getting communities to conform and even deliver policy implementation as they withdraw from welfare delivery.

- For others it acts as a resource for communities and interests to resist governments and markets and support their independent economic and social development.

- Coleman and Putnam have more recently popularised social capital in response to concerns about the erosion of family and civic life, especially in USA.

- Trust, reciprocity and norms of civic engagement have been placed at the centre of studies of social capital and claims about its capacity to restore communities, economies and even society at large.

- The stock of social capital is seen as both a cause and an effect especially in developing area regeneration, social enterprise and entrepreneurship.

- The concept is a difficult one to measure and evaluate and international audits have difficulty comparing the stock of social capital across very different cultural, political and economic contexts.

CASE 7.2

Holywood Old School Preservation Trust

Holywood is a small town close to Belfast and the Old School is one of the older buildings in it. It was built in 1845 and was located just over the road from the then new church which had just been built to replace the Old Priory, which the town had outgrown. Like the church, the school was one of the first buildings to be constructed above the early town on what is now Church Road and it is possible that much of the material for its roof actually came from the Old Priory. However, just after it was built, the railway came to Holywood and the town expanded again as it was now in commuting distance from Belfast. One result was that the new school was soon too small and another 'new' school was built and the former new school became the parish office and then was used by the Scouts.

After about 160 years of its life the condition of the building had deteriorated to the extent that it was no longer used by anyone and it seemed to be under threat of demolition to provide a development site. However, the Church, which owned the building, agreed to work with the Holywood Conservation Group to form a Building Preservation Trust which would restore the building and then to use it to provide accommodation for a variety of community uses.

The Holywood Old School Preservation Trust was formed. It first looked at the feasibility of a restoration project and established that the building could be restored and should then be able to raise enough income from its users to cover its operating costs. The Trust next addressed the task of raising the money necessary for the restoration work, which took it about two years. After a further year, at the time of writing, the restoration work had just been completed.

While this was not a major restoration project, and the Trust was only a relatively small community business, nevertheless it successfully made progress in achieving its objectives. To get to this stage it has researched its potential market and developed a business plan; has selected, interviewed and appointed competent conservation architects as its professional advisers; has identified potential sources of funding and has written successful applications to a number of them (and some unsuccessful ones to others). It has also launched a campaign of local events which has generated a lot of support and a significant contribution to its funds. What has helped it to do this?

Amongst the trustees was a business consultant who had formerly worked for the region's small business agency. During his career he had worked with small businesses and had administered funding schemes and helped others to administer their schemes. He did not know all the possible funders but, he suggested, he was not frightened of funding applications and he did understand what funders were looking for in them and how they were likely to be assessed. He prepared the Trust's business plan and wrote the Trust's funding

---

CASE 7.2 (cont'd)

applications. He had also done some work for the local council and was able to use that connection to ask the council's premises officer to help the Trust select its professional advisers.

Another trustee had originally trained as a solicitor but never practised. Instead, after raising a family, she had become interested in conservation and had tried to save the old, attractive, but not actually listed, next-door building from the developers. Through this she had met others engaged in conservation and then also served on the committee of the local architectural heritage society. This in turn had introduced her to members of other building preservation trusts, conservation architects and representatives of conservation funding bodies. She was therefore able to get advice from other groups about forming a trust and about different aspects of a building's restoration. She also knew who to ask to prepare a suitable list of conservation architects to tender to be the Trust's professional advisers.

The other trustees included a retired insolvency lawyer, an insurance manager, a carpet supplier and someone who had for many years been organising fundraising events, each of whom brought their own experience and/or contacts to the task. Between them the trustees had

- some experience of directing and advising social enterprises;
- an insight into how to write funding applications;
- an understanding of the need for careful financial control;
- introductions to the good conservation architects in the area;
- a good contact with another nearby building preservation trust which was happy to talk about what was involved and to explain what had worked, or not worked;
- contacts with like-minded people and bodies who could and did offer advice and encouragement;
- a network which included several people on the boards or committees of funding organisations or were their advisers. These people were often happy to explain the funders' requirements to the Trust and/or were in a position to vouch for it;
- experience of what was involved in running fund-raising events and credibility in asking others to support them;
- credibility in the town and support for their project. For instance, a request for support to the borough council was supported by the local Councillors;
- friendship with many people in the town who could be encouraged to help with fund-raising activities.

Source: Discussions with the trustees of the Holywood Old School Preservation Trust.

Questions, Exercises, Essay and Discussion Topics

1. From Case 7.2 prepare an inventory of the social capital of the Trust. How does this inventory compare with the various definitions of social capital given earlier?

2. Trace the origins and development of social capital.

3. Why has social capital become an important political and policy concern across the globe?

4. What are the different interpretations of social capital and its role in local development?

5. Describe some of the methodologies for measuring social capital and what are their limits in auditing the stock of social capital across time and place?

6. What is the link between social capital and the development of the social economy?

SUGGESTIONS FOR FURTHER READING

S. Baron, J. Field and T. Schuller, *Social Capital: Critical Perspectives* (Oxford: Oxford University Press, 2000).

D. Halpern, *Social Capital* (Cambridge: Polity Press, 2005).

R. Putnam, *Bowling Alone: The Collapse and Revival of American Community* (New York: Simon and Schuster, 2000).

References

1. S. Szreter, Social capital, the economy and education in historical perspective, In S. Baron, J. Field and T. Schuller (eds), *Social Capital: Critical Perspectives* (Oxford: Oxford University Press, 2000), pp. 56–77.
2. M. Cattel, 'Having a laugh and mucking in together; using social capital to explore dynamics between structure and agency in the context of declining and regenerated neighbourhoods', *Sociology*, Vol. 38, No. 5 (2004), pp. 945–963.
3. A. Portes, 'Social capital: Its origins and applications in modern sociology', *Annual Review of Sociology*, Vol. 124 (1998), pp. 1–24.
4. R. Forrest and A. Kearns, 'Social cohesion, social capital and the neighbourhood', *Urban Studies*, Vol. 38, No. 12 (2001), pp. 2125–2143.
5. S. Baron, J. Field and T. Schuller, *Social Capital: Critical Perspectives* (Oxford: Oxford University Press, 2000).
6. F. Fukuyama, *The End of History and the Last Man* (New York: Free Press, 1992).
7. W. Hutton, *The Stakeholding Society* (Cambridge: Polity Press, 1999).
8. A. Giddens, *The Third Way: The Renewal of Social Democracy* (Cambridge: Polity Press, 1998), p. 78.
9. Ibid., p. 127.
10. D. Halpern, *Social Capital* (Cambridge: Polity Press, 2005).

11. C. Calhoun, E. LiPuma and I. Postone, *Bourdieu: Critical Perspectives* (Cambridge: Polity Press, 1993), p. 4.

12. P. Bourdieu and L. Wacquant, *An Invitation to Reflexive Sociology* (Cambridge: Polity Press, 1996), p. 119.

13. F. Sabitini, *Social Capital, Public Spending and the Quality of Economic Development: The Case of Italy* (Milan: Fondazione Eni Enrico Mattei, 2006).

14. A. Portes, 'Social capital: Its origins and applications in modern sociology', *Annual Review of Sociology*, Vol. 124 (1998), pp. 1–24.

15. R. Putnam, '*E Pluribus Unum*: Diversity and community in the twenty-first century', The 2006 Johan Skytte Prize Lecture, *Scandinavian Political Studies*, Vol. 30, No. 2 (2007), pp. 137–174.

16. R. Putnam, 'Who killed civic America', *Prospect*, March Issue (1996), pp. 66–72, p. 66.

17. M. Leonard, 'Bonding and bridging social capital: Reflections from Belfast', *Sociology*, Vol. 38, No. 5 (2004), pp. 927–944.

18. A. Law and G. Mooney, 'The maladies of social capital I: The missing 'capital' in theories of social capital', *Critique*, Vol. 34, No. 2 (2006), pp. 127–143.

19. A. Kay, 'Social capital in building the social economy', In J. Pearce, *Social Enterprises in Anytown* (London: Calouste Gulbenkian Foundation, 2003), p. 75.

20. Performance and Innovation Unit, *Social Capital: A Discussion Paper* (London: Cabinet Office, 2002).

21. R. Putnam, 'Turning in, turning out: The strange disappearance of social capital in America' *Political Science and Politics*, Vol. 28 (1995), pp. 1–20.

22. A. Middleton, A. Murie and R. Groves, 'Social capital and neighbourhoods that work', *Urban Studies*, Vol. 42, No. 10 (2005), pp. 1711–1738.

23. World Bank; http://www.worldbank.org/poverty/scapita.

24. OECD, The Well-Being of Nations: The Role of Human and Social Capital (Paris: OECD, 2001).

25. Based on Performance and Innovation Unit, *Social Capital: A Discussion Paper* (London: Cabinet Office, 2002), p. 10.

26. Department for International Development (DFID), *Sustainable Development Guidance Sheets* (London: DFID, 1999), p. 1.

27. Department for International Development (DFID), *Sustainable Development Guidance Sheets* (London: DFID, 1999).

28. R. Putnam, *Bowling Alone: The Collapse and Revival of American Community* (New York: Simon and Schuster, 2000), p. 19.

29. M. Evans and B. Syrett, *Informal Economic Activities and Deprived Neighbourhoods* (London: Department for Communities and Local Government, 2006).

30. Performance and Innovation Unit, *Social Capital: A Discussion Paper* (London: Cabinet Office, 2002), p. 5.

31. F. Fukuyama, *The End of History and the Last Man* (New York: Free Press, 1995).

32. A. Kay, 'Social capital in building the social economy', In J. Pearce, *Social Enterprises in Anytown* (London: Calouste Gulbenkian Foundation, 2003), p. 78.

33. R. Putnam, *Making Democracy Work: Civic Traditions in Modern Italy* (Princeton: Princeton University Press, 1993), p. 167.

34. F. Fukuyama, *Trust: The Social Virtues and the Creation of Prosperity* (New York: Free Press, 1995).

35. Community Evaluation Northern Ireland, *Toolkit to Measure the Value Added of Voluntary and Community Based Activity* (Belfast: CENI, 2005).

36. R. Putnam, *Making Democracy Work: Civic Traditions in Modern Italy* (Princeton: Princeton University Press, 1993), p. 175.

37. R. Putnam, *Bowling Alone: The Collapse and Revival of American Community* (New York: Simon and Schuster, 2000), p. 23.

38. Ibid., pp. 402–403.

39. R. Putnam and L. Feldstein with D. Cohen, *Better Together Restoring the American Community* (New York: Simon and Schuster, 2003).

40. J. Cope, S. Jack and M. Rose, 'Social capital and entrepreneurship: An introduction', *International Small Business Journal*, Vol. 25, No. 3 (2007), pp. 213–219.

41. A. Anderson, J. Park and S. Jack, 'Entrepreneurial social capital', *International Small Business Journal*, Vol. 25, No. 3 (2007), pp. 245–272.

42. See for instance H.-H. Hohmann and F. Welter (eds), *Trust and Entrepreneurship: A West-East Perspective* (Cheltenham: Edward Elgar, 2005).

43. C. Chambers and F. Edwards-Stuart, *Leadership in the Social Economy* (London: School for Social Entrepreneurs, 2007).

44. R. Murray, M. Cooper and M. Sanfilippo, *Evaluation of the School for Social Entrepreneurs 1997–2007* (London: New Economics Foundation, 2007).

45. J. Farr, 'Social capital: A conceptual history', *Political Theory*, Vol. 32, No. 1 (2004), pp. 6–33.

46. E. Chell, 'Social enterprise and entrepreneurship: Towards a convergent theory of the entrepreneurial process', *International Small Business Journal*, Vol. 25, No. 1 (2007), pp. 5–26.

47. H. Johnstone and D. Lionais, 'Depleted communities and community business entrepreneurship: Revaluing space through place', *Entrepreneurship and Regional Development*, Vol. 16 (2004), pp. 217–233.

48. K. Birch and G. Whittam, 'Social entrepreneurship: The way to sustainable regional development', Paper read at the *Institute for Small Business and Entrepreneurship*, 31 October–2 November (Cardiff: ISBE, 2006).

49. J. Dees, The meaning of social entrepreneurship (2001), CASE, Duke University: http://www.fugua.duke.edu/centers/case/doicuments/dees_SE.pdf, quoted in Birch and Whittam (2006), p. 4.

50. K. Birch and G. Whittam, 'Social entrepreneurship: The way to sustainable regional development?', *ISBE Conference*, 2006, p. 7.

51. C. Howarth, 'Resisting the identity of social entrepreneur', Paper read at the *Institute for Small Business and Entrepreneurship*, 31 October–2 November (Cardiff: ISBE, 2006).

52. N. Miles and J. Tully, 'Regional development agency policy to tackle economic exclusion? The role of social capital in distressed communities', *Regional Studies*, Vol. 41, No. 6 (2007), pp. 855–866, p. 857.

53. Ibid., p. 863.

54. R. Forrest and A. Kearns, 'Social cohesion, social capital and the neighbourhood', *Urban Studies*, Vol. 38, No. 4 (2001), pp. 2125–2143.

55. J.-M. Callois and F. Aubert, 'Towards indicators of social capital for regional development issues: The case of French rural areas', *Regional Studies*, Vol. 41, No. 6 (2007), pp. 809–821.

56. F. Moulaert and J. Nussbaumer, 'Defining the social economy and its governance at the neighbourhood level: A methodological reflection', *Urban Studies*, Vol. 42, No. 11 (2005), pp. 2071–2088.

57. R. Kleinhans, H. Priemus and G. Engbersen, 'Understanding social capital in recently restructured urban neighbourhoods: Two case studies in Rotterdam', *Urban Studies*, Vol. 44, Nos. 5/6 (2007), pp. 1069–1091.

58. A. Crawford, ' "Fixing broken promises?": Neighbourhood wardens and social capital', *Urban Studies*, Vol. 43, Nos. 5/6 (2006), pp. 957–976.

59. M. Woolcock, 'Social capital and economic development: Toward a theoretical synthesis and policy framework', *Theory and Society*, Vol. 27, No. 2 (1998), pp. 151–208.

60. A. Amin, A. Cameron and R. Hudson, *Placing the Social Economy* (London: Routledge, 2002), p. 120.

61. Ibid., p. 125.

62. B. Arneil, *Diverse Communities: The Problem with Social Capital* (Cambridge: Cambridge University Press, 2006).

63. R. Putnam, *Bowling Alone: The Collapse and Revival of American Community* (New York: Simon and Schuster, 2000), p. 350.

64. W. Potapchuk, J. Crocker and W. Schechtler, 'Building community with social capital', *National Civic Review,* Vol. 86 (1997), pp. 129–139.

65. R. Putnam, *Making Democracy Work: Civic Traditions in Modern Italy* (Princeton: Princeton University Press, 1993), p. 130.

66. R. Putnam, '*E Pluribus Unum*: Diversity and Community in the Twenty-first Century', The 2006 Johan Skytte Prize Lecture, *Scandinavian Political Studies,* Vol. 30, No. 2 (2007), pp. 137–174, p. 138.

67. N. Ginsburg, 'Putting the social into urban regeneration policy', *Local Economy,* Vol. 13 (1999), pp. 55–71.

68. P. Burton, 'Power to the people: How to judge public participation', *Local Economy,* Vol. 19, No. 3 (2004), pp. 193–198.

69. J. Edwards, 'Urban policy: The victory of form over substance', *Urban Studies,* Vol. 34, Nos. 5/6 (1997), pp. 825–843, p. 831.

70. R. Putnam, *Making Democracy Work: Civic Traditions in Modern Italy* (Princeton: Princeton University Press, 1993), p. 167.

71. R. Levitas, 'Community, utopia and new labour', *Local Economy,* Vol. 15, No. 3 (2000), pp. 188–197, p. 196.

72. A. Law and G. Mooney, 'The maladies of social capital II: Resisting neo-liberal conformism', *Critique,* Vol. 34, No. 3 (2006), pp. 253–268.

73. M. Leonard 'Bonding and bridging social capital: Reflections from Belfast', *Sociology,* Vol. 38, No. 5 (2004), pp. 927–944.

74. M. Mayer, 'The onward sweep of social capital: Causes and consequences for understanding cities, communities and urban movements', *International Journal of Urban and Regional Research,* Vol. 27, No. 1 (2003), pp. 110–132.

75. P. Bourdieu, 'Forms of capital', In J. Richardson (ed.) *Handbook of Theory and Research for the Sociology of Education* (New York: Macmillan, 1986), pp. 248–249.

76. M. Taylor, 'Community participation in the real world: Opportunities and pitfalls in new governance spaces', *Urban Studies,* Vol. 44, No. 2 (2007), pp. 297–317.

77. P. Sommerville, 'Community governance and democracy', *Policy and Politics,* Vol. 33, No. 1 (2006), pp. 117–144, pp. 136–137.

78. J. Pearce, *Social Enterprise in Anytown* (London: Calouste Gulbenkian Foundation, 2003), p. 75.

79. Ibid., p. 76.

80. Community Evaluation Northern Ireland, *Toolkit to Measure the Value Added of Voluntary and Community Based Activity* (Belfast: CENI, 2005).

81. R. Putnam, *Bowling Alone: The Collapse and Revival of American Community* (New York: Simon Schuster, 2000), Chapter 16.

82. J. Onyx and P. Bullen, *Measuring Social Capital in Five Communities in New South Wales: An Analysis,* Working Paper No. 41 (Sydney: Centre for Australian Community Organisations and Management, University of Technology, Sydney, 1997).

83. W. Stone, *Measuring Social Capital* (Melbourne: Australian Institute of Family Studies, 2001).

84. S. Baron, J. Field and T. Schuller, *Social Capital: Critical Perspectives* (Oxford: Oxford University Press, 2000), p. 27.

85. K. Birch and G. Whittam, 'Social entrepreneurship: The way to sustainable regional development?' *ISBE Conference,* November 2006, p. 5.

86. A. Amin, A. Cameron and R. Hudson, *Placing the Social Economy* (London: Routledge, 2002), pp. vii and ix.

Promoting the Third Sector

Key Concepts

This chapter covers

- the reasons why the third sector, and in particular the social economy, is promoted;
- the various parties promoting the social economy, including governments;

(cont'd)

- the range of strategies followed by governments to promote the sector, and the various components of those strategies;

Learning Objectives

By the end of this chapter the reader should

- appreciate why the social economy is being promoted;
- understand who is promoting it;
- appreciate the range of promotional strategies and the different components in their evolution.

Introduction

Governments and other stakeholders are often interested in the third sector, or in the social economy within it, because they think that it has potential to help them to achieve some of their objectives. Therefore they are prepared to intervene to promote the sector and to encourage and support its establishment and development. This chapter explores the main issues associated with this promotion. In particular it looks at why the sector is promoted, who is promoting it, how and where it is being promoted and what the results of this promotion appear to be.

As indicated above, it is often not the whole of the third sector which is the focus of promotional efforts, but the social economy or the social enterprises of which it is composed. Instead of always dealing with the whole of the third sector, this chapter therefore chiefly addresses the social economy and sometimes social enterprises. However, as indicated in Chapters 3 and 4, definitions of these terms vary. In the absence of a single common terminology this chapter generally uses the terminology of the country whose policy is being considered.

Why the third sector is promoted

It is suggested in Chapter 1 that among the reasons why interest in the third sector, or at least in some of its components, has grown is the apparent potential of this sector of the economy to address some of the problems in, or of, society. Chapter 7, for instance, among other things, indicates why the social economy and social enterprises are sometimes seen as having a key role to play in regeneration and social cohesion strategies. The sector is seen therefore as having the ability to provide a variety of benefits in a number of areas including the following (and see also an expanded list in Chapter 9):

- the provision of goods, services and social benefits which the public sector does not adequately provide and a means for addressing some problems of the welfare state;
- the provision of jobs for people who might not otherwise be employed;

- the fostering of enterprise and economic competitiveness;
- the promotion of environmental sustainability, or ethical operations;
- the creation of social capital and social cohesion. This is sometimes seen as giving it the ability to reach parts that other initiatives cannot reach, in particular when trying to tackle disadvantage through urban and rural regeneration projects (see also the comments on social capital in Chapter 7).

Government interest

Many of these areas are of interest to governments. As a result, many governments have shown an interest in promoting the third sector or at least the social economy. As the section 'Paradigm Differences' in Chapter 4 indicates, a country's perception of what particular benefits it would like to get from the third sector often influences which bits of the sector it wishes to support and how it attempts to define them. A recent review, commissioned by the UK's Social Enterprise Unit (SEnU), reported in March 2006 on the social economy policy objectives of a number of European countries and the USA.[1] It not only confirmed similarities but also noted some differences, not least in respect of UK policy. The review recognised that, while in Europe social enterprises and the wider social economy have multiple objectives, it is possible to identify a tradition and a prevailing interest in the use of social enterprise as a means of

- integrating disadvantaged members of the community into employment (e.g. the long-term unemployed and the disabled);
- augmenting the delivery of public services, especially in the areas of health and social care.[2]

The contribution of social enterprise to social inclusion and cohesion (at the level of the individual and local areas) is shared as a common policy interest across a number of countries including the USA (and arguably more in other countries than in the UK), the report asserts. Also, the role of social enterprises in delivering public services is also well established in the countries reviewed and 'has attained a renewed vigour and purpose under UK policy'.[3]

The UK differs in at least one significant way from other countries in the emphasis it often puts on the potential of social enterprises to contribute to economic competitiveness and development, both regionally or nationally. This is re-enforced by an expectation that they should be financially self-sustainable, generally through some form of trading activity. This aspect seems to be less of a concern in other countries where the sector's contribution is often seen as a response to market failure and with that there is a greater willingness to recognise the additional costs associated with addressing such market failures. It appears that financial sustainability is not therefore, for them, a main aim. Moreover, other countries often retain a broader perspective on the social economy in terms of focus and approach, placing emphasis on a wider range of characteristics of the sector such as democratic control, citizen initiative and user participation.

The development of government policy for the sector

While many governments want to encourage the social economy, support for it is still a developing policy field. Thus, according to Graefe, 'it is difficult to foresee what directions policy will end up taking, what its results will be, and who will stand to benefit most'. This, he suggests, will 'depend crucially on the relative ability of the interested actors to embed their vision for the social economy in state policy' and, in this, there are two conflicting visions:

> On the one hand, there is the project borne by the social economy's champions, seeking to re-embed footloose capital, to spark local economic and social regeneration, and to counter social exclusion. On the other hand, there are those backing stage accumulation strategies of a more neoliberal bent who seek to employ the sector as a cut rate welfare state and a basin of low wage jobs.[4]

Because of these conflicting visions, interpretations of the focus of, and approaches to, policy and its consequences can differ. It is also apparent that there is no single good or bad, or right or wrong, policy framework; the different organisational models and their varying dominance in the sector, which are apparent in different countries, offer routes for the achievement of different policy goals.

It is also worth noting by way of introduction that any meaningful policy framework, whether on a supra-national, national or local level, requires clarity in terms of objectives and targets. This is true in the field of public policy in general and in policies to assist social enterprises in particular. Thus policy makers should, as far as possible, be explicit about the contribution which they seek from their social enterprises. They should clearly articulate in what ways (and to what extent) they think that social enterprise can contribute and to which policy goals.

However, therein lies a problem: often the objectives are either not explicit or not quantified, which makes it difficult not only to implement but also to understand and evaluate strategies. Moreover, within the social economy itself, measurement of its impact is at a very early stage of development. In the UK, the (then) DTI, for instance, has contended that while it was building 'intellectual capital about the sector,... rhetoric rather than a robust evidence base continues to inform most arguments for growth and support'.[5] Nevertheless this chapter seeks to provide an overview of what is generally known about these issues.

Other interests

Other organisations, as well as governments, are also interested in promoting part or all of the third sector. Some of these are organisations formed specifically to assist the sector and to promote its interests, and examples of them are given in Table 8.1. Some are organisations whose interest in promoting the sector appears to lie in its potential to provide a counter to the supposed power and influence of either the private or the public sectors. Such politically linked agenda are related, for instance, to the different paradigms of the social economy already noted above and a range of their interests is discussed below.

Table 8.1   Examples of the different types of national or regional social enterprise support agencies in the UK

Type	Example
Social enterprises	Social Enterprise Coalition
	Community Action Network
	Social Economy Forum
	Social Economy Network (Northern Ireland)
	The Community Development Finance Association
Community businesses	CBS Network
	Community Enterprise Wales
Worker co-operatives	Industrial Common Ownership Movement
	UK Co-operative Council
	Co-operative Futures
Housing co-operatives	Confederation of Cooperative Housing UK
Employee-owned enterprises	Employee Share Ownership Centre
	Job Ownership
Development trusts	Development Trust Association
Social firms	Social Firms UK
Intermediate labour markets	ILM Network UK
Credit unions	Association of British Credit Unions

Source: Based on D. Smallbone et al., *Researching Social Enterprise*, SBS Research Report RR004/01 July 2001, p. 23, with some additions.

Who is promoting the social economy

The social economy and its sub-sectors are being promoted by various people and organisations:

Governments

The social economy is promoted by government bodies at international, national, regional and local levels. For instance,

- At an international level the European Commission has stated that it wishes to 'promote social enterprises across Europe'[6] and examples of its actions include the 'Promoting social entrepreneurship in Europe' project in 2004 and the launch of a study on national policies and good practices in social enterprises in Europe (scheduled for 2005 but subsequently postponed until 2007).

- At a national level the UK government, in its 'Scaling New Heights : Action Plan', describes social enterprise as a force for changing society for the better.

- At a regional level in Northern Ireland the Department of Enterprise, Trade and Investment established a social economy branch and led the preparation and publication in 2004 of a cross-departmental strategy: 'Developing a Successful Social Economy'.

- At a local level in the late 1970s the Community Business scheme began in Paisley. It then extended to other parts of Glasgow and became, in the 1980s, the largest social enterprise development programme in the UK.[7]

Umbrella bodies

There are many organisations and groups which champion the sector and lobby for it, seeking to give it visibility and voice. Some recent research undertaken for the Home Office has revealed that there are at least 256 umbrella bodies in the UK representing the sector at a national level,[8] and in April 2007 the UK Cabinet Office set aside £2.4 million for three years 'as additional support to the social enterprise sector to raise its own profile and influence public debate'.[9] Some of the different types of these bodies are illustrated in Table 8.1 and include the following:

- The Social Enterprise Coalition (SEC), which was formed with UK government support in 2002 'to address the lack of a coherent, representative voice for social enterprises', bringing together 'the range of existing umbrella bodies operating in the sector'.[10] The SEC, describing itself as 'the UK's national body for social enterprise' purports to lead 'a combined membership of over 10,000 organizations'.[11]

- The Social Economy Network in Northern Ireland, which is a membership-based, government-funded organisation comprised of social economy enterprises and networks. It has a mission to build an active social economy which aims for excellence in meeting community need. Its responsibilities include being a voice for its members on relevant issues and to stimulate government action in support of the sector and influence its policies and programmes.

- The Community Development Finance Association (CDFA), which is the umbrella body or trade association for Community Development Finance Institutions (CDFIs), which are recently established specialist financing bodies for social enterprises (and SMEs).

- The National Council for Voluntary Organisations (NCVO), the Association for Chief Executives of Voluntary Organisations (Acevo), the Institute of Fundraising and the Charity Finance Directors' Group, which are also sector representative bodies which lobby, share best practice and measure performance on behalf of their members. They cover bodies across the third sector spectrum.

Other organisations

There are a range of other organisations which for a variety of reasons promote the third sector or its components, often because they are social economy organisations themselves operating within the sector and/or generating income from it. Examples of them include the following:

- The new economics foundation (nef), founded in 1986, is an example of an independent 'think and do tank'[12] organisation that describes itself as wishing to 'promote innovative solutions that challenge mainstream thinking on economic environment and social issues'.[13] Thus it promotes the third sector, inter alia, as a means of finding innovative solutions.

- The Charity Bank ('Banking for the Common Good'), launched in October 2002, is the first ever charity to be granted a banking licence and the world's first not-for-profit bank. It aims to increase the capacity of the charitable/ non-profit sector by remedying the gap in their financial services not filled by the traditional banking sector. Its goal is to move the sector away from grant-dependency to self-sustainability with a pool of capital which could be ever recycled into the sector and to make a cultural shift within the sector.

- Social Firms UK aims 'to create employment opportunities for disadvantaged people through the development and support of Social Firms. Social Firms are market-led businesses that are set up specifically to create good quality jobs for people severely disadvantaged in the labour market'.[14] Social Firms UK recognises that many organisations lack the resources to identify viable business opportunities or to turn an idea into a business. 'Flagship Firms' is the name of its programme of franchising, licensing and replication which offers business opportunities, perceived as having the potential for successful ventures by social firms, to those seeking new businesses.

- UnLtd is a charitable organisation set up in 2000 to promote social entrepreneurship. In 2002 it was granted a £100 million legacy by the Millennium Commission which it has invested to fund its Millennium Awards scheme in perpetuity. UnLtd is also the lead delivery partner of The Big Boost programmes funded by The Big Lottery Fund, which gives awards to young people to set up community projects. UnLtd's awards programme gives both practical and financial support to social entrepreneurs.

- The School for Social Entrepreneurs was established to develop the competences of aspiring social entrepreneurs utilising the principles of 'action learning'. It offers a training and mentoring service with the aim of accelerating the numbers, growth and quality of social enterprises.

The sector itself

To advocacy from the sorts of promotion and support organisations listed above can be added the exhortations of others in the sector itself. Indeed, some have argued that, due to the voluntary sector's 'babble of tongues',[15] there are now 'too many overlapping voices struggling to be heard'[16] and so, overall, there is a lack of a consistent message and of effective leadership.

Where, and how, the social economy is promoted

The reasons why governments consider intervention to support the social economy and/or social enterprises to be appropriate have been discussed. This section looks at some of the places where they are promoted, and how.

The social enterprise sectors of different countries have distinctive characteristics, reflecting the needs, and uniqueness, of each country's political economy.

Nevertheless, there is considerable similarity in the experience and development of the sector and associated policies across many countries, with each tending to face the same broad strategic issues. This section considers the promotion of the social economy in a number of European countries and in the USA.

Policy in the UK

The UK policy framework is considered in some depth as England has been described as having 'a more advanced state of social economic policy initiatives than many other countries'.[17] Indeed since the time the Labour government came into office in 1997 a number of initiatives have been launched to facilitate the growth and transformation of the social economy, financially, legislatively and rhetorically. (The UK government has used the terms 'social economy' and 'social enterprise' in a range of policy initiatives designed to stimulate, support and develop the 'third sector').

Three broad policy themes have emerged in the areas of

- Philanthropy: involving initiatives to stimulate the giving of time and/or money.
- Voluntary and community sector: involving initiatives to facilitate the sector to build its organisational infrastructure and relationships with government.
- Social enterprise: involving initiatives to stimulate a broader range of social enterprises (such as social businesses, co-operatives and friendly societies) and to support social entrepreneurs.

Because the UK Government has focused on different parts of the third sector in different ways, with reforms remaining largely independent of each other, it can be said to have resulted in 'a loss of momentum to construct a single social economy framework'.[18]

Some key stages in the evolution of the UK policy

Late 1990s – policy action teams
While social enterprise has existed in various forms for many years, as noted in Part I, and was the subject of policy initiatives at the European level in the 1990s, a significant step change took place in the UK in the late 1990s. This occurred as a result of the work of a number of Policy Action Teams (PATs) which, in 1999, produced reports to contribute to the National Strategy for Neighbourhood Renewal.[19]

Three of the reports drew attention to social enterprises in the context of disadvantaged communities. One report in particular, PAT 3, emphasised the role of social enterprise as a means of facilitating enterprise development and community self-help. This message was re-enforced by two further reports, one by the Bank of England and the other by the Social Investment Task Force, which asserted that social enterprise could lead to more jobs, increased supplies of local goods and services and money flows, and thereby reduce the extent of social exclusion. This led to one of three general focus areas for social enterprise policy:

- One focus area was that of economic competitiveness and enterprise.
- A second policy focus, which emanated from the PAT reports, articulated a link between economic regeneration and the extent of social and political engagement of members of local communities, and indicated that this link might be given further impetus if those members can be engaged in voluntary and community action and organisations. In effect social enterprises could generate greater social cohesion and social capital.
- The third focus of policy which developed was the delivery of public services. Social enterprises offered an alternative to private and public sector providers – a third way. The sector could, perhaps, offer better, more economic or more accessible services especially where those needing them could not meet their full cost and government would not, or could not, fill the gap.

2001 – Social Enterprise Unit

There was, therefore, a growing interest in strengthening the social enterprise sector and thus the Social Enterprise Unit (SEnU) was established in October 2001 as the policy-making body for social enterprise in the UK. It was formed within the (then) DTI's Small Business Service section and was tasked with being the focal point 'for strategic decision-making across Government'.[20]

The SEnU set up eight Working Groups which identified 'the major barriers to growth of the social enterprise sector'[21] (see Table 8.2), and in tackling the barriers three key outcomes were to be sought:

- create an enabling environment;
- make social enterprises better businesses; and
- establish the value of social enterprise.[22]

Later, in May 2006, the SEnU was absorbed into the newly created Office of the Third Sector (within the Cabinet Office) which was established 'in recognition of the increasingly important role the third sector plays in both society and the economy'[23] and its remit was described as:

- acting as a focal point for policy making affecting social enterprise;
- promoting and championing social enterprise;
- taking action needed to address barriers to growth of social enterprises; and
- identifying and spreading good practice.[24]

2002 – social enterprise strategy

The Working Groups' reports were completed in February 2002 and this was followed, in July 2002, by the publication of a social enterprise strategy from the

Table 8.2   Major barriers to growth of the social enterprise sector in the UK

- poor understanding of the particular abilities and value of social enterprise;
- little hard evidence to demonstrate the impact and added value of social enterprise;
- fragmented availability of accessible, appropriate advice and support;
- difficulty accessing and making use of what is perceived to be limited appropriate finance and funding available;
- limited account taken of the particular characteristics and needs of social enterprise within an enabling environment;
- complexity and lack of coherence within the sector, combined with widely varying skills and knowledge bases.

Source: DTI, *Social Enterprise: a strategy for success* (2002) p. 9.

(then) DTI. This document was entitled 'Social Enterprise: a strategy for success' (SES 2002) and it stated that 'the Government's vision is of dynamic and sustainable social enterprises strengthening an inclusive and growing economy', adding that 'successful social enterprises can play an important role in helping deliver on many of the Government's key policy objectives'.[25] This cross-departmental strategy set out a three-year programme designed to promote and sustain social enterprise activity and served as the policy framework for the UK (together with the strategies which have been developed by the devolved administrations of Scotland, Wales and Northern Ireland):

> The strategy sets out a programme for the next three years illustrating how, working with other stakeholders, we will promote and sustain social enterprise activity. Key partners in the delivery of the strategy will include central government and its agencies, Government Offices, the devolved administrations, Region Development Agencies, local authorities, the Co-operative Movement, the Social Enterprise Coalition, practitioners and intermediaries, as well as other key stakeholders in the social enterprise sector.[26]

Following the publication of 'Social Enterprise: a strategy for success' in 2002, the UK Government reviewed progress on its implementation and its action plan in October 2003. It recorded its actions as having fallen into three areas as follows:

- Improving the evidence: for example, mapping the sector, social accounting tools;
- Structures and networking: for example, joint working and partnership; facilitating networking; integrated business support; awareness raising; trade fairs; and
- Technical assistance: for example, capacity-building asset transfer, support for CDFIs; other specialist finance (grants and loans); provision of incubation space; web-based services; trade promotion; increasing capability of Business Links Operators to support social enterprise.[27]

These areas bear a general similarity to the types of initiatives taken over the last 10–15 years to support the SME sector. They centre around evidence gathering and awareness raising, improving the flows of advice, information and finance, and assisting structures and networks.

A fuller review of the government's progress in delivering its strategy was published in 2006 drawing upon an independent review by consultants GHK.[28] The latter noted that continued support for enterprise and economic competitiveness was apparent in a variety of ways ranging from the (then) DTI's public service agreement (PSA) targets (which specify increased productivity, enterprise and competitiveness) to the Action Plan for Small Business (which included social enterprise), and to the remit and funding changes relating to RDAs. It concluded that, since 2002

> developments in the broader policy environment concerning economic competitiveness, social cohesion and public service delivery have all acted to re-enforce the potential role of the social enterprise sector in the delivery of government objectives for the UK economy and society.[29]

2006 – social enterprise action plan

This review was followed in 2006 by the government's three-year strategy document for the way forward, entitled 'Social enterprise action plan: Scaling new heights'.[30] This document included a review of progress made since the launch of SES 2002 and laid out the government's plans for continuing support for social enterprises. It restated government support for the sector as contributing to its vision of a fairer, more just society and identified the contribution of social enterprise as

- Meeting social needs, by using business success to meet social or environmental ends and providing opportunity and skills for marginalised groups.
- Encouraging ethical markets, by responding to new markets driven by increasing ethical consumerism and raising the bar by adopting pioneering ethical practices.
- Improving public services, by shaping new service designs, pioneering new approaches and winning contracts to deliver services.
- Increasing enterprise, by attracting new entrepreneurs who want to make a difference to society or the environment and encouraging more women, under-represented groups, and young people to start their own business.[31]

It recognised that government does not create social enterprises, but stated that 'government, working with social enterprises and the organisations that represent them, can create the conditions that enable social enterprises to thrive, and government can tackle the market failures that would otherwise frustrate them'.[32] Specifically (see also Case 8.1) it said the government will

- foster a culture of social enterprise;
- ensure that the right information and advice are available to those running social enterprises;
- enable social enterprises to access appropriate finance;
- enable social enterprises to work with government.[33]

2007 – 'Final report'

Then, in July 2007, the UK government published the 'final report' of the joint Cabinet Office – Treasury review of the future role of the third sector in social and economic regeneration. (Note the change in vocabulary from 'social enterprise' in the 2006 action plan to 'third sector' in the 2007 report, which further reflects the Cabinet Office's move away from the 'better business'-focused approach apparent in the language of the (then) DTI). This report was described as setting out 'a new agenda on social action' and as presenting a 'vision of a partnership in which government empowers and enables individuals and organisations working for positive social change'.[34] It effectively re-emphasises the thrust of its earlier strategy documents.

The review identified four major areas of common interest between the sector and the government: an enabling voice and campaigning, strengthening communities, transforming public services and encouraging social enterprise. To these were added supporting a thriving, healthy third sector to make the five main themes of the review for which an agenda was set out (see Illustration 8.1), in what could be criticised as a mix of ends and means ('drivers', 'objectives' and 'approaches' – see Figure 8.1).

Illustration 8.1   The Five Themes of the 2007 'Final Report'

Enabling voice and campaigning

- A new focus on enabling the third sector's role in campaigning and providing voice for many vulnerable groups, including investment in innovative consultation approaches, work to protect the right of organisations to campaign and mechanisms to ensure Ministers hear the views of third sector organisations on policy.

Strengthening communities

- A new £50 million local endowment match fund enabling local independent foundations to develop community endowments to provide sustainability in future grant making, building on the £80 million small grants programme for community action and voice announced in Budget 2007.

- At least £10 million of new investment in community anchor organisations and community asset and enterprise development, building on the £30 million Community Assets Fund announced in the 2006 Pre-Budget Report.

- £117 million of new resources for youth volunteering, building on the work of v, alongside other volunteering programmes.

Transforming public services

- Building capacity of third sector organisations to improve public services, through the Futurebuilders Fund, training for public sector Commissioners and work to build the evidence on opportunities for the third sector.

Illustration 8.1   (cont'd)

Encouraging social enterprise

- Additional investment to raise awareness of the social enterprise business model, and support for government departments to investigate areas for social enterprise delivery-including getting social enterprise into the Key Stage 3 and 4 curriculum framework from 2008.

Supporting a thriving, healthy third sector

- Better mechanisms to drive best practice in funding the third sector, including in the expectation that when Government Departments and their agencies receive their 2008–11 budgets, they will pass on that three year funding to third sector organisations that they fund, as the norm.

- A new programme to build the third sector evidence base, including £5 million on a new national research centre.

- A new third sector skills strategy.

- Over £80 million of new investment for third sector infrastructure development through Capacitybuilders, with new programmes on voice and campaigning, social enterprise and a focus on reaching down to the smallest community groups.

- Continued focus on the Compact as a means to build the relationship between the third sector and all levels of Government.

Source: Taken from www.cabinetoffice.gov.uk – press release, accessed 10 August 2007, and HM Treasury/Cabinet Office, *The future role of the third sector in social and economic regeneration: final report,* HM Treasury, July 2007.

The components of the UK policy

The evolution of the UK's social enterprise policy which is summarised above can be studied in more detail in the various documents published for or about it (see Further Reading section at the end of this chapter). However, anyone attempting to follow it from those documents might be confused by the various steps in policy development and the variety of items or components that are presented for each step. Figure 8.1 has therefore been prepared as a model of an overall framework for this process together with examples of some detail of the different components. Brief explanations of the components then follow.

Political drivers
The political drivers can be interpreted as the core political reason for having a particular policy, albeit sometimes this is rarely highlighted. In the case of the

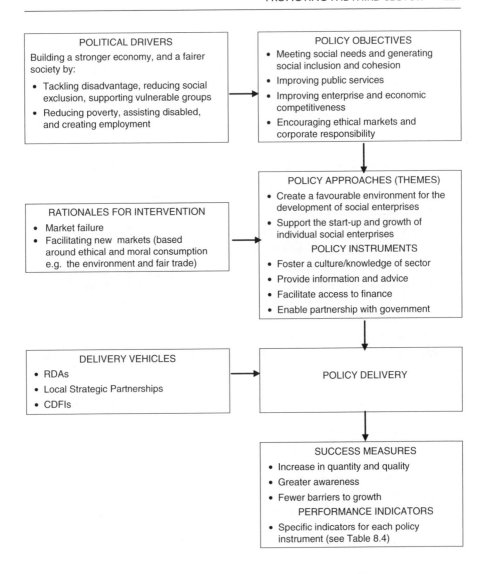

Figure 8.1   A diagram of the UK policy framework for social enterprises

UK government's published social enterprise policy the following statements can be found:

- 'The Government's vision is of dynamic and sustainable social enterprise sustaining an inclusive and growing economy.'[35]

- The vision is 'dynamic and sustainable social enterprises, contributing to a stronger economy and a fairer society'.[36]

- 'The Government recognises that social enterprises contribute to its vision "of a fairer, more just society..."'[37]

Policy objectives

The policy objectives are the overall aim of the policy in question and they can be stated qualitatively, quantitatively or in both ways. Sometimes, however, the overall aim is described as a vision or mission statement while the term objectives is confined to quantified targets that enable one to determine when the mission has been accomplished. In the case of the UK's policy the following are presented:

- *Social Cohesion.* Social enterprise is perceived as adding to the contribution of the community and voluntary sector in the regeneration of disadvantaged communities: 'empowering individuals and communities, encouraging the development of work habits and increasing employment diversity'.[38]
- *Public Service Delivery.* Social enterprise activity is seen as being a means to improve the quality and efficiency of public service delivery.
- *Economic Competitiveness.* A role is seen for social enterprise in its efforts to support enterprise (including the number of people going into business), especially in disadvantaged areas, and sustainable improvements in the economic performance of UK regions.
- *Ethics and Responsibilities.* Social enterprise is seen as setting an example in encouraging an ethical approach to business and to corporate responsibility.

Rationales for policy intervention

Although a government may identify certain objectives, government intervention to achieve them may, be counterproductive unless there is a good justification for it. The justification frequently used (whether adequately assessed or otherwise) is that of 'market failure'. The implication is that a gap needs to be filled because of the lack of private provision and inadequate public service delivery (and, inter alia, that the benefits of intervention exceed the costs of so doing).

There appear to be two factors that provide the rationale for intervention in support of social enterprises in the UK:

- *Market failure.* The social economy is seen as capable of making available products and services that would not otherwise be available in particular places or for particular people. 'Social enterprises create new goods and services and develop opportunities for markets where mainstream business cannot, or will not, go.'[39]
- *New markets.* With shifts in public attitudes towards greater social and environmental responsibility, social enterprises are perceived as being in the vanguard in meeting ethical consumers' needs, the private and public sectors being slower to respond.

Policy approaches and instruments

To achieve the objectives of intervention two broad approaches are generally available. One concentrates on the creation of an environment favourable to the establishment and growth of social enterprise and the other supports the actual start-up and growth of individual enterprises. Within each approach a number of specific instruments can then be used. The two approaches are not mutually exclusive and both can be seen in the policy instruments in the UK which include the following (see also Table 8.3). (Policy instruments can be further detailed in specific actions and the 'key actions' presented in the 2006 *Social enterprise action plan: Scaling new heights* are listed in Case 8.1.)

Table 8.3   A taxonomy of policy instruments

Among the range of policy instruments potentially available to achieve government objectives for the social economy are the following, all of which have been, at one time or another, deployed by the UK government:

Raising the profile and providing information

- Research/evidence-based publications
- Award schemes and best practice dissemination campaigns
- Information and advice (e.g. procurement toolkit, working with private sector)

Advocacy and lobbying

- Informing and involving government departments, such as the Cabinet Office and Office the Third Sector, the Department of Business, Enterprise and Regulatory Reform
- Liaison with representative organisations (e.g. Social Enterprise Coalition)

Deregulation and simplification

- Legal form (e.g. Community Interest Company)
- Legislative exemptions
- Procurement procedures

Sectoral and problem-specific policies

- Rural enterprises
- Inner city enterprises
- Ethnic enterprises
- Procurement (a National Procurement Strategy)

Financial assistance

- Community Development Finance Initiative
- Local Enterprise Growth Initiative (LEGI)
- Grants
- Loan funds
- Venture capital and other funds (e.g. Futurebuilders, Adventure Capital Fund, and Unltd)
- Tax relief (CITR)

Indirect assistance

- Influencing mainstream business support
- Training for advisers, staff, volunteers and public sector purchasers
- Mentoring
- Network development

- *Fostering a culture of social enterprise*, for instance, through publications, award competitions and support for networks such as the Social Enterprise Coalition.
- *Providing access to finance*, for instance, through organisations such as Community Development Finance Institutions (CDFIs), through tax relief schemes such as the Community Investment Tax Relief (CITR) and through guidance on best practice in funding.
- *Providing information and advice*, for instance, through publications, business advisers and key business support agencies.
- *Enabling partnership with government*, for instance, by providing advice on creating better working relationships between government and the sector, not least in the area of procurement.

Delivery vehicles

In order to undertake the work of implementing its policy a government needs delivery vehicles. In the case of the UK government's social enterprise policy the principal delivery agent, at least in England, has been the Regional Development Agencies (RDAs) through their Business Links and other partners. However, other organisations, such as the Social Enterprise Coalition, have also had a part to play.

Policy delivery

Having put all that together, policy delivery should then take place. The effectiveness of that delivery can then be assessed through success measures and/or performance indicators.

Success measures and performance indicators

In its *Social enterprise action plan: Scaling new heights*, the UK government identified a trend indicator, which was 'an upward trend in the number of businesses

Table 8.4   Performance indicators for 'Scaling new heights'

Strategy: Encourage growth in social enterprise in four ways:			
Fostering a culture of social enterprise	**Ensuring that the right information and advice are available**	**Enabling access to appropriate finance**	**Enabling social enterprises to work with government**
Performance indicator	Performance indicator	Performance indicator	Performance indicator
Levels of involvement in social enterprise through employment and awareness	Measurement of penetration and satisfaction rates for social enterprises using Business Link	Comparison of social enterprises' access to finance with matched samples of commercial businesses	Assessment of social enterprises/third sector organisations' experience of government procurement
Source: DTI Household Survey	*Source:* RDAs	*Source:* Additions to the DTI's survey on small business finance	*Source:* Office of the Third Sector (which will consult on the most appropriate measure)

Source: Cabinet Office/Office of the Third Sector, *Social enterprise action plan: Scaling new heights*, November 2006, p. 62.

that fit the Government's definition of social enterprise',[40] as well as performance indicators for each of the four ways (policy instruments) in which it planned to encourage growth in social enterprises (see Table 8.4).

CASE 8.1

Key Actions in a Strategy to Promote Social Enterprise

At the end of 2006 the UK government launched its 'Social enterprise action plan: Scaling new heights'. The points articulated and/or actions planned under each of the main items in the action plan are summarised as follows:

Fostering a culture of social enterprise

It seeks to raise awareness of social enterprise and demonstrates that financial success is consistent with social and environmental benefit. It will aim to

- build the evidence base on the role and impact of social enterprises and
- use such evidence to raise various groups' awareness, for example, young people, businesses, employees, potential founders

Proposed actions include:

- development of a new research programme to build further evidence on the economic, social and environmental value of the sector
- review research on ethical consumer markets and their effect on social enterprises
- using the evidence and work with partners, to raise awareness and under-standing of the sector across a range of audiences
- development of a programme to support social enterprise 'ambassadors' who will raise awareness and work on policy with government
- supporting a campaign to promote social enterprise
- ensuring improved guidance material for schools on social enterprise and exchange of best practice by schools in this field
- seeking a higher profile for social enterprise business models in school courses
- promoting social enterprises learning and the tertiary sectors and as a career option
- encouraging links between social enterprise and the conventional private sector

Ensuring that the right information and advice are available to those running social enterprises

It restates that it wants to enable social enterprises to be 'successful businesses' by ensuring that 'entrepreneurs' have access to good advice and information.

CASE 8.1 (cont'd)

The challenge, it says, is to ensure that they are 'able to access the support they need, in the market or through government programmes'.[41] The government further notes that 'in many instances, social enterprises need very similar advice and support to mainstream businesses' although in some cases 'more specialist help may be needed'.[42] It identifies the start-up phase (and the need to choose a suitable legal form and account for double/treble bottom lines) and issues relating to finance, marketing and governance as areas of specialist advice.

Problems in meeting needs are identified as:

- uneven support provision from region to region
- the complexity of the support landscape
- some organizations not regarding themselves to be within the remit of Business Link
- making sure that mainstream business advisers can meet the needs of social enterprises

Proposed actions include:

- funding for Regional Development Agencies (RDAs) to improve Business Link's capacity to broker business support for social enterprises
- improving information and guidance on the Business Link website for the sector
- ensuring Capacitybuilders,[43] in its strategic plan, fully integrates support for social enterprise infrastructure
- identifying social enterprise networks, national to local and sectoral, with a view to meeting any gaps in provision
- commissioning a review to assess the skills needs of the sector and the extent to which they are met by mainstream providers

Enabling social enterprises to access appropriate finance

It seeks to ensure that social enterprises have adequate access to capital to operate and grow – a frequently cited barrier to growth for the sector. In particular, it examines access to debt finance, equity finance and tax incentives for investment.

Proposed actions include:

- Regional Development Agencies (RDAs) to review the extent of existing investment in the sector through Community Development Finance Institutions (CDFIs) and consider disseminating good practice models

CASE 8.1 (cont'd)

- expanding financial awareness
- ensuring the Small Business Service's interventions to assist SMEs to access finance are inclusive of social enterprises
- reviewing the operation of Community Investment Tax Relief[44] (CITR)
- training for the sector
- reviewing research and test project outcomes and consulting on how best to use their results and any future funding

Enabling social enterprises to work with government

It wants to encourage social enterprises to be involved in the design and delivery of public services and public policy generally, where they may have particular expertise.

It seeks to address three main issues:

- improving the way in which public services are delivered (in particular, removing barriers to social enterprises delivering them on contract)
- considering how social enterprises can work in partnership with government to achieve social and economic objectives (and to remove barriers to them having a greater role)
- enabling the sector to raise its profile and credibility with policy makers (so that their potential may be recognised)

Proposed actions include:

- development and implementation of an action plan for the third sector addressing barriers to its delivery of public services
- consult on and review the state of knowledge and best practice in the use of 'social clauses' in contracts
- promoting greater awareness by social enterprises of the government portal (supply2.gov.uk)
- enabling social enterprises to benefit from the London 2012 Olympics by researching opportunities, ensuring an appropriate procurement policy and assisting a start-up programme
- promoting ways in which public funding can be used to develop sustainable solutions in the sector including providing guidelines on 'clawback'[45]
- offering strategic funding support for a wider range of national partners representing the sector

Source: Cabinet Office/Office of the Third Sector, *Social enterprise action plan: Scaling new heights*, November 2006.

Social economy policy in the EU

The Development of EU Policy

1989 – Social Economy Unit
The first significant EU official recognition of the social economy could be said to have occurred in 1989 when the European Commission established a dedicated unit to handle the social economy portfolio. Called the 'Social Economy Unit', it was created within DG XXIII, which was responsible for 'Enterprise Policy, Distributive Trades, Tourism and Social Economy'. For this the European definition of the social economy included co-operatives, mutuals, associations and foundations (CMAFs), as well as social enterprises.

From 1994 – Multi-Annual Programme
Two strands have been identified[46] in the subsequent development of policy for the social economy in the EU, and they are similar to those in the UK. The first strand emerged in February 1994 within the areas of enterprise policy when the Commission agreed a Multi-Annual Programme (MAP) of work for the period 1994–1996. It sought to lay down the infrastructure seen as necessary for the development of the sector and to stimulate innovation within it. The MAP resulted in three European CMAF Statutes, strengthening the role of the social economy as a vehicle for EU policies, a representative body to act as a dialogue partner (a consultative committee) and improved statistics. It also led to pilot projects to assist financing the sector and communication.[47]

The Enterprise and Industry DG (see below) has developed subsequently MAPs for enterprise and entrepreneurship, and support of social enterprises is a part of those programmes (albeit a small part). Mirroring the subsequent emphasis in the UK's Social Enterprise Strategy, the MAP 2001–2005, for example, sought, for social enterprises, to:

- raise the degree of understanding and visibility;
- review the regulatory framework;
- better assess their economic impact.

From the mid-1990s – employment policies
The second strand of policy development came from within the area of employment policy, reflecting mid-1990s concerns about 'jobless growth'. The social economy was thought to have the potential to create jobs in areas such as personal services, culture and the environment, and local economic development initiatives were also seen as having a significant role for social enterprise.[48] A pilot action called 'Third System and Employment' (TSE) was introduced (1997–2001) and the evaluation of this action identified a range of barriers to the development of the sector (see Table 8.5), similar to those articulated in the UK (see Table 8.2).

Table 8.5   Barriers to the development of the social enterprise sector in the EU

External Barriers

- Political preferences for market or state solutions.
- Inadequate social and fiscal policies.
- Inappropriate contracting procedures.
- Inappropriate legal frameworks for third sector activity.

Internal Barriers

- A lack of managerial and professional skills.
- A lack of quality control systems for social services provided by private organisations.
- A lack of co-ordination, leading to price competition among service deliverers.
- Difficulty in accessing finance.
- An inadequately developed system of second-level support organisations.

Source: Adapted from GHK, *Social Enterprise: An International Literature Review*, a report submitted to SBS/SEnU, March 2006, p. 6, quoting Campbell, M., *The Third System, Employment and Local Development – Volume I – Synthesis Report*, Leeds Metropolitan University (August 1999).

Out of the employment considerations emerged the EU initiatives named Adapt and Employment followed by EQUAL. This initiative, funded through the European Social Fund, has tested and promoted new means of combating discrimination and inequalities in labour markets, frequently through transnational co-operation. While it has not taken the lead in policy for the social economy, it has, nevertheless, been the EU's most significant source of financial support for it (€300 million from 2002 to 2008 – a figure matched by national contributions).

Some of the recommendations which have emerged from EQUAL 'development partnerships' (DPs[49]) are again very similar to those already being implemented or considered in the UK, such as:

- ensuring that public procurement tender includes social criteria to enable social enterprises to have access to public markets;
- developing measures of social added value;
- improving legal frameworks;
- developing a braided support structure combining specialist with mainstream business support;
- having a department in government which has a clear responsibility for liaising with the social enterprise sector.

The job creation potential of the social economy (including meeting new needs) has been regularly commented upon by the EU. Nevertheless it has been suggested that, as the employment strategy has developed, 'the social economy has been progressively sidelined'.[50] Table 8.6 provides examples indicating a diminishing emphasis on the social economy in official EU documents over time and, in the Integrated Guidelines for Growth and Jobs (2005–2008),[51] explicit reference is made only once to 'the social economy' in contrast to the increasing emphasis placed by the UK government on both the social economy in general and social enterprises in particular.

Table 8.6   Examples of the apparently diminishing emphasis on the social economy in EU employment strategy

2000	The European Charter for Small Enterprises has no specific reference to the social economy or social enterprises.
2001–2002	European Employment Guideline (EEG) 11 sought to 'promote measures to enhance the competitive development and job creation capacity of the social economy especially the provision of ... needs not yet satisfied by the market'.
2001–2002	In EEG 10 the social economy was mentioned only as a tool for creating jobs at local level as part of reducing regional disparities.
2004	Launch of Promoting Social Entrepreneurship in Europe project, which was to lead to a study on social enterprises in Europe in 2005, but it has not yet materialised.
2005	In the Implementation Report on the European Charter for Small Enterprises: Consultation on National Reports, no reference is made to the social economy, social enterprise or third sector.
2005–2008	The Integrated Guidelines for Growth and Jobs (which have subsumed the EEGs) mention the social economy 'but the mention is not prominent'.

Source: Based on GHK, *Social Enterprise: An International Literature Review*, a report submitted to SBS/SEnU March 2006, p. 9.

2000 – Directorate General for Enterprise and Industry

While these two strands continued to guide support into the twenty-first century, the Social Economy Unit itself was downgraded. In 2000, a Directorate General for Enterprise and Industry was created through a merger of DGIII (Industry), the Innovation Unit of DGXIII (Information Technology) and DG XXIII (Enterprise Policy, Distributive Trades, Tourism and the Social Economy). The Social Economy Unit was subsumed into this new DG, where it became one of the responsibilities of the Unit for Small Enterprises, Crafts, Co-operatives and Mutuals (Unit ENTR/E3).

Sector representative bodies

There are a significant number of bodies representing the social economy sector at EU level, more so than in the UK. Some of the best known are listed in Table 8.7.

Table 8.7   Social enterprise sector representation at EU level

Name of organisation	Description or membership	Roles
CEP – CMAF (DEC – CMAF)	The European Standing Conference of Co-operatives, Mutuals, Associations and Foundations.	A joint representative body serving as an interlocutor for the EU Commission on policy for the social economy.
European Platform of Social NGOs	Comprises representative federations and networks of NGOs active in the social sector.	Subsidised by the Education and Training DG to promote social justice and participative democracy on behalf of its members.
Intergroup on the Social Economy and Subsidiarity	An informal association of members of the European Parliament representing all political groups.	Aims to offer a single voice to the Commission on the Social Economy and promote co-operation across countries.

EESC Liaison Group	The European Economic and Social Committee is a non-political body which forms a platform for views on EU issues to be forwarded to EU decision-makers.	The Liaison Group offers the EESC a co-ordinated approach to civil society organisations and networks and a means to monitor joint initiatives.

'Family'-specific federal bodies:
  CEDAG (Associations)
  EFC (Foundations)
  AIM (Health Mutuals)
  ACME (Mutual insurers)
  and various co-operative
  federations, including
  CECODHAS (social
  housing)
  EUROCOOP (consumer
  co-ops)
  COGECA (agriculture)
	All members of the CEP – CMAF, the European Standing Conference (see CEP – CMAF above).	

CECOP	European Confederation of Workers' Co-operatives, Social Co-operatives and Participative Enterprises.	Represents small and medium-sized worker controlled enterprises.
ENSIE	European Network for Social Integration Enterprises	Represents work integration social enterprises.
CEFEC	Confederation of European social firms, employment initiatives and social co-operatives.	Represents enterprise with an emphasis on assisting people with disabilities.

Some comments on EU policy

As described in Chapter 4, the EU has indicated that it considers social enterprises to be one of the categories of organisation included in the social economy. However, beyond that it has no agreed definition of a social enterprise. Whether or not the EU has a coherent policy (or, as some might contest, any policy) towards social enterprises is somewhat unclear. Jeremy Kendall has observed that in relation to EU policy and the third sector there is 'sustained policy salience but contested policy substance' and that 'the topic will stay alive, as a contested and fraught domain characterised by competing interests and ideas'.[52] He also adds that

- Definitions of the third sector are politically constructed, as they determine who benefits from subsequent regulatory and funding decisions.
- Most policy refers to the 'vertical' policy field (referring to social issues such as poverty or employment), though certain 'horizontal' issues (cross-cutting issues that cover all organisations under consideration) have emerged, such as legal status, citizenship, consultation, funding and volunteering.
- The most important level of interaction between the third sector and government is at the local level, as this is where the policy is delivered, not at national or European.[53]

However, it has also been said that a 'policy towards social enterprise is slowly emerging' and that 'there is evidence of a more joined-up view', illustrated by 'the treaties of Maastricht and Amsterdam, the Commission communication on voluntary organisations (*COM (1997) 241 final of 6 June, 1997*), the management of the Structural Funds and the governance debate'.[54] The European Commission is exploring how the social economy can contribute to

- efficient competition in markets;
- potential job creation and new forms of entrepreneurship and employment;
- meeting new needs;
- citizen participation and voluntary work;
- enhanced solidarity and cohesion;
- the integration of the economies of the candidate countries.[55]

Policy towards social enterprise is easier to identify and articulate in the UK than at an EU level. UK policy also has a coherence which derives in part from the consensus which largely exists as to what constitutes the concept of 'social enterprise'. In Europe, there is no such consensus and the differing national conceptions have tended to produce a fragmentary approach towards policy with considerable fluctuations in the resources made available over time.

Social economy policy in other European countries

The following is a summary, based substantially on the findings of the GHK report,[56] of some of the features of the social enterprise policy in four European countries:

France

- The idea of the 'social economy' first grew in France in the nineteenth century but was subsequently eclipsed by the co-operative and public sectors. The French model has, however, been influential on broader European thinking.
- French policy now tends to use the term 'social and solidarity economy' rather than 'social enterprise'.
- Cohesion within the sector has been encouraged and facilitated through simple legal frameworks.
- There are positive examples of the integration of provider and user voices within enterprises. For instance, strong stakeholder relationships including democratic ownership and the involvement of both customers and employees can enhance the sustainability of enterprises.
- The social benefits delivered by the social and solidarity economy have been recognised through economic instruments for the sector, for example, 'cheques domiciles': vouchers for services provided by social enterprises.

Germany

- Policy in Germany has followed a relatively strict division between co-operatives (pursuing self-help) and welfare organisations (performing a public duty). The family of co-operative organisations is strong but has a weak attachment to the idea of social enterprise.

- Within government the main policy drivers of support for the sector are to reduce unemployment, to integrate disabled people into the workforce and to combat poverty, social exclusion and racial discord. However, there is no co-ordinated government dialogue with social enterprises and development has been hindered by the absence of a long-term vision for the sector.

- Innovation in the sector is hindered by regulations and procedures which constrain the ability of social enterprises to trade in the open market and in areas of the economy that are 'additional' to the activities of existing businesses.

- As long as social enterprise is seen primarily as a means for short-term job creation, instead of as a contributor to local economic development, community development and social capital, innovation and self-sufficiency in the sector may be hampered.

Italy

- The role of the co-operative movement is anchored in Italy's constitution and it is large and well organised. In contrast, associations in Italy are relatively badly structured. The country has been responsible for some innovative partnership ideas but it is the co-operative family that has been the engine for innovation. There are, many examples of multi-stakeholder structures (involving employees, users, volunteers and supporters) within the sector.

- Although the terminology varies, the social economy is normally thought of as including all co-operatives, along with mutuals, associations and foundations. The third sector, or third system, is the part of this that works for the public benefit and does not distribute profit.

- Italian government policy towards the third sector has historically been unsystematic and pragmatic. Since the 1990s, however, a more stable government framework has grown within which the third sector has been able to work more coherently.

- Tax relief is used to reflect the social benefits delivered by the sector, and the social co-operative sector is working to transform the business advice system and to establish the legitimacy of social enterprise among business advisers. The sector thus benefits from an advisory support system which takes social enterprise seriously.

Poland

- In Poland the term 'social economy' is chiefly associated with the country's associations and foundations. The social economy in Poland had rich traditions between the wars but became a tool of centralised planning under communism.

- The main motivation of the Polish government to support the development of social enterprises has been as a source of jobs to counter high unemployment. However, the government does recognise the useful role of the social economy in tackling a wide range of issues including entrepreneurship, employment, youth unemployment, drug abuse, social inclusion and promoting democracy.

- The term 'social enterprise' is not much used in Poland, where the term 'third sector' is more common.

- European networks are being used to develop the sector, and public finance is available for sector development. Regional initiatives and local actions have stimulated the growth of the sector carried out within the framework of a coherent regional policy.

Points from a comparison

Various conclusions have been drawn from a comparison of the policies of European countries including the UK. The following are some of the points suggested in the GHK review[57] or, where indicated, from other sources:

- The economic and political dynamics of a given country tend to dictate the scope, nature, treatment and even recognition of the 'social economy'.

- The role of the organisations in the social economy of countries within the EU is increasing. However, due to differences in definitions used, comparable data for the various activities in which they are involved are not available.

- There is no 'right or wrong' policy framework. There is considerable diversity of organisational models in the social enterprise sector and certain models can best fit certain policy goals.

- There are common aims for social enterprises and the social economy in the fields of social cohesion and public service delivery. Unlike the UK, there is less of a concern about its role in promoting economic competitiveness.

- In most countries, the *de facto* policy ministries are those which regulate and fund the sector. In countries where policy is highly decentralised (e.g. Germany and Spain) regional and local authorities play an important role in policy creation and in the nature of relationships with the sector. 'Only the UK, France and Italy have appointed a specific authority in charge of co-ordinating, at least in part, the national policy for the sector.'[58]

- There is strong belief that the social economy needs and builds human and social capital and that it is an instrument to address social and economic exclusion.

- Some governments encourage social enterprises to become more self-sufficient (UK, France, Belgium).

- There is a perceived need for micro-finance as a necessary mechanism to support social economy enterprises.
- The role of regional structures is important in developing the sector, linking national strategy with local activity. In the UK, this suggests a valuable role for RDA's and the Devolved Administrations.
- There is less interest in evaluating the social benefits of the sector in other European countries than in the UK and the DIES[59] in France.
- The main national policy instruments used in support of the sector are[60]

  – special legal forms and regulations
  – favourable tax system
  – grants and subsidies
  – incentives for fund-raising
  – support for voluntary work and job generation (e.g. paid days off work, tax exemptions on expenses).

A way forward?

A review of EU and European national systems of support for the social enterprise sector would suggest, for those wishing to advance the sector, seven principles of good practice:

1. Political commitment
   There needs to be genuine belief that the sector has a strategic and long-term role to play in the social and economic systems of the country, such belief exhibiting itself in appropriate support policies.
2. A clear focus for the sector
   There should be a recognition that the sector has a distinctive contribution to make and agreement on what that contribution is and its clear articulation.
3. Vertical and horizontal Integration
   There should be a strategic approach appropriate to the needs of the social economy at the local level, recognising and integrating horizontal issues common to the sector and vertical issues common to its various areas of involvement (e.g. employment, healthcare). In addition, co-operation and integration of social enterprises themselves should be facilitated to further their common objectives and meet their common needs.
4. Independent financial resources
   Access to financial resources (other than grants) should be facilitated, for instance, borrowing against assets to enhance the prospects of sustainability.
5. Skills, education and training
   There should be a support and advisory system that can deliver critical mass whilst recognising the distinctiveness of the sector applied to the various stakeholders

including staff, board members, volunteers and supporters. Education *about* the
social economy should rest alongside education *for* the social economy.

6. Social entrepreneurship
   There should be recognition and support for the phenomenon of the
   social entrepreneur as a catalyst in developing innovative ways of addressing
   social problems.

7. A shared vision
   Processes which lead to a shared vision should be in place comprising
   appropriate structures in the public sector and in the social economy, maintaining shared objectives, resources and dialogues addressing common issues.

Policy in the USA

The third sector is claimed to be the fastest-growing part of the US economy
and the USA has one of the highest levels of voluntary sector activity anywhere
in the world (at almost 10 per cent of the economically active working for a civil
society organisation).[61] The third sector in the USA is said to comprise a mix
of 'nonprofit' or 'not-for-profit' organisations and co-operatives.[62] The terms
'social economy' and 'social enterprise' have not been much used, and neither
is the term 'social entrepreneurship', although there is now a rapidly growing
social entrepreneurship movement developing around universities, foundations
and not-for-profit organisations.

In the USA, as in other countries, the role of government in supporting the sector
needs to be interpreted within the particular political, economic and social characteristics of the country. Indeed some would draw a sharp contrast between the UK/US
social enterprise approach to the sector and the European social economy approach.
In the former, the social or not-for-profit enterprise has its rationale as a business
in the market context (albeit with more socially informed values and for which it
uses its surpluses). It is suggested that on 'the basis of US experience it can even
claim to be becoming "fashionable" – merging in with new corporate management
methods (to privilege trust and worker empowerment), the drive for good corporate
citizenship... as a vehicle to add a second (social) and third (environmental) bottom
line to good corporate practice... an alternative business vehicle'.[63] The European
approach differs in that the social economy has its roots in political economy as
opposed to economic sociology or business management. In this context, the social
enterprise is more than 'just another kind of business'.

In the USA, organisations in the sector generally have higher levels of commerciality than their counterparts in Europe. Moreover, there is a much higher
level of corporate philanthropy than in European countries with philanthropic
foundations serving as important investment vehicles for third sector activity
(for instance, the Schwab, Ashoka and Skoll Foundations). Government support
is mainly in the form of grants and tax incentives, although it is also important
as a contractor of services, not least in healthcare. In addition, tax concessions
support worker buyouts and succession buyouts leading to further expansion

Table 8.8   A comparison of not-for-profit sources of income (2003)

Country	Fees (%)	Government (%)	Philanthropy (%)
Developed Countries	45	48	7
UK	45	47	9
USA	57	31	13

Source: Lester, M, Salamon, S, Wojciech Sakolowski, and Regin List 'Global Civil Society: An overview' (Baltimore: John Hopkins Center for Civil Society Studies, 2003) reproduced in 'GHK Social Enterprise: An international Literature Review' submitted to SBS/SEnU (March 2006), p. 59.

of the sector. Table 8.8 contrasts the sources of income for US not-for-profits compared to the situation in the UK and other developed countries. It shows that the US not-for-profits have much higher levels of fee-earning income, a much lower level of government support (less than one-third of their income) and receive almost double the level of philanthropic giving, compared to similar enterprises elsewhere.

The conclusions[64] to be drawn about support for the third/social enterprise sector in the USA include the following:

- Corporate philanthropy, which is supported by tax breaks, has a significant influence on sector development.
- The sector benefits from high levels of commerciality and is also driven by increasing social entrepreneurship.
- There are some government grants for the sector (about 8 per cent of the revenue of reporting charities) and government contracting for services plays a dominant role in the health care sector.
- A significant support role is played by an extensive array of diverse structures at State level and trade associations.
- Government support for employee ownership also assists the expansion of the sector.

Conclusions

This chapter is about promoting the third sector through interventions which are designed to encourage, support, focus and/or grow it. It started by considering why there is an interest in promoting the sector and then looked at who is promoting it. Much of that promotion is instigated by governments and therefore a considerable section of the chapter is devoted to government strategies for the sector and particularly for the social economy within it. Governments in different countries approach the sector in different ways and with different perspectives, sometimes placing a different focus on its potential and attempting to help it by somewhat different means.

Nevertheless it is clear that there has been, is and will continue to be considerable interest in the sector from international governmental organisations such as the EU, from national governments and from regional and local government bodies also. This chapter therefore suggests a model of how, in these government strategies, political drivers and objectives, rationales, approaches and themes, instruments and delivery vehicles, and success measures and performance indicators, can be linked, although not all strategies will formally acknowledge all these components.

As the first part of this chapter explains, these interventions are generally undertaken because of the apparent potential of the third sector to address some of the problems in, or of, society. Governments and others therefore believe that the third sector has the potential to help them to achieve some of their social, and economic, objectives, and thus they promote it in order to make it stronger and able to deliver more. But do these promotions work? Is the third sector, or at least some of its components, stronger as a consequence, and are they as a result delivering more? That question is considered in the next chapter.

The Key Points of Chapter 8

- The third sector, or parts of it, are perceived to provide benefits such as augmenting welfare state provision and generating jobs, enterprise, social cohesion, environmental sustainability and ethical operations.

- Governments and others have an interest in some, if not all, of these benefits and so they promote and encourage the social economy. Government support can be at the international, national, regional and local levels.

- To understand government strategy it can be useful to have a model linking policy drivers and objectives, rationales, approaches and themes, instruments, delivery vehicles, success measures and performance indicators (or their equivalents).

- The UK is viewed as being one of the countries with advanced social economy policies and has published a series of strategies/action plans over recent years describing its goals, plans and performance.

- Policy development in the UK has centred around fostering a culture of social enterprise, easing access to finance, providing information and advice as well as enabling partnership with government.

- At the EU level, social economy policy developments have tended to be embraced within enterprise and employment policy but with a diminishing emphasis and in a somewhat fragmentary way.

- Different European countries have different regulatory frameworks and organisation structures within which policy is applied. These result mainly from their unique political, economic and social histories. Social objectives are often common, however.

- Some lessons can be drawn about the social economy sector by reviewing its development and promotion across a number of countries, as can some tentative principles of good practice.

Questions, Exercises, Essay and Discussion Topics

1. Does the social economy need to be promoted any more than other areas of the economy? Discuss.

2. What categories of organisation promote the sector? Are there too few or too many voices for the sector?

3. Identify the main components of a cohesive strategy for policy support for the sector.

4. Describe the main policy instruments used by the UK government to promote social enterprises. How do they relate to the 'key actions' listed in Case 8.1?

5. Are the commonalities of policy across countries greater than the differences?

6. Describe some best practice principles to guide policy support or social enterprises.

SUGGESTIONS FOR FURTHER READING

Some key publications relevant to the development of the social enterprise sector in the UK:

1999   Bank of England, *Finances for Small Businesses in Deprived Communities*

1999   OECD, *Social Enterprises*, OECD, Paris (http://www.oecd.org)

1999   HM Treasury, National Strategy for Neighbourhood Renewal: Policy Action Team 3, *Enterprise and Social Exclusion*, London

1999   HM Treasury, National Strategy for Neighbourhood Renewal: Policy Action Team 9, *Community and Self Help*

1999   HM Treasury, National Strategy for Neighbourhood Renewal: Policy Action Team 14, *Access to Financial Services*

2000   Social Investment Task Force, *Enterprising Communities: Wealth Beyond Welfare*

2002   DTI, *Social Enterprises: a strategy for success*

2003   A Review of the Scottish Executive's Policies to promote the Social Economy (www.scotland.gov.uk/library5/social/rose-00.asp)

2003   Bank of England, *The Financing of Social Enterprises*. A special Report by the Bank of England

2003   DTI, *Guidance on Mapping Social Enterprise*, ECOTEC Research and Consulting Ltd

2003   DTI, *A Progress Report on Social Enterprise: a strategy for success*

2003   DTI, *Private Action, Public Benefit: The Role of the Voluntary and Community Sector in Service Delivery*

2005	HM Treasury, DTI, Home Office, *Exploring the Role of the Third Sector in Public Service Delivery and Reform*, London
2005	GHK, *Review of the Social Enterprises Strategy: Summary of DTI Findings*, London, Small Business Service
2005	DTI, *Survey of Social Enterprises across the UK*
2006	GHK, *Social Enterprise: International Literature Review*, London
2006	Office of the Third Sector, Cabinet Office, *Social Enterprise Action Plan: Scaling New Heights*
2006/7	DTI, *Finance for Small and Medium-Sized Enterprises: Comparisons of Social Enterprises and Mainstream Business*
Jul 2007	Cabinet Office, *The Future Role of the Third Sector in Social and Economic Regeneration: Final Report*, HM Treasury

References

1. GHK, *Social Enterprise: An International Literature Review*, a report submitted to SBS/SEnU, London, March 2006.
2. Ibid., p. iv.
3. Ibid., p. 68.
4. P. Graefe, 'The social economy and the state: Linking ambitions with institutions in Quebec, Canada', *Policy and Politics*, Vol. 30 No. 2, p. 248.
5. DTI, *A Progress Report on Social Enterprise: a strategy for success* (October 2003), p. 49.
6. http://cc.europa.eu/enterprise/coop/social-cinafagenda/social-enterp, accessed 29 August 2007.
7. A. Amin, R. Hudson and A. Cameron, *Placing the Social Economy* (London: Routledge, 2002), p. 61.
8. http://www.thirdsector.co.uk/News/DailyBulletin/613394/Umbrella-groups-need-this, accessed 21 August 2007, p. 1.
9. Cabinet Office, *Social Enterprise: Scaling New Heights*, Action Plan Draft 0.8 Nrv2 off, p. 45.
10. Cabinet Office, Office of the Third Sector, *Social Enterprise Action Plan: Scaling New Heights*, November 2006, p. 60.
11. http://www.socialenterprise.org.uk/page.aspx?SP=1346, accessed 19 August 2007.
12. http://www.neweconomics.org/gen/m1i1aboutushome.aspx, accessed 19 August 2007.
13. Ibid.
14. http://www.socialfirms.co.uk, accessed 19 August 2007.
15. http://www.thirdsector.co.uk/News/DailyBulletin/613394/Umbrella-groups-need-this, accessed 21 August 2007, p. 1.
16. Ibid.
17. Canadian Government draft of 'Europe-Social Economy; Synthesis and Analysis of Environmental Scans', Unpublished Circa 2005.
18. Canadian Government Europe-Social Economy, p. 45.
19. Neighbourhood Renewal Unit, PAT Reports, www.neighbourhood.gov.uk.
20. DTI, *Social Enterprise: a strategy for success* (2002), p. 8.
21. Ibid.

22. Ibid.

23. http://www.sbs.gov.uk/sbsgov/action/layer, accessed 15 April 2007.

24. GHK, *Review of the Social Enterprise Strategy*, a final report submitted to the Small Business Service (2002), p. 5.

25. DTI, *Social Enterprise: a strategy for success* (2002), p. 8.

26. Ibid.

27. DTI, *A Progress Report on Social Enterprise: a strategy for success*, (October 2003), p. 7.

28. GHK, *Review of the Social Enterprise Strategy*, a final report submitted to the Small Business Service, 2005.

29. Ibid., p. 12.

30. Cabinet Office/Office of the Third Sector, *Social Enterprise Action Plan: Scaling New Heights*, November 2006.

31. Ibid., p. 13.

32. Ibid., p. 3.

33. Ibid., pp. 3–5.

34. www.cabinetoffice.gov.uk – press release, accessed 10 August 2007.

35. DTI, *Social Enterprise: a strategy for success*, July 2002, p. 7.

36. Cabinet Office/Office of the Third Sector, *Social Enterprise Action Plan: Scaling New Heights*, November 2006.

37. Cabinet Office, *Social Enterprise: Scaling New Heights*, Action Plan Draft 0.8 Version for DA Committee November 2006, p. 9.

38. DTI, *Social Enterprise: a strategy for success*, July 2002, p. 20.

39. Ibid.

40. Cabinet Office/Office of the Third Sector, *Social Enterprise Action Plan: Scaling New Heights*, November 2006, p. 62.

41. Scaling New Heights, p. 38.

42. Ibid.

43. Capacitybuilders is an arm's-length implementation body implementing the Government's Change Up Programme, itself set up to support voluntary and community organisations.

44. Community Investment Tax Relief gives individual and corporate investors in Community Finance Development Initiatives (CDFIs) 5 per cent tax relief on their investments, each year for five years.

45. 'Clawback' is a common way of ensuring that monies which have paid as grants are used appropriately. A condition of the grant gives the funding body a charge over the grant-aided asset and may require that the funder receives a percentage of the proceeds (the clawback) from any sale of the asset.

46. GHK, *Social Enterprise: An International Literature Review*, a report submitted to SBS/SEnU March 2006, p. 5.

47. COM (1997) 241 final of 6 June 1997 'Promoting the Role of Voluntary Organisations and Foundations in Europe'.

48. See *Local Development and Employment Initiatives: An Investigation in the European Union*, SEC564/95.

49. DPs are strategic partnerships bringing together geographical and sectoral representatives who agree on a common work programme to meet EQUAL's objectives.

50. GHK, *Social Enterprise: An International Literature Review*, a report submitted to SBS/SEnU March 2006, p. 9.

51. COM (2005) 141 final of 12 April 2005. Quoted in GHK ibid, p. 9.

52. J. Kendall, Third Sector European Policy: Organisations Between Market and State, the Policy Process and the EU, TSEP Working Paper No. 7, London 2005.

53. As reported in GHK, *Social Enterprise: An International Literature Review*, a report submitted to SBS/SEnU March 2006, p. 7.
54. Ibid.
55. Ibid., p. 8.
56. Ibid.
57. Ibid., p. 66 et sec.
58. 'The European Observatory for SMEs, Sixth Report Executive Summary', EIM Zoetemeer (1999), p. 14.
59. The DIES is the French Interdepartmental Delegation for Social Innovation and the Social Economy. Established in 1981, it serves to create a favourable policy environment for the associative sector.
60. 'The European Observatory for SMEs, Sixth Report Executive Summary' EIM Zoetermeer (1999), p. 14.
61. GHK, *Social Enterprise: An International Literature Review*, a report submitted to SBS/SEnU March 2006, p. 62.
62. C. Gunn, *Third Sector Development: Making up for the Market* (USA, Cornell University, 2004), p. viii and p. 2.
63. P. Lloyd, 'Rethinking the Social Economy'. A paper based on a Forum sponsored by the Belfast Local Strategy Partnership and The Queen's University of Belfast (January 2006), p. 7 and 8.
64. Based on GHK, *Review of the Social Enterprise Strategy*, a final report submitted by GHK to SBS London (2005).

The Impact of the Third Sector: Benefits, Audits and Evaluations

9

Key Concepts

This chapter covers

- the range of benefits the third sector might deliver;
- how those benefits might be measured;
- some indications of the scale of the third sector;
- some of the issues associated with evaluations of government promotion of the third sector, and some of their findings.

Learning objectives

By the end of this chapter the reader should

- understand the variety of impacts attributed to the third sector;
- be aware of some methods suggested for auditing the impact of third sector organisations;

(cont'd)

- appreciate the indicated scale of the third sector;
- understand some of the issues involved in evaluations of government efforts to promote the third sector, and some possible limitations of their findings.

Introduction

As Chapter 1 indicated, some economic textbooks, even modern ones, still give the impression that there are only two significant sectors in a mixed economy: the private sector and the public sector. Yet, as Chapter 2 shows, for as long as there have been distinct private and public sectors, there has also been a third sector.

Attempts have been made, under the so-called 'communist systems', to produce a society in which all activity was public sector activity, done through or by the state, but these have not lasted. 'Market' economies with private sectors, in some form or other, have proved to be more efficient at co-ordinating many aspects of human endeavour than single sector 'command' economies. Indeed communist societies still had private sector activity, although it might have been illegal, or at least unofficial, and they still had some third sector activity carried out neither by the state nor purely for personal gain. At the other extreme, even the most capitalistic of societies have had third sector activity in their economies.

Third sector activity is clearly old and it clearly endures, but why? Why do we seem to need it and why do people engage in it? What impact does it have and what benefits does it deliver? Does it deliver the benefits that are claimed of it and does it justify the variety of support provided for it? To try to answer such questions this chapter considers some of the things that third sector organisations are at least reported to do and considers how they might be 'audited' to assess their contribution. It also considers what is sometimes expected of the sector from its governmental supporters, how such support programmes might be evaluated and what is known about their impact.

Benefits

What does the third sector deliver?

Asking what the third sector delivers is a bit like asking what the public sector delivers: it depends on both where the question is being put and who is being asked to respond. That is because the relative strengths of different parts of the third sector differ from country to country and, within countries, can differ from region to region. It is also because different people have different views on what the third sector and its components can, or should, do. Nevertheless the list below attempts to indicate the wide range of things that have, at one time, or in one place, or another, been attributed to the third sector or to one of its components.

The list is not exhaustive and some of the things listed address more than one of the impact areas under which they are categorised. For instance, the creation of jobs has both an economic and a social benefit but, to avoid a very long list, is only listed under one of them. Also, if the whole is considered to be more than the sum of its parts, such a list might be considered to be an unwarranted disaggregation of the sector. The format of the list, however, is not intended to suggest that the third sector can be split into separate impacts but that the totality of its impact can be considered to have aspects of all the things listed (see Illustration 9.1).

Illustration 9.1   The Contribution of Social Enterprise – A View from the Social Enterprise Coalition

Social enterprises are dynamic businesses with a social purpose, working all around the UK and internationally to deliver lasting social and environmental change. They operate across an incredibly wide range of industries and sectors, from childcare and social housing to fair trade and farmers' markets.

The social enterprise sector is extremely diverse, encompassing co-operatives, development trusts, community enterprises, housing associations, football supporters' trusts, social firms and leisure trusts, among others.

As innovators, social enterprises are often at the leading edge, pioneering ground-breaking ways of doing business and meeting new challenges. Their added value comes from the engagement of stakeholders and the way in which profit is used to maximise social and environmental benefits.

Social enterprise offers the government a range of solutions to meet its goals – whether on sustainable economic development or public service reform.

A business model

Social enterprise is a distinct way of doing business that seeks to meet social and environmental needs rather than maximising shareholder value. It has a role in creating wealth and employment and in enhancing choice and diversity in a more plural, resilient and sustainable economy.

Thriving communities

Social enterprises are able to harness the power of local communities – catalysing regeneration and promoting active citizenship. Development trusts have pioneered sustainable

Illustration 9.1   (cont'd)

approaches to development and an increasing number of housing associations are taking an enterprising approach. Housing co-operatives have a proven track record in community empowerment and cost-effective property management, and in rural areas community-owned shops and pubs are vital to locking in long-term prosperity.

An essential element of many of these approaches is community ownership of buildings and land. It can transform even the most struggling community – energising local people and providing the long-term foundation for enterprise and renewal. By locking in land value, community ownership can support the development of mixed-income housing, vital local services and public space, enabling community involvement in local planning decisions and preventing people and businesses being priced out of an area.

Public services

There is an ongoing debate around increasing choice through diversity of provision and how to make services more centred on the needs of the individual and local communities. So far the discussion has mostly been split between improving direct provision by the state through additional resources and targets, and the introduction of private companies who can bring market-based efficiencies. What has been largely missing from this debate is the role that social enterprise can play in providing quality services that are truly value for money.

By combining the entrepreneurial drive of a business approach with a public service ethos, social enterprise brings together the best of the public and private sectors. The debate around choice needs to focus on social enterprise as a practical new way to deliver public services.

Within a number of key areas – for example childcare, social care and health – there is the potential for social enterprises to play a bigger and more strategic role delivering public services. They are certainly not the only solutions social enterprise has to offer, but they represent areas where a fresh look at service delivery could reap real rewards.

Education and entrepreneurship

Entrepreneurship is a set of life skills such as self-confidence, self-reliance and the ability to bring resources together to innovate and create change. Enterprise teaching in schools must be about developing these skills rather than a narrow focus on 'teaching business', and should incorporate social entrepreneurship and social enterprise into the mainstream enterprise curriculum.

Incentives to work

Many social enterprises, for example social firms (businesses set up specifically to create employment for disabled people), help disadvantaged groups into meaningful work.

> ### Illustration 9.1   (cont'd)
>
> Other social enterprises, particularly those in disadvantaged areas, are set up by people on benefits as a way of creating community benefit and employment. However, in many instances 'traps' within the benefits system, particularly for those receiving incapacity benefits, actively discourage people from entering employment or from donating their time voluntarily in order to set up a social enterprise.
>
> Research shows that people with a financial cushion are more likely to apply for a job in contrast to those living from week to week. Therefore a benefit system that works in favour of those who choose to move towards employment is a vital component of any attempt to increase levels of employment among disadvantaged and marginalised groups.
>
> *Source*: Based on Social Enterprise Coalition, *There's More to Business: A Manifesto for Social Enterprise*, www.socialenterprise.org.uk, accessed 15 October 2007.

Within the third sector there are organisations which have

- An *economic impact*, through

  - producing goods and services;
  - fostering enterprise and competitiveness;
  - creating employment, often focusing particularly on the socially excluded;
  - training people and assisting them into employment;
  - facilitating economic/social development by providing grants (e.g. from foundations) and low-cost loans (e.g. from credit unions – see Illustration 9.2).

- A *social impact*, through

  - supplementing the public sector social services and addressing welfare state problems by, for instance, providing affordable childcare, domiciliary and day-care;
  - fostering innovations in services and often playing a pathfinder role in the introduction of new or improved services later taken up by the public sector;
  - providing an alternative social service business model;
  - aiding regeneration by reaching areas and people other initiatives cannot or do not reach;
  - fostering social inclusion and social cohesion and the building of social capital;
  - enhancing civic involvement through the use of volunteers.

Illustration 9.2   The Potential of Credit Unions in the UK

The Credit Unions Taskforce was established by HM Treasury in 1998 with a remit to explore ways in which banks and building societies can work more closely with credit unions; increase their effectiveness; look at ways to widen the range of services provided to credit union customers; and encourage the expansion of the movement. The Taskforce noted the small size of the sector compared to other countries, the small scale of organisations, the lack of financial management skills and the absence of national co-ordinating machinery. The Taskforce also found that there had been an opening up of the sector when a Deregulation Order came into force on 1 September 1996 and in 1998 when the Government proposed a package of measures designed to lift some of the restrictions in the Credit Union Act 1979. These were designed to allow credit unions to borrow money from banks and other credit unions.

The UK credit unions are now classified under two types: type 1 is comprised of the smaller credit unions, while type 2 includes the larger organisations. Since November 2006 many type 2 credit unions have been authorised to offer their members debit card accounts. For the first time this will enable credit unions members to obtain funds from any Link Automatic Till Machine (ATM).

The Task Force highlighted the potential of credit unions to help areas in decline. It noted that in around 10% of households there is no one with a bank account and this affects about 2.5–3.5 million adults, virtually all of whom are outside the labour market. Financial exclusion is therefore an important part of social exclusion and the Taskforce suggested that credit unions could help because:

*   They are open to lower income groups in particular.
*   They instil in their members a sense of self-reliance and an understanding of the virtues of thrift.
*   They provide low-cost credit.

Source: Based on *Credit Unions of the Future: Taskforce Report* (London: HM Treasury, 1999 © Crown Copyright), pp. 2–3.

*   A *local impact*, through
    *   contributing to enterprise in areas with low levels of private entrepreneurship;
    *   creating and managing workspace;
    *   facilitating community ownership of land, buildings and other resources, putting them to community use;
    *   providing local facilities, such as shops and pubs for remote communities;
    *   re-using old buildings and thus preserving parts of local history which might otherwise be redeveloped;
    *   providing local public amenity space.

- An *environmental* or *cultural/artistic/sporting impact*, through

  - promoting and practicing environmental sustainability;
  - operating recycling schemes when there isn't enough financial return for the private sector;
  - facilitating artistic activity;
  - facilitating sports activity.

- An *educational impact*, through

  - providing mainstream education in third sector schools and colleges;
  - complementing traditional approaches and subjects (e.g. Young Enterprise).

- A *political impact*, through

  - advocating, or helping to deliver, a fairer society, democratic participation, and involved citizenship;
  - facilitating greater stakeholder engagement and pluralism (see Illustration 9.3);
  - providing an alternative economic approach and showing that business does not have to be solely concerned with profit maximisation and personal enrichment;
  - providing a counter culture (or a way of reintroducing socialism?);
  - providing an alternative paradigm. (Do some people seek the support of the third sector in their aspirations to reduce the power of either the private or the public sectors?)

- A *moral* and *ethical impact*, through

  - promoting religion and spirituality, a more caring society and/or the development of a set of moral and/or ethical values;
  - enhancing the philosophy of giving in society as opposed to receiving.

Illustration 9.3   Community Bodies 'Are More Engaging'

An evaluation of the Northern Rock Foundation's Money and Jobs grant programme, said that disadvantaged people involved in the programme are getting richer 'both financially and in terms of personal wellbeing'. It also said that community-based organisations are 'in general, better at this engagement than statutory agencies and therefore make a distinct and valuable contribution to social and economic provision, including current government labour market policies'.

Source: Based on a report on www.thirdsector.co.uk, 21 August 2007.

- A *personal impact*, through

  - helping their founders and operators to achieve personal goals and to 'self-actualise'.

Audits of the third sector

Tools for measuring the impact of social economy enterprises are at an early stage of development. Some tools are being developed and assessed – but they are not being used by many organisations. Also there are many different aspects of impact to be measured which cannot easily be reduced to a single common dimension in the way that private sector returns can all be summarised in terms of money.

In many cases there is no legal requirement to produce and declare social accounts. An exception in the UK is the case of Community Interest Companies (CICs) (see Illustration 5.1), which must file an annual CIC report with their accounts to show that they are still satisfying the Community Interest Test. Otherwise all that is available are the relatively few voluntarily published social reports and/or accounts, and even these have not been consistently reviewed and summarised. Furthermore, many of them are not produced by third sector organisations but by private sector businesses to fulfil a commitment to demonstrate corporate social responsibility.

Other researchers have also found little quantitative data and have relied instead on anecdotal evidence. For instance, under the heading 'evidence for impact' Smallbone et al., in their 2001 report on researching social enterprise, referred to case studies, not statistics:

> Part of the case for encouraging and supporting social enterprises is based on their wider social contribution which can include helping to reduce social exclusion, encouraging environmentally friendly practices, contributing to community regeneration and offering work and educational experiences to young people. This can be illustrated with *selected examples* drawn from our enterprise case studies[1] (our italics).

Despite this lack of information there are a number of brochures and other documents produced for or about the third sector by bodies wishing to advance its interests. These, however, are often designed to promote the sector, rather than to evaluate it, and as a result sometimes appear to be subjective in their assessment.

Benefit audits

Chapter 5, in the section entitled 'Measures of success', looked at some of the methods by which individual social enterprises, and other third sector organisations, can try to measure their success. Some of those methods have been referred to as social auditing but, unlike financial auditing, they often cover the initial accounting for success, rather than the subsequent verification of that accounting which is the role of the financial auditing function.

Those measures of success are often like the financial accounts of a business in that they assess what the organisation has delivered rather than its value as an investment. There are, though, some techniques which do look at this additional dimension of what an organisation's backers might have got in return for the resources which they put into the organisation. An example is Social Return on Investment (SROI), which was pioneered in the 1990s by the Roberts Enterprise Development Fund, a San Francisco-based venture philanthropy fund, as a means to illustrate the value generated through an investment in its programmes.[2] It has been taken up by the new economics foundation (nef), based in London, which describes SROI as an innovative approach which 'places stakeholders – the people that matter – at the heart of the measurement process' and 'shows how social and environmental outcomes translate into tangible monetary value, helping organisations and investors of all kinds to see a fuller picture of the benefits that flow from their investment of time, money and other resources. This investment can then be seen in terms of the "return" or the value created for individual, communities, society or the environment.'[3]

The approach of nef involves assessing the net present value of the benefits produced, allowing for the 'deadweight' of what would have happened anyway, and looking at the ratio between that net present value and the net present value of the investment used to create it. As nef's guide says, 'those who invest in an organisation can learn more about how their input directly contributes to social value creation'.[4] This is, however, a relatively recent development and, while the nef guide includes a case study of SROI application, it does not yet appear to have been widely used and there is not a compilation of audits using it upon which a wider assessment of the overall value created by the sector might be based.

The scale of the third sector

One overall aspect of the third sector, relevant to the amount of benefit it delivers, and for which some assessment attempts have been made, is its size. Earlier chapters have on occasion given some indications of its scale in particular countries, or of the scale of some of its components. What follows is a wider collection of statistics, almost all about the social economy, from different parts of the world. The UK example also serves to illustrate how difficult it is to get reliable figures as it shows significant differences between the figures reported by different government sources for the same year.

UK

Jeremy Kendall, in his book on the voluntary sector, included an assessment that in 1995 there were nearly 1.5 million full-time equivalent employees in the

UK's 'broad non-profit sector', and an additional 1.6 million full-time equivalent volunteers.[5] On a narrower basis the Small Business Service (SBS) in 2005 published *A Survey of Social Enterprises Across the UK*.[6] This survey followed an earlier DTI exercise to assess the feasibility of mapping social enterprise which concluded that while social enterprises may take a range of legal forms, companies limited by guarantee and Industrial and Provident Societies were the most popular. Therefore the survey, instead of claiming to describe the total population of social enterprises, focused only on these two legal forms but excluded some on the basis that their Standard Industrial Classification meant that they were unlikely to include much social enterprise activity.

Despite its shortcomings this survey was ground-breaking in its attempt to survey social enterprises across the UK and appeared to be the most complete survey to date. Among its findings were the following:

- There were around 15,000 social enterprises in the UK registered as companies limited by guarantee or Industrial and Provident Societies.

- In terms of the overall business population that meant that social enterprises accounted for 1.2 per cent of all enterprises with employees in the UK.

- The annual turnover of these social enterprises was just under £18 billion approximately, which was just under 1 per cent of the turnover of all UK businesses.

- These social enterprises employed 475,000 people, of whom two-thirds were employed full-time. A further 300,000 people worked for the social enterprises on a volunteer basis.

- The typical social enterprise employed 10 people. Almost half (49 per cent) employed fewer than 10, 38 per cent employed between 10 and 49, 11 per cent between 50 and 249, and 2 per cent employed 250 or more.

Nevertheless in 2006 the UK government's social enterprise action plan stated that there were an estimated 55,000 social enterprise across the country and that they had an annual turnover of more than £27 billion and contributed more than £8 billion a year to GDP.[7] These figures were repeated in the UK government's 2007[8] report setting out its vision for the third sector, and which added that the estimate that there were 55,000 social enterprises was for the year 2005 and that they had then accounted for around 5 per cent of all businesses with employees at that time (see also Illustration 9.4). It also indicated that in England and Wales at the end of 2006 there were 168,000 registered charities (and an estimated 110,000 unregistered charities), and that at the end of 2005 there were over 8100 registered Industrial and Provident Societies.

The UK government's 2007 report also indicated that in 2006 there were 567 registered credit unions with just under half a million members. The Association of British Credit Unions Ltd (ABCUL) reported that in 2005 it has almost 400 credit unions as members and they provided financial services to

---

Illustration 9.4   Other UK Figures

Under the headline of 'Third sector workforce expands', a news bulletin reported that the UK Voluntary Sector Workforce Almanac 2007, published by the Workforce Hub, showed that the sector grew from 483,000 employees in 1996 to 611,000 by the end of 2005 – an increase of 26 per cent. The rise, it said, means that the voluntary sector accounts for 2 per cent of all UK employees.[9]

This was extended in the UK Civil Society Almanac 2008, published by NCVO, (which, as well as indicating that in 2005/06 the UK paid voluntary sector workforce was 611,000, indicated that this was part of a total paid workforce headcount of 1,367,000 in 865,000 civil society organisations in the UK, which between them had a total income of £108.9 billion.[10]

---

over 404,000 people. Membership of ABCUL credit unions had trebled since 1995, when it stood at 130,000. In the ten-year period, money saved by credit union members has increased from £57 million to £380 million and the amount of money on loan grew from £54 million to £353 million, a similar sixfold increase. The average ABCUL credit union member had £439 in shares in 1995 and over £939 in 2005.

In mid-1999 the Treasury indicated that the structure of the credit union movement in the UK was as shown in Table 9.1:

Table 9.1   The structure of the credit union movement in the UK

Region	No of credit unions	Members	Assets (£ in million)
England & Wales	524	130,000	69
Scotland	135	95,000	55
GB Total	659	225,000	124
Northern Ireland	174	267,000	321
UK Total	833	492,000	445

Source: *Credit Unions of the Future: Taskforce Report* (London: HM Treasury, 1999), p. 4.

Europe

The European Commission estimated in 2007 that around 10 million people were employed in the social economy in the European Union, that European co-operatives had a total of 78 million members and that at least 109 million Europeans were insured with mutual insurers.[11]

CECOP (European Confederation of Workers' Co-operatives, Social Co-operatives, and Participative Enterprises) is an international non-profit association with its headquarters in Brussels representing small and medium-sized worker-controlled enterprises across 42 member countries of the Council of Europe. CECOP's members include 37 national and regional federations of co-operative enterprises representing around 83,000 enterprises employing 1.3 million workers.[12]

France

In 2006 it was estimated that in France[13]

- The social economy employs some 7 per cent of the workforce.
- There are some 1.6 million associations, of which probably 700,000 are active and of which 200,000 are recognised as being of public utility. They employ 1.3 million people, which is 5 per cent of the working population. Half the jobs are in the health and care sector.
- The 6000 non-financial co-operatives have 3 million members and employ some 180,000 people. This includes the 1500 workers' co-operatives employing 23,000 people. The four co-operative banks employ a further 130,000 people.
- The health mutuals number over 900 and employ some 57,000 people. Insurance mutuals number 13 and employ 21,000 people.
- There are 2500 work integration enterprises which offer around 38,000 full-time equivalent integration places.

USA

The third sector was reported in 2004 to be the fastest-growing part of the US economy, and makes up 10 per cent of economic activity (somewhat more than that on the basis of employment and somewhat less than that on the basis of the value of economic transactions).[14] A study published in 2002, for instance, found that in New York, the third sector accounted for 11.5 per cent of economic activity in the city and 14 per cent of its employment and that, during the 1990s, non-profit organisations were the fastest-growing source of jobs and their share of employment outranked that of the city's financial, insurance and real-estate sectors.[15] Other indications of the scale of the third sector in the US are given in Table 9.2.

The development of credit unions in the USA was fastest in the industrialising north-east, especially Massachusetts, at the start of the twentieth century. By 1925, 15 States had passed credit union laws and by 1935, 39 States had legislation covering 3300 organisations with 641,800 members. During the formative years of the movement in the USA the formation of leagues enabled stronger development by pooling financial resources, organisational skills and legal services. The Credit Union National Association (CUNA) was formed in 1934 and

Table 9.2   The third sector in the US economy

Type of organisation	Indications of scale
Public benefit and service providers	
Health care	In 1987 85% of medical and surgical hospitals and 64% of home health care services were nonprofits.
Education	Nonprofits account for 69% of four-year colleges.
Social service providers	By some estimates nonprofits account for 90% of social service employment.
Civic organisations	From 1977 to the mid-1990s the number of organisations grew by 68% and employment in them by 48%.
Art and culture organisations	Art and Culture Organisations form 8% of nonprofit organisations.
Religious organisations	There are approximately 200 religious denominations and religious organisations make up approximately a quarter of public-serving nonprofits.
Research and testing organisations	Relatively small in number.
Funding intermediaries	
Foundations	
Member-serving nonprofits	
Labor unions	
Business and professional organisations	
Political organisations	
Political action committees	
Mutual benefit and co-operative organisations	
Credit Unions	Approximately 30% of Americans are credit union members.
Mutual Insurance Companies	
Consumers' Co-operatives	
Workers' Co-operatives	
Agricultural Co-operatives	

Source: Adapted material from C. Gunn, *Third Sector Development: Making up for the Market,* Copyright © 2004 by Cornell University. Used by permission of the publisher, Cornell University Press.

developed a Mutual Insurance Society, which is now one of the largest in the country with assets of more than $1.5 billion.[16] By 2005 in the United States, credit unions had a membership of 86 million and they can apply to the National Credit Union Administration for Low-Income Credit Union (LICU) status. LICU status enables the credit unions to benefit from national programmes to build capacity in disadvantaged areas. As of the end of 2005, the National Credit Union Administration insured more than $515 billion in deposits at 8695 non-profit co-operative US credit unions.[17]

Table 9.3 Some figures for the Canadian economy

Sector:	Private sector	Social economy			Public sector	
Organisation type:	For-profit business	Common interest SEEs	Public service SEEs	Other NGOs	Near government organisations	Government organisations
Number of Employees:		2 million, plus volunteers, in 2003				
		155,389 in 2004	740,000 in 1999			821,000 in 2004
Share of GDP:			2.5% in 1999, excluding volunteers		4.3% in 1999, excluding volunteers	
	87.4% in 1999			0.9% in 1999		5.8% in 1999

Source: Canada, PRI (Policy Research Initiative), *What We Need to Know About the Social Economy: A Guide for Policy Research* (Ottawa: PRI, 2005), p. 4.

Canada

A rough estimate recorded in 2005 showed that the social economy accounted for about 2.6 per cent of the total Canadian economy, which was larger than the contribution of aerospace (0.6 per cent), mining (1.0 per cent) or the pulp and paper industries (1.3 per cent) and about the same size as that of oil and gas extraction (2.5 per cent)[18] (and see Table 9.3).

Evaluations

Audit techniques, such as SROI, try to indicate to 'investors' in third sector organisations what social or other benefits those organisations have delivered as a result of their investments. Among the most significant contributors to the third sector have been governments and their interest in the sector and their methods of involvement are described in Chapter 8. Governments, however, have generally sought to promote not just individual third sector organisations but the overall sector, or at least sub-sectors within it such as the social economy. Further, while governments might be pleased to see the general benefits which the sector delivers, they have usually contributed in order to achieve specific objectives such as the delivery of certain services or increases in employment in disadvantaged areas.

Audit techniques designed to identify the range of benefits delivered by individual organisations are not then particularly helpful to governments promoting an overall sector in order to achieve specific benefits. It is not just a question of whether governments get a social return on their investments, but whether, if there is a return, it is the return they wanted, and whether it is an adequate return for the investment of public money. They therefore carry out evaluations to indicate what they get for their money.

Issues around evaluation methodology

Evaluations are carried out to assess such initiatives to see what they have achieved and/or how they might be improved. Evaluations are not, however, an easy or an exact science, if indeed they are a science and not an art.

Evaluation has been defined as 'the retrospective analysis of a project, programme, or policy to assess how successful or otherwise it has been, and what lessons can be learnt for the future'.[19] This definition indicates two aspects of evaluations: the assessment of success or otherwise, which looks primarily at the impact of a project, programme or policy; and the lessons to be learnt, for instance to improve delivery of a project, programme or policy, which will look primarily at their processes. These two aspects of evaluations have also been described in the following ways:

1. *Improving and Proving.* Evaluation, it has been said, has two primary aims:

   - an *improving* and *learning* aim to provide information that will help those involved to learn and so improve the design, operation and outcomes of policy initiatives;

   - a *proving* aim to examine what difference the policy initiative has made to the individuals or firms or to the wider economic and social parameters it seeks to influence.[20]

2. *Formative and Summative.* Formative evaluation is undertaken to provide information that will be used to improve a programme; summative evaluation is evaluation used to form a summary judgement about how a programme operated.[21]

Overall, it is the impact, proving and summative aspect of evaluations which indicates if programmes are achieving their purposes. However, conducting such evaluations is not easy:

- Assessing whether a programme achieved its purposes is only possible where that purpose has been clearly stated and clear impact targets have been specified.

- While the process of delivering a programme can be observed as it happens, it can then take some time before the subsequent impact will become apparent. Despite this, for reasons such as a requirement to justify further funding or because they have to be paid for in a limited budget period, there is often an incentive to commission evaluations before sufficient impact time has elapsed.

- Assessing the real impact of a programme requires an understanding of what is going on and insight into the nature of the relevant cause and effect.

Other reasons why evaluations of public sector programmes might not be available or reliable have been indicated by Curran, who suggested that, at least in the field of small business policy, evaluations have been of two main kinds:

- evaluations sponsored by government funding departments and/or agencies delivering the policy, conducted by private sector for-profit bodies. Most small business support evaluation in the UK is probably of this type and often the results never enter the public domain;
- evaluations by independent (usually academic) researchers on a not-for-profit basis, sponsored by other than those funding or delivering the initiative. The results are normally made public with the aim of promoting constructive discussion.

The distinction between the two, according to Curran is important. 'The first kind is much more likely to be favourable to the policy or programme than the second kind. Where those conducting the evaluation are dependent on the initiator or deliverer for their fees and future similar work, there will be pressures to be less critical. This is less likely if evaluation is by researchers not reliant on policy makers or deliverers for their funding and the results are open to peer scrutiny. One result of such a poor record is that generally small business initiatives receive more favourable recognition for promoting small businesses, employment and economic performance than they merit.'[22] An official view on policy evaluation is given in Illustration 9.5.

Illustration 9.5   An Official View on Policy Evaluation

Assessing the impact of a policy is usually done through a policy evaluation. The UK government's guide to appraisal and evaluation (the Green Book) describes evaluation as 'the retrospective analysis of a project, programme, or policy to assess how successful or otherwise it has been, and what lessons can be learnt for the future. The terms "policy evaluation" and "post-project evaluation" are often used to describe evaluation in those two areas.'[23]

Evaluation, according to the Green Book,

examines the outturn of a project or policy. When carried out it adds value by providing lessons from experience to help future project management or development of a specific policy. It may also contribute to the quality of wider policy debate. ... The evaluation itself should normally follow this sequence:

i.   Establish exactly what is to be evaluated and how the past outturns can be measured.

ii. Choose alternative states of the world and/or alternative management decisions as counterfactuals. (The decision on exactly what should be compared

---

Illustration 9.5   (cont'd)

with what needs clear thinking... The outturn of any complex activity will never be exactly as projected in advance. However the reasons for the outturn being in some respects better or worse than expected may be attributable to the 'state of the world'. Or it may be attributable to actions under the control of the responsible body.)

iii. Compare the outturn with the target outturn, and with the effects of the chosen alternative states of the world and/or management decisions.

iv. Present the results and recommendations.

v. Disseminate and use the results and recommendations.[24]

The core of an evaluation should be the extent of the net benefit, or *additionality*, attributable to the intervention in question. Implicit in the foregoing, however, are two concepts that are often ignored in evaluation studies: the *deadweight* and *displacement* effects. They have the effect of reducing the net benefit of interventions. *Multiplier* effects have the opposite effect. They enhance the benefits and should also be considered. *Effectiveness, efficiency* and *economy* are measures of different aspects of the process.

Additionality. This is the measure of the net benefit: the benefit which accrued as a result of the measure, whether intended or not, which would not otherwise have accrued.

Deadweight. This is a measure of 'what would have happened anyway' without the measure. Because of deadweight, even the direct effects alone of intervention are often not easy to ascertain. It may be possible to show that an enterprise has received assistance and has subsequently improved, but to what extent is that improvement due to other factors and would have happened anyway, even had there been no intervention?

Displacement. This is a measure of 'how much of the gain in one area is offset by losses elsewhere'. It may be that an enterprise directly benefits from intervention and increases its employment as a result. However, if the employment in another enterprise is reduced because the first enterprise wins the contract, the total employment between the two may not increase and therefore overall there may be no benefit. The increase in activity in one merely displaces activity in another, albeit the quality of the jobs may change. While, superficially, more solid enterprises may appear to be beneficial, this is so only if there is net social or economic benefit as opposed to redistributing existing benefits. (In addition, the benefits of a measure should exceed the cost of the measure.)

Multiplier effects. There can be additional benefits from the indirect or side effects of intervention. If an increase in activity in a directly affected enterprise results in an increase in activity in another enterprise, for instance because it is a subcontractor, that is a beneficial *multiplier* effect, which increases the extent of the additionality.

Illustration 9.5   (cont'd)

Effectiveness, efficiency and economy. This is a trio of measures concerned with value for money. *Effectiveness* is the extent to which an intervention achieved its aims; *efficiency* measures the amount of direct output that the inputs achieved; and *economy* is concerned with the cost of those inputs.

Source: Based on chapter 13 of S. Bridge, K. O'Neill and S. Cromie, *Understanding Enterprise, Entrepreneurship and Small Business* (Basingstoke: Palgrave Macmillan, 2003).

What is expected of the third sector?

Evaluations of the third sector therefore need to start with some idea of what was expected of the project, programme or policy being evaluated, which will in turn be linked to what is expected of the sector itself, or of components of it. At least three approaches to this aspect of the third sector have been suggested in earlier chapters:

The paradigm approach

In Chapter 4, in the section on different paradigms, it is suggested that there are three broad choices for what people might expect of the third sector and in particular of the social economy:

- Two of these choices see it as a source of benefits such as jobs and welfare provision:
  - One of them, in an economic/entrepreneurship approach, sees social economy organisations as 'businesses' that can assist community regeneration. It puts an emphasis on their financial sustainability.
  - The other is a socio-economic policy approach which puts less emphasis on self-sufficiency and sees the sector as 'patching up' the inadequacies of the welfare state.
- A third approach is a political/ideological approach which envisages a social economy sector significantly strong to lever institutional change and to promote more democratic structures and citizen participation in decision-making.

Therefore, if a judgement is to be made about the effectiveness/impact of the sector, it is important to be clear about what ambitions are set for it. For instance, each of the following options offers a different framework within which to assess the impact of the social economy:

- Is it an attempt to produce an 'alternative business model' – a better business as the UK government would describe it?

- Is it a temporary or cut-rate mechanism for plastering over weaknesses in the welfare state?

- Is it to produce an improved model for better integration of service delivery to those in need?

- Is it a 'whole society' approach which ultimately aims to create a new political-cultural landscape in which democratic participation, citizenship, trust, integrity and respect are more fully embedded?

A policy framework approach

A policy framework by which to understand the related objectives, approaches, themes, rationale, instruments and measures for the UK government's approach to the social economy is described in Chapter 8. This suggests that, in attempting to assess the impact of the social economy in an economy/society as a whole, whether driven by government or other support bodies, an evaluation might consider one or more of the following:

- the impact of the social economy on the ultimate objectives of a more successful economy or a fairer society;

- the social economy's contribution to political drivers such as generating social inclusion and cohesion, improving public services and improving economic competitiveness;

- the extent to which the specified success measures, such as greater awareness of the sector, more and better social enterprises, and fewer barriers to growth, have been attained;

- the achievement of the sector in terms of the performance indicators for each of the policy instruments such as new legal forms, greater financial support, more success in its tendering for government contracts, or more, louder and coherent voices speaking for the sector;

- any specific indicators specified in policy documents. For instance, the UK government has chosen to consider change in the number and quality of social enterprises, greater awareness of the sector and evidence of fewer barriers to growth.

An expected benefits approach

A third approach to assessing the impact of the third sector is to benchmark its performance against what many of its advocates surmise as its particular benefits to an economy or society at large. These benefits are described in Chapter 1 and summarised in Chapter 8. They include

- the provision of goods, services and social benefits which the public sector does not adequately provide;

- the provision of jobs for people who might not otherwise be employed;

- the fostering of enterprise (and economic competitiveness);
- a means for addressing some problems of the welfare state;
- the creation and retention of social surplus;
- the promotion of environmental sustainability, or ethical operations;
- the creation of social capital and social cohesion;
- other development help;
- a mechanism for a counter-culture;
- the ability to reach parts that other initiatives cannot reach, in particular in tackling disadvantage. As Chapter 7 indicates, the social economy, and in particular the social enterprises within it have been seen as having a key role to play in regeneration and social cohesion strategies.

In terms of assessing the impact of the sector, however, the problem is also made more difficult because

- Not all of the benefits suggested apply to all third sector organisations. A clear perception is needed of what each segment of the sector is expected to deliver.
- There is recognition that the third sector not only complements some public sector provision where it adds value, but also leads the way in other aspects of meeting the needs of disadvantaged people and it goes where public provision may follow subsequently. Thus it has a 'pathfinder' role and, through the learning gained by an organisation's initiation of new service delivery, new or improved public provision may develop. So what may appear initially as experimental and offering little tangible benefits may be the forerunner of considerable societal gain. Indeed the gains may often differ from those originally anticipated (making it sometimes inappropriate to assess impact only against a predetermined objective).
- There are, on the other hand, areas where the third sector displays innovation without expectation that the public sector should then seek to complement or replace its services. There is no suggestion, for example, that credit unions, local enterprise agencies or ethical retailers should be the forerunners of state provision (albeit many lessons may be learned which could affect the nature of other pubic sector provision).

The results of evaluations: how effective is government promotion of the third sector?

Broadly speaking, the different approaches summarised above encompass the different reasons governments have for wanting to promote the third sector. Chapter 8 looked at the different ways in which governments have sought to promote, support and encourage the third sector, but to what extent have they got a return for their efforts? It has been suggested that sometimes the subsequently declared targets for government programmes are based on 'anything they happen to hit' but, on other occasions, clear 'SMART'[25] objectives are specified for government-funded projects, and evaluations are then carried out to establish what happened.

What have such evaluations revealed about the effectiveness of government policy in addressing the objectives set for it? In considering the effectiveness of UK government policy Table 8.4 provides a useful starting point as it identifies the UK government's own suggested indicators for judging the success of its policy interventions. The performance indicators suggested in Table 8.4 are not SMART as they are not expressed quantitatively nor bound by timescales. Given the relative lack of knowledge of the sector's starting point, however, it might be argued that attempts at quantification would be inappropriate. Indeed, without previous experience of the efficacy of the interventions and instruments used, quantified outputs could be regarded as meaningless, if not foolish.

Of importance also in any form of evaluation of policy impact is the relationship between success measures/performance indicators and ultimate policy drivers and objectives. In the case of the UK, the policy seeks to achieve, through the social economy in part, a fairer and more prosperous society, although there are different perspectives as to how, and to what extent, the social economy can advance these objectives (see Chapter 4). Is it by making 'better businesses' in the sector which can offer a more cost-effective alternative to the welfare system? Or is it by creating a fully integrated private–third–public sector continuum with the potential to create a different kind of economic system? Those are different means, and evaluations will need to know which one to consider.

In the UK a comprehensive review of the government's social enterprise strategy from 2002–2005 was carried out in 2005 by a firm of consultants on behalf of the (then) DTI. The findings of that review were summarised in 'Scaling New Heights' from which Table 9.4 was derived.

The review report itself reveals a cautious assessment of the progress made and it draws a distinction between 'progress in achieving the outcomes of the social enterprise strategy' and 'the contribution of the social enterprise strategy to the progress made', recognising that there are influences at work other than those led by government through its strategy. It concludes[26] that the social enterprise strategy has resulted in

- putting the sector 'on the map' among policy makers;
- the development of consultative forums (e.g. the Social Enterprise Coalition) which are crucial for a cohesive approach to the sector;
- a common 'jump off' policy for government departments, Devolved Administrations and RDAs;
- better understanding of how social 'enterprise' can deliver social benefit;
- greater legitimisation of the sector in the eyes of other stakeholders arising from the leverage of additional funds.

Table 9.4   The Government's progress report

Issue	Independent review findings
Size of the sector	Respondents reported growth of the sector
Awareness of social enterprise	Increasing awareness of social enterprise, including high-profile examples of successful social enterprises
Business improvement and development	Availability of appropriate support has increased, and new and better tools have been developed to support the sector
Improving profile and credibility of social enterprise	Significant improvement, particularly in social enterprises' profile among policy makers
Underpinning evidence	The volume and quality of data and information on the sector have increased – in particular through the Department of Trade and Industry's Survey of Social Enterprise in the UK

Source: Cabinet Office/Office of the Third Sector, *Social Enterprise Action Plan: Scaling New Heights,* November 2006, p. 21.

However, it is not easy to find hard evidence in the report that the government's own success measures have been attained. The Cabinet Office itself acknowledges this, stating that it is 'difficult to know without baseline figures', but it adds that

- 'The *perception* is that social enterprise is growing.'
- 'There is *more* awareness of it and interest is growing.'
- 'Departments *are beginning* to look at how social enterprise might help them deliver their objectives'[27] (Authors' italics).

The report itself is cautious in its conclusions on the social enterprise strategy outcomes, frequently using qualifying terms.[28] For instance, it notes that

- 'The operating environment has become more conducive for the sector. Nevertheless, improvements in the enabling environment remain patchy. . . . reflecting differential prosecution of the SES objectives across governmental activity.'
- 'The review has identified a strong perception of growth and some concrete evidence of growth. The perceptions of growth may overstate the actual increase in activity because of pre-existing activity being redefined as social enterprise.'

It also notes that while the term 'social enterprise' has become 'a widespread part of the lexicon of government activity across and within, the United Kingdom, awareness does not necessarily imply understanding'.[29] In looking for concrete evidence of achievement against the success measures and performance indicators, there is much more evidence of initiatives having been taken than of proven results in the areas of growth, awareness (as understanding) and removal of growth barriers. In short, it is easier to identify and measure inputs and activities than results at this stage and, to a significant extent, this is because many of the interventions are only beginning to have track records.

That report was relatively positive, as far as it goes, and seems to suggest that the UK government might have made a reasonable start. Others, in looking at different initiatives or at different aspects of policy, have been less complimentary (and two such examples are summarised in Case 9.1). None of these reports however have looked at the longer-term impacts of the initiatives.

That may not be surprising because it does take time both for overall changes in a sector to become apparent and for objective assessments of them to be made. It was, for instance, in the late 1970s and the 1980s that much government attention was paid to small businesses, yet it is only now that independent assessments of the overall effectiveness of that policy are becoming available. Unfortunately the evidence in that case does not seem to be positive.

Five years ago one book which included an introduction to such initiatives still concluded that 'there appears to be no strong body of evidence to say that intervention works, but also there is no clear evidence that it doesn't'.[30] Now, however, a number of commentators have indicated that the balance of the evidence is that the policies have not worked. For instance,

> Our review of business policy instruments...indicates that, with a few exceptions, results are unimpressive – and even for the exceptions, they are fairly marginal in their effects. There is no reason to suppose that if most subsidy and assistance programmes were abolished altogether, it would make a significant difference to the shape and prosperity of the SME sector anywhere.[31]

CASE 9.1

Examples of Critical Assessments of Third Sector Initiatives

Community businesses in Glasgow

Hayton, who commented on the Glasgow Community Business scheme, defined a community business as 'a trading organisation which, through the sale of goods or services, aims to become self sustaining'. Nevertheless he was critical of this experience of promoting community business because of the poor sustainability of the businesses started, the scheme's cost-effectiveness, the type of jobs created, their costs and the extent to which the businesses were causing displacement. He also found that many of the enterprises established were not actually community businesses and classified them into the following four categories:

- community businesses owned and controlled by local residents with a remit to create jobs for local people by setting up commercially viable trading organisations;

- enterprises that were essentially conventional private sector companies with ownership and control vested in those who owned the company rather than the wider community;

CASE 9.1 (cont'd)

- 'Businesses' that were Urban Programme-funded projects that had been set up to run for the duration of the grant;
- 'Businesses' whose objective was to create a service for a community rather than jobs. Effectively these were voluntary sector projects which, after an initial period of public subsidy, were able to survive as they relied upon unpaid labour. They had no intention of becoming commercially viable.

Hayton argued that the pressure on business performance indicators in the scheme emphasised business start-up at the expense of support to existing companies. The lack of a clear business approach to the management and development of community organisations is a theme running through Hayton's critique. His conclusion about the scheme was that

> the main outcomes were that many initiatives that were not community businesses were supported and there was a high failure rate as the emphasis was upon new starts rather than providing development support.... Funding had ... been provided at a far higher level than the support framework was capable of absorbing effectively. The consequence was a failure to deliver. Community business obtained short-term benefits by over-selling but these were at the expense of the concept's longer-term credibility.

As a result of this failure it would appear that, at least in Glasgow, the term 'community business' became discredited to the detriment of the surviving organisations still known as community businesses.[32] Despite that, there are still many successful organisations which could be classified as community businesses.

Source: Based on K. Hayton, 'Scottish Community Business: An Idea that Has Had its Day', *Policy and Politics*, Vol. 28, No. 2 (2000), pp. 195–197.

Rural Development Agency support for Social Enterprises

As indicated earlier in the chapter, much of the UK government's social enterprise strategy has, in England, been implemented principally through the RDAs. It is therefore instructive to examine the lessons to be learnt from the RDAs from their work in supporting the sector.

According to one observer, a major difficulty for the RDAs in seeking mainstream support for the sector was 'revealed as the struggle for *clarity*. Chief Executives and Directors of Strategy found it difficult to grasp what *social enterprise* and *social economy* meant.'[33] They therefore found it difficult to put a value on these sorts of activities as against other more easily measured components of their 'target driven portfolio'.

The RDAs faced these issues at a difficult time for them, as they were facing significant organisational and strategic change. So, despite the impetus given by the publication of *Social Enterprise: a strategy for success*, confusion and complexity was dominant and the situation was compounded by

> ### CASE 9.1 (cont'd)
>
> - 'The DTI emphasis on trading social enterprise (sic) as the proper focus of attention – seeing social enterprises as relatively normal businesses operating in a marketplace.'
>
> - A complementary range of initiatives relating to the creation and development of CDFIs and patient capital initiatives.
>
> - A separate line of development arising from the legacy of EU Programme-driven and other bottom-up and partnership polices, focusing on social enterprise as a tool for regeneration and inclusion with a focus on participation and engagement and with an emphasis on grant-driven development rather than market-driven development, and
>
> - A long-standing interest, in what might be called the old co-operative movement, with an emphasis on democratic management but linked to the DTI social enterprise agenda.
>
> *Source*: Based on C. Stutt Consulting, *Finance for the Social Economy in Northern Ireland*, 2004, p. 39, www.colinstutt.com, accessed 7 October 2007.

Conclusions

While it is clear that some third sector organisations have created jobs and some have launched social innovations, some have contributed to local regeneration and some do represent significant entrepreneurial ventures, the overall extent of that has not been quantified. Similarly, some third sector organisations clearly supplement the public sector social services and address what they perceive to be gaps in its provision, and some have sustained themselves for many years. Yet there are others which have found that they were unable to survive in such roles because they could not generate enough income, from whatever sources they could find, to sustain them. Have third sector organisations levered institutional change and promoted more democratic structures and citizen participation in decision-making? Given that political parties are third sector organisations, it might then be argued that they have done so, but that expectation has been laid specifically on the social economy and social enterprises, and there again there appears to be no clear body of evidence (see Illustration 9.6).

The chapter does not say much either about the effectiveness of government interventions to promote the third sector because, it seems, there is not much to say. This is, at least in part, because recognition of the potential of the sector has only happened relatively recently, and so many of interventions to support it are relatively new and have not had time for their full impact to show. However, experience of other sectors where governments intervene to try to promote growth, such as that of small businesses, suggests that, despite the significant budgets devoted to this work, often there is little meaningful and reliable evaluation of its effects, and where there has been some overall evaluation, it is not indicating a significant impact.

Illustration 9.6   Don't Have Unreasonable Expectations of the Third Sector

In the preface to their book *Placing the Social Economy*, Amin et al state that

> Our evidence shows that it is naive and unreasonable to expect, as does UK, and increasingly EU policy, and increasingly also EU thinking, that the social economy can be a major source of jobs, entrepreneurship, local regeneration, and welfare provision. To do so, runs the risk of marked disappointment, a return to the vagaries of 'good acts' and 'good people' in combating social exclusion and meeting welfare needs, while legitimating cuts in state expenditure or state welfare remit. We find, instead, that social enterprises – in the right places and with the relevant support – have a role to play that is complementary to provision via state and market. As such, they can achieve something genuinely different. The more successful social enterprises analysed in our research are those that open up new possibilities and networks for people who had previously been confined to the limited resources of poor places....Therefore, our perspective is at odds with Third Way/New Labour thinking, which charges social enterprises with creating jobs, tackling social exclusion in the round, providing training, developing local services and local markets, and generally countering the effects of years of disinvestment and disengagement by public and private sectors alike. Furthermore, they are expected to become financially viable. Our findings demonstrate quite clearly that the social economy as it is currently constituted cannot deliver this range of outcomes. This is not only because of its own inherent limitations, but because of the different capacities of people and places to develop social economy activities – the poorest places having the least chance of doing so – and because these many problems cannot be tackled solely at the level of local communities.[34]

That does not mean intervention to support and promote the third sector is not effective, just that it is not possible at this stage to conclude the result of the various efforts is a stronger, bigger, better-organised and better-run, or more productive and contributing sector than would otherwise have been the case.

The Key points of Chapter 9

- There is no single clear assessment of what the third sector achieves. Nevertheless economic, social, local, environmental, cultural, arts, sporting, educational, political, moral, ethical and personal impacts have all been attributed to it.
- Measurement of the impact of the third sector is at an early stage and there is little quantified evidence for the extent of these impacts.

(cont'd)

- Many expectations of the third sector can be divided into three broad approaches: an economic/entrepreneurship approach seeking jobs and welfare provision with an emphasis on financial sustainability, a socio-economic approach also seeking jobs and welfare provision but primarily to compensate for welfare state inadequacies, and a political/ideological approach which seeks to lever institutional change.

- The third sector generally forms a significant part of economies but indications of its scale are partial and sometimes inconsistent.

- Despite significant recent government support for the third sector, or at least for parts of it, there is so far little evidence of what that intervention is achieving.

Questions, Exercises, Essay and Discussion Topics

1. According to what criteria would you seek to assess the impact of the third sector?

2. How would you categorise the impacts of the third sector?

3. Why are the achievements of the third sector difficult to assess?

4. Can the overall impact of the third sector be assessed by gauging its size?

5. What do you think will be the impact of government support for the third sector and why?

SUGGESTIONS FOR FURTHER READING

GHK, *Social Enterprise: An International Literature Review* (a report for the Social Enterprise Unit), March 2006.

References

1. D. Smallbone, M. Evans, I. Ekanem and S. Butters, *Researching Social Enterprise*, report to the Small Business Service RR004/01, July 2001, p. 32.
2. http://sroi.london.edu, accessed 4 April 2008.
3. New economic foundation, *Measuring Real Value: A DIY guide to Social Return on Investment* (www.neweconomics.org), accessed 4 April 2008, p. 2.
4. Ibid., p. 5.
5. J. Kendall, *The Voluntary Sector* (London: Routledge, 2003), p. 22.
6. *A Survey of Social Enterprises Across the UK*, a research report prepared for the Small Business Service by IFF Research Ltd, July 2005 (www.berr.gov.uk/files/file38343.pdf), accessed 25 November 2007.
7. *Social Enterprise Action Plan: Scaling New Heights*, Office of the Third Sector, Cabinet Office, November 2006, p. 3.
8. Cabinet Office, *The Future Role of the Third Sector in Social and Economic Regeneration: Final Report*, HM Treasury, July 2007.

9. Source: www.thirdsector.co.uk/News/DailyBulletin, 31 October 2007.

10. Source: www.ncvo-vol.org.uk/publications, accessed 31 March 2008.

11. http://ec.europe.eu/enterprise/entrepreneurship/social_economy.htm, accessed 3 August 2007.

12. http://www.cecop.coop, accessed 31 October 2007.

13. GHK, *Social Enterprise: An International Literature Review* (a report for the Social Enterprise Unit), March 2006, p. 18.

14. C. Gunn, *Third Sector Development: Making up for the Market* (USA: Cornell University, 2004), p. viii.

15. Ibid.

16. http://en.wikipedia.org/wiki/Credit_union.

17. Current data from http://en.wikipedia.org/wiki/Credit_union.

18. *What We Need to Know About the Social Economy: A Guide for Policy Research*, Canadian Government, Policy Research Initiative (unpublished), July 2005, p. 3.

19. H. M. Treasury, *Appraisal and Evaluation in Central Government: 'The Green Book'* (London: The Stationery Office, 1997), pp. 96–97.

20. R. Scott, Personal correspondence based on the work for Northern Ireland's Department of Economic Development.

21. A. Purdon, C. Lessof, K. Woodfield and C. Bryson, *Research Methods for Policy Evaluation*, Department of Work and Pensions Research Working Paper No. 2 (London: HMSO, 2001), p. iii.

22. J. Curran, 'What is small business policy in the UK for? Evaluation and assessing small business policies', *International Small Business Journal*, Vol. 18, No. 3 (2000), pp. 38–39.

23. H. M. Treasury, *Appraisal and Evaluation in Central Government: 'The Green Book'* (London: The Stationary Office, 1997), pp. 96–97.

24. Ibid., p. 12.

25. Specific, Measurable, Achievable, Relevant and Time-bound.

26. GHK, *Review of the Social Enterprise Strategy*, a final report submitted by GHK to SBS, London (2005), p. 54.

27. www.cabinetoffice.gov.uk/thirdsector.

28. GHK, *Review of the Social Enterprise Strategy*, a final report submitted by GHK to SBS, London (2005).

29. Ibid., p. 53.

30. S. Bridge, K. O'Neill and S. Cromie, *Understanding Enterprise, Entrepreneurship and Small Business* (London: Palgrave Macmillan, 2003), p. 497.

31. G. Bannock, *The Economics and Management of Small Business* (London: Routledge, 2005), p. 133.

32. A. Amin, A. Cameron and R. Hudson, *Placing the Social Economy* (London: Routledge, 2002), p. 67.

33. Colin Stutt Consulting, *Finance for the Social Economy in Northern Ireland*, p. 38, www.colinstutt.com, accessed 7 October 2007.

34. A. Amin, A. Cameron and R. Hudson, *Placing the Social Economy* (London: Routledge, 2002), p. x.

Part III
Afterword

Looking Forwards 10

Key Concepts

This chapter covers

- some important perspectives of the third sector in relation to mainstream economics, the public and private sectors, and civil society;

- the main internal factors that might influence the future of the third sector;

- the potential influence of external factors such as expectations, promotion, help and acceptance;

- the likely impact of these factors on the future of the sector.

Learning Objectives

By the end of this chapter the reader should

- appreciate some of the issues involved in exploring the relevance of the third sector to mainstream economics, its potential as an alternative to the public and private sectors, and its relationship to the emerging concept of civil society;

(cont'd)

- understand some of the possible influences on the future of the sector;
- appreciate that current trends may not lead to significant change in the sector, and that any change may therefore come from currently unforeseen influences.

The past origins of the social economy and the third sector are explored to some extent in Part I of this book, which looks at their evolution and maps out the relationships that have developed between them, and between the third sector and the rest of an economy. Part II looks in more detail at the present situation of many organisations in the third sector, at some of the factors that are currently of relevance to them, and at some of the attempts that are being made to promote them and their impact on the sector.

This book concludes, in this chapter, with a look towards the future of the third sector. That future will depend both on where the sector is now and on the influences which act on it and which might change that position. Views on where the sector is now depend, to a considerable extent, on where people would like it to be, so this chapter considers views on the third sector in relation to mainstream economics, in providing an alternative to at least parts of either the public or the private sector, and in its relationship to the emerging concept of civil society. Influences which might act on the sector include both internal and external factors, and possibly relevant issues from both these areas are explored.

These issues, undoubtedly, will be clearer looking back from a future perspective than from a present appreciation which, inevitably, will be somewhat limited in its viewpoint, biased and ignorant of a future of currently unforeseen developments. Future projections will therefore be something in the nature of an extrapolation from apparent trends and from some issues which can currently be foreseen which are potentially relevant to the future of the third sector. It is not therefore an attempt to predict specific changes in the sector but instead to highlight some of the issues that might continue to be relevant to it and to consider what their impact might be.

Different perspectives on the third sector

This chapter starts with some questions about the current position of the social economy and/or the third sector. These are questions which are based on, or follow on from, some of the points already considered in previous chapters but they are considered here both to add to what has been said before and because they do have relevance to projections about the sector's future.

Is the third sector peripheral to mainstream economics?

Perhaps the most crucial area of modern life in which culture exercises a direct influence on well-being and international order is the economy. Although economic activity is inextricably linked with social and political life, there is a mistaken tendency, encouraged by contemporary economic discourse, to regard the economy as a facet of life with its own laws, separate from the rest of society.[1]

If economic activity is considered from a perspective informed by classical economics, it might be seen as a separate area of human activity subject to its own particular modes and rationales of behaviour. The laws of economics are universal, it is suggested, and the motivation behind them is the pursuit of 'utility'. The basic definition of that utility has been linked to the pursuit of pleasure, or the avoidance of pain, but utility-maximising behaviour is essentially selfish and is often related to money. The label 'capitalism' for the dominant economic system further encourages us to see the provision of capital for financial return as a fundamental driver of the system and often the key elements in an economic analysis are the firm and the profit it makes.

From that perspective the social economy might appear to be a peripheral area, not in the mainstream and not essential to an economic system. As Fukuyama has commented, 'the very change in the name of the discipline from "political economy" to "economics" between the eighteenth and late nineteenth centuries reflects the narrowing of the model of human behaviour at its core'.[2] But economic activity can also be viewed as an aspect of a wider pattern of human interactions. As Fukuyama has also pointed out, 'Adam Smith well understood (that) economic life is deeply embedded in social life'[3] and it is therefore relevant to look at economic activity from a social perspective not as separate from other activity but as an integral part of human interaction. Looked at in that way, the third sector is no less central than other aspects of an economy. After all, those areas of activity referred to as the social economy and the third sector have existed for as long as distinguishable public and private sector activity.

If economics is solely, or at least mainly, about the financial return for effort, then organisations in the third sector, and the social economy within it, are deviant because they do not necessarily seek to maximise their financial return. If, however, economics is about human effort for utility, and with a much wider interpretation of utility than is sometimes applied, then the social economy and the rest of the third sector are equally valid forms of economic effort. Economics does not just have to be about the pursuit of financial return. An understanding of economics has been used, for instance, to inform our understanding of relationships between other forms of life which do not use money. The application of economic approaches to ecological studies are to be found, for example, in works such as *Economics in Nature – Social Dilemmas, Mate Choices and Biological Markets*,[4] yet we do not think of those relationships which appear to follow economic laws as separate from other areas of biological activity.

Perhaps, therefore, we should more often consider that the key elements in a human economic system are not firms and profit, and the relationship between them, but instead the individuals behind those firms, together with their needs and the social relationships that influence them.

Individuals have a variety of needs which vary at different times and stages, as Maslow has pointed out,[5] but Maslow did not include money in his hierarchy of needs. Instead wanting money is a form of proxy for needs because it can be used to satisfy some of the needs in Maslow's hierarchy, especially the lower ones. At the top of his hierarchy is self-actualisation and that can take many forms including scientific or geographic exploration, artistic or sporting achievement, or the sense of satisfaction that comes from helping others, and these cannot simply be bought with money. If those forms of self-actualisation are people's objectives then, for them, the relevant 'utility' will have a much wider application than just the pursuit of money and, with it, pleasure.

Social economy and other third sector organisations have often been defined negatively as 'non-profit' or 'not-for-profit', which again serves to diminish them from an economic perspective. In reality, of course, they have a much wider range of purposes than the pursuit of financial profit and if they were defined positively by what they were 'for', rather than negatively for what they are 'not for', then they might be viewed in a much more positive light. But what they are together 'for' includes such a wide range of 'utilities' that it is easier to talk about what they are not for, so the width of their benefit to society may be a disadvantage when it comes to valuing them.

Third sector organisations are often distinguished from private sector organisations by their legal structure. For instance, a survey of social enterprises in the UK, referred to in Chapter 3, took as its sample enterprises which were registered as Companies Limited by Guarantee or Industrial and Provident Societies. However, Chapter 2, in looking at the people behind the venture, suggests that the choice of legal form for an organisation is not necessarily pre-determined, but is a choice made by the organisation's founders between the options that seem to be available for giving their enterprise a legal existence. That might not be a clear choice as none of the options may be ideal (see also Case 3.1). Enterprises, it has been suggested, are goal realisation devices,[6] and thus both private and third sector organisations can be seen to have common origins in people choosing the enterprise route as the way to achieve their goals, with the choice of the legal form to take for those enterprises then determining whether they are seen as private or third sector. Of course some private sector enterprises were always very clearly private sector ventures, and some third sector enterprise were very clearly different from that. But there are some enterprises between them which might have gone either way, and to regard some as being economically peripheral, just because they went one way rather than the other, is not appropriate.

Is the third sector an alternative to the public or private sector?

> By traditionally presenting itself as an alternative to the market and to public production, the social economy has always claimed to play a pioneering role as compared to these other two means of allocation resources.[7]

Another view of the third sector and particularly of the social economy is that it has the potential to provide an alternative to at least parts of either the public or the private sector. This view has been referred to earlier, for instance in Chapter 4, and comes from different political viewpoints. The social economy is seen by some as more market driven than the public sector and thus as better able to deliver a range of public services, or is seen by others as more equitable than the private sector and thus as a preferable vehicle for much economic activity.

Borzaga and Tortia[8] suggest that, in explanations of the emergence of social economy forms of enterprise in market conditions, the approach mainly linked to Hansmann stands out. His theory, they suggest, explains the birth and development of a significant number of co-operatives and non-profit organisations when there are market failures and suggests that their role is supposed to lessen when markets become more competitive and failures become less frequent. That approach tends to present the social economy as an alternative, or at least as a supplement, to the private sector. As Lloyd quotes, 'Is the social economy predominantly seen as the basis for a radical grand narrative or a more limited "toolkit" to fix the social problems that arise out of the return to increasingly unfettered market forces?'[9]

But, as Lloyd also acknowledges, the social economy has been seen as a 'service gap filler' and as

a tool in providing policy solutions (that) came from attempts to address three long-standing but always changing problems:

i)   a rising demand for social, personal and community services;

ii) a need to find ways to meet these demands while constraining levels of direct state expenditure and rates of taxation; and

iii) the persistence of spatially localised pockets of deprivation where these service gaps are extreme regardless of the economic cycle.[10]

It can of course be pointed out that the third sector is not going to take over from the public or the private sector. Those sectors may not be perfect but, overall, they have not failed, and seem very unlikely in either case to be replaced by the third sector. Further, all three sectors have always been there, and have coexisted, since separate economic sectors first became distinguishable. With the exception of tribal and communist economies, human society generally seems to have had mixed economies which incorporate all three sectors.

Despite this, aspects of the third sector are sometimes presented as adding something extra to the other two and it might appear, as a result, that the role of, or at least scope for, the third sector and in particular the social economy is now rising. That seems to have happened at times in the past, as reported in Chapter 4, and therefore, if the third sector is now growing relative to the other sectors, it may be cyclical and not a long-term future trend.

Is the third sector just another label for civil society?

> The *Civil Society Almanac* is an indispensable guide to the sector…It gives an essential overview of where civil society organisations get their money from, how they spend it and how the sector is changing.
>
> This ground breaking research looks at higher education, museums, housing associations, co-operatives, trades unions, political parties and more.[11]
>
> National Council for Voluntary Action
> 'giving voice and support to civil society'

There are many different definitions of civil society, or civic society as it is sometimes called. One of these is provided by the Centre for Civil Society at the London School of Economics which, it says, captures the multi-faceted nature of the concept:

> Civil society refers to the arena of uncoerced collective action around shared interests, purposes and values. In theory, its institutional forms are distinct from those of the state, family and market, though in practice, the boundaries between state, civil society, family and market are often complex, blurred and negotiated. Civil society commonly embraces a diversity of spaces, actors and institutional forms, varying in their degree of formality, autonomy and power. Civil societies are often populated by organisations such as registered charities, development non-governmental organisations, community groups, women's organisations, faith-based organisations, professional associations, trades unions, self-help groups, social movements, business associations, coalitions and advocacy groups.[12]

While the original formulation of the concept of 'civil society' might apparently be traced to the nineteenth century,[13] it came to prominence in the late 1980s and 1990s when it became seen as a way of controlling the state. It was civil society, it has been suggested, that mobilised against the state in Eastern and Central Europe and sparked the 'velvet revolution'[14] and it was pressure from civil society that led to the end of apartheid in South Africa. Civil society therefore had to be autonomous of the state and, in the eyes of some, even critical of it.

However, like so many issues in this area, the concept of civil society is not only narrowly defined but is variously contested. One commentator, for instance, has identified three different uses of the term:

- As a *description* of varieties of association,
- As a *value* advocating the advantages of co-operation
- As a *democratic ecosystem* – a public sphere in which engagement with the whole future and shape of society takes place (or could take place).[15]

The concept of civil society therefore can be very wide and not easily summarised in just a few paragraphs. Nevertheless, what are, or might be, its links with the third sector? That depends, to some extent, on which use of the term 'civil society' is being considered. If civic society is used to describe varieties of association, then those varieties of association often listed as being in civil society are also listed as being in the third sector. Civil society has been described, for instance, as 'a complex welter of intermediate institutions, including businesses, voluntary associations, educational institutions, clubs, unions, media, charities and churches (which) builds in turn, on the family, the primary instrument by which people are socialised into their culture and given the skills that allow them to live in broader society and through which the values and knowledge of that society are transmitted across the generations':[16] a list of components very like lists of third sector components.

If, though, the term 'civil society' is used as 'a value advocating the advantages of co-operation' then that might be beyond what is indicated by the third sector, but not possibly beyond the objectives of some advocates of the social economy. As indicated previously, some advocates of the third sector, and particularly of the social economy, look to it to offer a challenge to liberal market forces. So both civil society and the social economy can be associated with advocacy.

If the term 'civic society' is used to indicate a 'democratic ecosystem' then that ecosystem might be said to provide a channel for, and/or a source of, social capital. Social capital has been described as 'the ability of people to work together for common purposes in groups and organisations',[17] and working together for common purposes in groups and organisations is what civil society does. As links are sometimes drawn between social capital and the social economy, as described in Chapter 7, this provides another connection between civil society and the third sector.

Thus, whichever of the suggested uses of the term 'civil society' is considered, links can be found between it and the third sector, and, indeed, the terms are sometimes used interchangeably. However, taken overall, the term 'civil society' might be considered to differ from the third sector, not in the range of organisations it encompasses, but in the wider social and political dimension which for many is the reason for considering it. Therefore, while some people do appear to be looking for a political impact from the third sector, and from the social economy within it, that is not generally highlighted as its main feature. Instead the concept of the third sector, as the third sector of the economy, focuses on its economic impact. This suggests not that what are labelled 'the civil society' and 'the third sector' are different things, but that those labels emphasise different aspects of what is being considered. The third sector and civic society are clearly linked and might thus be considered to refer to two different facets of the same components of organised human society.

Looking at the future of the third sector

Internal factors

The first group of factors to be considered are those that are largely internal to the sector. They include the nature of the sector and the organisations in it, the tensions in the sector, the sometimes contentious issue of funding, and the sector's own efforts to advance itself.

The nature of the sector

Like the private sector, the health of the third sector as a whole does not depend on the health of all of its parts. Third sector organisations can suffer from ill health, fail and cease to exist but, unless they all fail at the same time, it does not mean that the overall health of the third sector is failing, just as in an ecology the deaths of some component parts and their replacement by new forms of life is a process which is not only natural, but is even essential for the long-term well-being of the system. Even if many current third sector organisations appear to be in good health, it seems safe to predict that soon some of them will cease to operate. However, if other existing organisations prosper and grow while, at the same time, new organisations are continually being founded as people seek vehicles through which to try to address perceived needs, the future of the sector will thus remain healthy.

It is also clear that the third sector is a very heterogeneous sector (as Pearce's diagram in Figure 2.1 indicates) and therefore it is unlikely that all the organisations in it will respond to the same factors. It is also clear that, at its boundaries, there are no big gulfs and/or sudden changes between it and the other economic sectors. Instead there is a progression with overlaps and similarities and, for instance, while some organisations in the third sector are very different from many private sector businesses, there are also enterprises, especially in that part of the third sector often referred to as the social economy, which have a lot in common with many organisations in the private sector. Therefore trying to consider the future of the third sector in isolation is unlikely to be helpful. The third sector will be affected by many of the same issues as the private sector, and that applies particularly to the social economy which is often the part of the third sector uppermost in people's minds.

Tensions in the sector

There are clearly tensions in the third sector. As well as tensions between it and other sectors, for instance, when some private sector organisations see it as unfair competition and some public sector organisations see it as threat, there are also tensions between different objectives within third sector organisations. On the one hand, third sector organisations are not in the private sector because they do not exist principally to make money, but they do have to acquire money in order to survive. This tension may be most obvious in social enterprises which need to balance the generation of sufficient income to secure financial sustainability with the attainment of the enterprises' social (or other non-financial) goals, and it seems reasonable to suggest that this will continue to be an issue. Social enterprises have often reported tensions when pursuing social and economic goals simultaneously and some people still appear to see a social enterprise as a potentially unstable mix of an organisation with a social purpose and a business with a social mission, with current trends, such as the emphasis on sustainability, pushing it in the business direction.[18] This social-economic tension can either be resented as a force which has the potential to weaken a social enterprise and to tear it apart or be accepted as a natural part of third sector existence which can serve instead to strengthen an organisation and focus its efforts.

Indeed both social enterprises and private sector businesses are enterprises, and the 'mushroom' theory presented in Chapter 2 suggests that all enterprises have similar origins in that they are formed by their founders to achieve something. Enterprises may differ in their goals but both third and private sector enterprises can have multiple goals, and both have to survive financially if they are to achieve them. In many fundamentals third sector enterprises, and especially social enterprises, are no different from private (or public) sector enterprises.

> My opinion is that any voluntary sector organisation *must* operate along business lines. The only difference between a social enterprise and normal enterprise is simply that there are no shareholders that receive a dividend, but there are 'shareholders' in terms of the members and the community at large who may benefit from the initiatives that are put together.[19]

Among other characteristics shared with private sector enterprises are the issues involved in employing people, the need to satisfy the requirements of external stakeholders, the requirements of commercial and company law, and the need for leadership. Even size can often be a common characteristic as in both the private and the third sectors many enterprises are small and, as such, the latter are not very different from other small businesses. Social enterprises may be a newly recognised sector but the difference between them and other small businesses is often no greater than that between other different sectors within the small business ambit.

Funding issues

Funding issues will continue to be a problem for many third sector organisations. Except for those organisations established with a sufficiently large endowment to provide a continuing income, there will always be a necessity to generate sufficient income to cover operating costs. Sometimes it seems that the people behind third sector organisations feel that this is in some way unfair and that, because they are doing useful work, they should be provided with a continuing supply of resources. In particular, some grant schemes have been criticised for only offering relatively short-term funding thus leaving the recipients of the grants in the lurch when the term of the grant funding comes to an end, without a guarantee of any further funding.

One group of organisations which are particularly sensitive to withdrawals of grant funding are those social economy organisations which were created not so much through market forces and the ideas of particular social entrepreneurs, but through government encouragement and the availability of government grants and subsidies. They might call themselves social enterprises but it is said they are probably best labelled 'quasi-public' organisations and have a different logic underpinning them.[20] They may feel that there is a strong case for state funding for their continuation but they may find that they are disappointed.

Indeed, many private sector businesses have an even more hand-to-mouth existence and also have no source of guaranteed income beyond their current orders. They usually realise that they need continually to sell their output in order to renew their sources of income. Therefore, unless government or other external support for the sector includes guaranteed sources of medium- or long-term funding, it is clear that third sector enterprises also may have to accept that selling must be a continuous process at the heart of business, rather than just an occasional once-off separate chore. They may try to 'sell' their benefits to philanthropists, they may try to support their work by trading, they may try joint venturing or they may try a combination. But if they do not thus help themselves they may find that no one else will.

The sector's own efforts

The sector's own efforts at advancement, not just as separate organisations but also with a sector-wide voice, could, of course, be influential in its future. If the sector can articulate and communicate some sector-wide (or sub-sector-wide) goals, or if organisations in it can combine to exploit the advantages of scale, that could be influential. Similarly, the sector's own efforts to identify and publicise the benefits it provides could help to bring it more to public attention and gain it more tangible support. As yet, however, there is not much evidence of a breakthrough in this direction.

External factors

The above examination of factors internal to the third sector suggests a future of largely more of the same as no significant internal changes are foreseen. If there is to be change it seems that it will largely be due to external factors such as the expectations people have of the sector; the extent to which they might continue then to promote, fund, guide and/or otherwise seek to influence it; encroachment on or by the sector and the wider public perception of the sector.

Expectations of the sector

An important factor relevant to the future of the third sector will be the expectations its various stakeholders have of it, because they will have an impact on the support that might be made available to it. Clearly some of these expectations will be internal coming from of those who are working in the sector and these can probably be presented in a hierarchy, not unlike Maslow's hierarchy of human needs. There will be people whose immediate requirement is employment which provides them with an income and whose next level of need is probably security of employment. However, there will also be people who, as well as an income, also want to feel that they are contributing to society in a useful way. Particularly among the people in the sector who have been responsible for starting or developing third sector organisations, there will be some who are clearly seeking self-actualisation. Those people who just want an income could also seek it in the private or public sector, but for those who are seeking esteem or self-actualisation the third sector might be the only sector in which they think they will find it.

There are stakeholders external to the sector who also have a range of aspirations for the sector. They include people in government responsible for the public sector but who will, in general, support the third sector, or parts of it, because they perceive that it can deliver the sort of benefits which they believe are needed. The benefits they seek may cover a range of issues including

- a way of addressing social exclusion and the tackling of deprivation,
- the creation of more employment,
- assisting with more political aspirations such as
  - providing a vehicle able to deliver more effective or efficient personal and social services than a public sector which is thought to be inefficient and too large;
  - the development of an alternative economic system which avoids the perceived excesses of an unrestrained private sector.

There can be an important tension here between the view of the third sector as a radical alternative to the state or private markets and that of the sector as a more conservative agent of governments in the delivery of a range of services. This is especially so for the social economy which many think offers an arena which allows the disadvantaged to resist the globalisation of economics and culture by developing their own resources, assets and skills. This tension has been referred to earlier but how, or whether, it is resolved could influence the sector's future.

In any case it is clear that the sector cannot meet all the different expectations that people sometimes have of it (see Illustration 9.6). Further, the sector is not a single co-ordinated entity, which might therefore easily be steered in a particular direction, but a convenient way of referring to a very heterogeneous set of organisations which have their own disparate aims and objectives and will continue to pursue them.

Promotion of the sector

Unless, and until, it becomes much clearer that it cannot meet expectations and deliver the benefits sought from it, the third sector, or at least parts of it, can expect to continue to be promoted by the government. There are likely to continue to be various government strategies designed to encourage the development of more, bigger and/or better third sector organisations but it will be important for the sector to recognise that, for governments, such a result will be a means to an end, but not the end itself. Instead the outcomes sought might include increasing employment as well as countering social exclusion and improving the lot of deprived communities, although that might not always be made clear.

Funding and guidance for the sector

In the public sector, organisations are generally assured of an income stream from public funds for the foreseeable future. In the private sector they depend upon their own earning efforts. Special sources of funding, together with guidance on how best to access the funding that is available, would obviously be a particular help to the third sector and especially to those organisations which have not learnt how to secure funding on a continuing basis. However, as Chapter 6 indicates, there are already particular sources of funding and advice which have been made available to the third sector in the UK and there is no reason to expect that there will be many more.

It might be argued that helping those third sector organisations which have not learnt how to secure funding with special sources of funding and advice would be unfair on those organisations which have invested in their fund-raising efforts. In any case it is more logical to tie sources of funding to the outputs and outcomes sought and so to award available funding on the basis of tenders for the efficient supply of those outputs rather than indicating that funding would be available as grants for any suitable organisation that wants it. There is evidence that grants can lead to dependency and, if that leads to fewer grants being available in the future, those organisations which have learnt how to fund-raise in other ways will be better placed to survive.

Encroachment

Another issue for the third sector might be described as encroachment. If it is increasingly appropriated by government (see Chapter 8) to deliver a wide range of programmes and service outcomes, it might lose its edge as a potential radical and radicalising alternative to the power of public sector politics. As indicated in Chapter 5, the public sector can become closely involved in the third sector when it tries to control how the contracts it places are performed or when it is involved in the establishment of third sector organisations to deliver those contracts, and this might lead to third sector organisations adopting public sector cultures and attitudes. At the same time an increasing emphasis on corporate social responsibility (CSR) in the private sector might seem to be an example of third sector attitudes encroaching on the private sector or it could lead to a bigger private sector influence on some of the social values of the third sector.

Acceptance of the sector

A further area in which the third sector might like help is acceptance. In recent years it has increasingly been accepted by governments which have tried to promote and support it because of the benefits which they believe it can provide. However, it would also help the sector if it had gained wider public recognition and acceptance, both for the value it adds to society generally and for the benefits it can provide for individual participants. It would, for instance, be a considerable help to the sector if it had greater recognition as a source of valid and rewarding careers: careers which might not be among the highest paid in financial terms, but careers which have very considerable potential to make a positive contribution to society. Whether or not the sector develops an appropriate 'brand image' and receives more recognition and acceptance is uncertain at this time.

The impact

> I have seen the future and it's very much like the present, only longer.
>
> Kehlog Albran
>
> *Source: Quotations for Our Time*, compiled by L. Peters (London: Magnum Books, 1981).

Will the third sector deliver?

What will be the impact of the third sector? Chapter 9 in particular looks at the benefits that it might deliver and how they might be assessed, but it suggests that there is not much evidence to quantify the extent of the benefits being delivered. An issue for the future of the sector is the extent to which it does, or at least appears to, deliver the benefits sought from it. For instance,

- *Employment.* It is clear that it does provide a considerable amount of employment, although how much is often still not clear despite better surveys being conducted on the sector.
- *Addressing exclusion and deprivation.* There does not seem to be clear evidence that third sector organisations have an inherent ability consistently to address issues of exclusion and deprivation.
- *Social Capital.* Social capital can be viewed as a cause or an effect in the development of the social economy, but the evidence for the links seems to be more rhetorical than demonstrable. The performance of the sector may be due more to the efforts of individual social entrepreneurs than to the stock of social capital, and organisations in the sector may not, in turn, produce social capital which, in any case, may not prove to be the antidote to deprivation in the way that has been suggested.
- *Political alternatives.* It is the satisfying of the more quasi-political expectations of the third sector that is probably hardest to predict. Among the trends that are apparent are that some private sector organisations are becoming more like social enterprises in order to win public sector contracts, which might suggest that the third sector is having a civilising influence on at least part of the private sector. It would also seem that some third sector organisations are becoming, or at least want to appear to be, more like private sector organisations in their efforts to earn money to replace grants as the

latter dry up, which might be thought to be a trend in the other direction. In the view, for instance, of the Centre for Employment and Enterprise Development (CEED) based in St Pauls, Bristol, 'CEED does not seek to create an alternative to capitalism – quite the opposite. What CEED seeks to demonstrate is that anyone, regardless of their ethnic background, gender, or postcode can develop successful careers, given the appropriate level of training and support. As such it raises important questions as to how "success" is to be defined and about the factors that underpin success.'[21]

* *The evidence.* A significant problem in analysing these benefits and making predictions from that analysis is often the lack of clear and convincing evidence. That lack of evidence might, itself, be a factor in the sector's future. Thus the sector's own efforts to demonstrate and measure its impact, for instance, through using the new measurement tools which are becoming available, might be important.

Will it still be popular?

The current interest in the third sector has some of the characteristics of a fashion, and fashions often do not last. Government interest in the sector has been triggered by an appreciation of the potential of the sector to deliver particular benefits. That interest is likely to be maintained only if the sector seems to be delivering those benefits more effectively than others and also if government support for the sector seems to increase the amount of benefit thus delivered.

So far there does not appear to be a lot of evidence that either of those requirements is being met, although much of the relevant evaluation work may still be at an early stage. Many attempts to promote the social economy and social enterprises have come up with very similar support mechanisms to those devised to support small businesses in general and there is little evidence that those small business promotion strategies have been able to make a clear overall difference. Government support can, however, often be rather like the proverbial oil tanker which takes a long time to turn around once the need for a change in direction is perceived.

If there is evidence that the third sector can deliver on its expectations then government interest in it might increase, and government interest also stimulates other areas of interest such as that in business schools and universities. If, on the other hand, third sector organisations prove not to be able to deliver the outcomes sought, or at least if promotional efforts do not produce a proportional increase in those outcomes, then the third sector might find that it eventually ceases to attract government support, and ceases to be promoted in the way that is being done at present. Thus the current level of interest might increase or wane, but would that make a lot of difference to the sector as a whole, as opposed to just those organisations selected for special assistance?

What might change it?

If the discernable current trends are not likely to lead to significant change in the third sector, what would change it? Historically, it has generally responded to structural changes in society, such as political changes in the nineteenth century and economic developments in the twentieth. But what will be the next such change and what will be its effects? It could be that society will increasingly encourage and welcome voluntary action, and become more dependent on it, and that could have a big effect on the third sector.

However, the third sector is only a part, and an integral part, of the bigger economic picture. What happens in the whole of an economy is likely to affect all its sectors, and what happens in one sector is likely to affect the others. Thus the third sector may not shape its own destiny but will respond to how society organises itself economically and how the private and public sectors develop in response to that.

That at least might be the situation in the UK, but the third sector will be influenced by different factors in different countries, because it is in each of those countries the third sector of that country's economy. The influence of the society of a country on its third sector and the influences of the sectors of a country's economy on each other are likely to be stronger than the links between the third sectors of different economies.

Will the sector survive?

The above summaries suggest that there is little foreseeable reason to expect any major overall changes in scale, make-up and direction of the third sector. There has been a third sector for as long as the other two sectors of an economy have been distinguishable as separate areas of activity. It seems likely that this will continue, as will the existence of cracks in what the public and private sectors do which the third sector can fill. Perhaps the future of the third sector will depend more upon the private and public sectors, and on how it reacts to their evolution, than on forces operating directly on it. Undoubtedly, the sector has contributed much, and clearly has much still to offer.

The Key Points of Chapter 10

- Among the issues being raised about the social economy and/or the third sector are the extent to which it is relevant to mainstream economics, the extent to which it can or should provide an alternative to either the public or the private sector, and the extent to which it is related to, or coincides with, the emerging concept of civil society. Such issues are relevant to speculations on the future of the third sector.

- Among the main internal factors which might influence the future of the third sector are the nature of the sector and tensions in it, including especially tensions around funding issues.

- Among the main external factors which might influence the future of the third sector are the expectations that people and governments have of it, the attempts that are thus being made to promote it and the help being given to it, and the extent to which it is gaining wider acceptance.

(cont'd)

- There does not yet appear to be much evidence either that the sector can deliver some of the things expected of it or that attempts to promote it can increase its outputs. Therefore interest in it might wane.
- Current trends may not lead to significant change in the sector, thus any change may come as a consequence of other developments in the public and private sectors, or from currently unforeseen influences.

CASE 10.1

A Selection of Reports on Trends and Influences

Study to focus on union service fears

A new research project will consider why trade unions are uneasy about government plans to contract more charities to deliver public services.

The study, led by chief executives body Acevo, will examine relations between unions and third sector organisations. It will also look into concerns raised by the unions – they say charity workers have poorer working conditions and greater job insecurity than their public sector counterparts.

Andy Ricketts, Third Sector Online, 25 September 2007

CSR 'starting to lose its add-on tag'

Companies have started to implement their corporate responsibility strategies throughout their operations, rather than seeing them as a separate add-on or sales promotion, according to Business in the Community.

'Businesses are realising that, because of the rising tide of consumer expectation and general stakeholder expectations, it's very important to make internal strategies more public and market them,' said Sue Adkins, the charity's director, at the 27th International Fundraising Congress in Amsterdam. 'Businesses have to connect what they say inside with what they do outside.'

She cited a Sainsbury's media campaign that used the slogan 'Same price different values' and promoted issues such as being energy-efficient, and Marks & Spencer's Look Behind the Label marketing campaign, which highlighted a number of causes, including genetically modified food, animal welfare, reducing hydrogenated fats or climate change.

Emma Rigby, Third Sector Online, 30 October 2007

Report: 'service delivery threatens independence'

The third sector's increased role in public service delivery is stifling its distinctiveness and damaging its contribution to civil society, according to new research by the Carnegie UK Trust.

CASE 10.1 (cont'd)

The trust's report, *The Shape of Civil Society to Come*, claims that the concentration of resources in a smaller number of large organisations threatens the sector's independence and autonomy. It goes on to criticise the 'conformity of governance' among voluntary and community groups that are using corporate and enterprise models necessitated by government contracting, which it says leads to a loss of diversity.

Helen Warrell, Third Sector, 31 October 2007

'Don't become cowardly,' charities told

The sector must guard against turning into a cowardly arm of government, according to Sean Bailey, a prospective Conservative candidate and co-founder of young person's charity My Generation.

Bailey made the comments during a debate at the NCVO's political conference. 'We are becoming cowards, an arm of government – you can see it in the terminology we use, phrases such as: "best practice" and "value for money,"' he told the audience. 'The sector is currently a very hot thing, but it's up to us to make sure we secure lasting policies'. 'Will we become second-tier civil servants, or innovative people who know what we are about rather than told what we are about?'

But newspaper columnist Yasmin Alibhai-Brown disagreed. 'Professionalisation of the sector was long overdue,' she said. 'I saw many voluntary projects in the 80s die because of a lack of professionalisation.' She also advised charities not to let themselves be manipulated by MPs. 'The sector should not allow itself to be used for political photo opportunities,' she added.

Indira Das-Gupta, Third Sector Online, 23 November 2007

Source: www.thirdsector.co.uk, accessed on the dates indicated.

CASE 10.2

A Study of the Social Economy in Four Places

In their book *Placing the Social Economy*, Amin et al. looked at the social economy in four different city locations in the UK: Bristol, Glasgow, Middlesbrough and Tower Hamlets in London. While their conclusions do not necessarily apply to all manifestations of the social economy everywhere, they do raise some points relevant to future projections for the sector and its potential to meet the expectations placed on it.

Does a social enterprise have to originate in a local community?

Amin et al. question, for instance, whether a social enterprise has to be based in a local community? They comment that in Tower Hamlets the social enterprise Bromely-by-Bow is 'seen by many as a model of future social enterprise development' but 'does not see itself as a local community project in the strict sense' in that 'it is not community-owned, it was set up and is

CASE 10.2 (cont'd)

run by professionals from elsewhere, and it provides high-level, integrated services which could not possibly have been developed using local capacities alone'.[22]

Does social enterprise do best in areas with social exclusion?

They also question the link between social enterprise and social exclusion: 'Despite the common expectation that the social economy flourishes in areas of marked social exclusion, paradoxically, of our four case areas, the prosperous city of Bristol has the most extensive and successful social economy.'[23]

Just as social exclusion can be seen to have a distinct geography tied to particular places, so we can conclude that the social "inclusion" represented by social economy also has a distinct, though different, geography, one that does not match that of social exclusion. The social economy, despite being routinely linked in policy discourse to poor places, seems to require resources, outlets and capabilities that do not correspond to the geography of social need. They go beyond the local community. Where such access does not exist, the task may well fall to local authorities and local communities, both of which, however, seem ill-equipped to mobilise the social economy in a significant way.[24]

Is social enterprise always welcome?

Amin et al. quote a case in Tower Hamlets, where a third sector housing association was not universally welcomed because the transfer of housing to the social enterprise was resented as 'privatisation' although the social enterprise was bringing investment to the estates and rents were lower.[25]

This case raises the question that if 'nationalisation' is the transfer of an enterprise from the private to the public sector and 'privatisation' is the transfer of an enterprise from the public to the private sector, what are the relevant words to describe transfers to and from the third sector? If they do not exist then will inappropriate words, such as 'privatisation', continue to be used which will convey the wrong meaning or have the wrong associations?

Questions, Exercises, Essay and Discussion Topics

1. Identify five reasons for suggesting that the third sector is not likely to change significantly for the foreseeable future.

2. Identify, with reasons, the five factors most likely to lead to change in the third sector.

3. To what extent do you think that public acceptance of the third sector will grow?

============ **SUGGESTIONS FOR FURTHER READING** ============

A. Noya and E. Clarence (eds), *The Social Economy, BUILDING EXCLUSIVE ECONOMIES* (OECD, 2007).

References

1. F. Fukuyama, Trust: The Social Virtues and the Creation of Prosperity (New York: Free Press Paperbacks, 1996), p. 6.
2. Ibid., p. 13.
3. R. Noë, J. A. R. A. M. van Hooff and P. Hammerstein (eds), *Economics in Nature – Social Dilemmas, Mate Choices and Biological Markets* (Cambridge: Cambridge University Press, 2001).
4. Ibid., p. 18.
5. A. Maslow, *Motivation and Personality* (New York: Harper, 1954).
6. For instance, L. Hunter speaking at a University of Ulster seminar on 'Developing a Strategy and Vision for Social Entrepreneurship', Coleraine, 10 September 2007.
7. X. Greffe, 'The Role of the Social Economy in Local Development', in A. Noya and E. Clarence (eds), *The Social Economy, BUILDING EXCLUSIVE ECONOMIES* (OECD, 2007), p. 95.
8. C. Borzaga and E. Tortia, 'Social Economy Organisations in the Theory of the Firm', in A. Noya and E. Clarence (eds), *The Social Economy, BUILDING EXCLUSIVE ECONOMIES* (OECD, 2007), pp. 38–40.
9. P. Lloyd, 'The Social Economy in the New Political Economic Context', in A. Noya and E. Clarence (eds), *The Social Economy, BUILDING EXCLUSIVE ECONOMIES* (OECD, 2007), pp. 67–68.
10. Ibid., p. 77.
11. National Council for Voluntary Action (NCVO), *The UK Civil Society Almanac 2008*, executive summary from www.ncvo-vol.org.uk/publications, 31 March 2008.
12. London School of Economics Centre for Civil Society (www.lse.ac.uk/collections/CCS/introduction.htm, accessed 31 March 2008).
13. For instance, G. W. F. Hegel, *Elements of the Philosophy of Right*, 1827 (translated by Dyde 1897).
14. N. Chandhoke, *The Taming of Civil Society* (www.india-society/com/2005/545, accessed 28 March 2008).
15. M. Edwards, reported in N. Chandhoke, 'What the Hell is "Civil Society"?' (OpenDemocracy, 2005), www.opendemocracy.net, accessed 29 March 2008.
16. F. Fukuyama, *Trust: The Social Virtues and the Creation of Prosperity* (New York: Free Press Paperbacks, 1996), pp. 4–5.
17. J. Coleman, 'Social Capital in the Creation of Human Capital', *American Journal of Sociology*, 94 (1988), S95–120, quoted by F. Fukuyama, *Trust: The Social Virtues and the Creation of Prosperity* (New York: Free Press Paperbacks, 1996), p. 10.
18. For instance, see P. Seanor, M. Bull and R. Ridley-Duff, 'Contradictions in Social Enterprise: Do They Draw in Straight Lines or Circles?', a paper presented at the *30th isbe conference*, Glasgow 2007.
19. A director of a social enterprise (CEED) quoted by A. Amin, A. Cameron and R. Hudson, *Placing the Social Economy* (London: Routledge, 2002), p. 103.
20. P. Lloyd in *Rethinking the Social Economy* (Queen's University Belfast CU2: Contested Cities – Urban Universities, 2006), p. 13.
21. A. Amin, A. Cameron and R. Hudson, *Placing the Social Economy* (London: Routledge, 2002), p. 104.
22. Ibid., p. 113.
23. Ibid., p. 97.
24. Ibid., p. 115.
25. Ibid., p. 110.

Index

In this index case studies are indicated by c.; figures by fig.; illustrations by ill.; tables by tab.; in italics. E.g. Amicus, 130 (c.5.4). Published documents are presented in italics